AGAINST DOGMATISM

AGAINST DOGMATISM

Dwelling in Faith and Doubt

MADHURI M. YADLAPATI

UNIVERSITY OF ILLINOIS PRESS

Urbana, Chicago, and Springfield

© 2013 by the Board of Trustees
of the University of Illinois
All rights reserved
Manufactured in the United States of America
1 2 3 4 5 C P 5 4 3 2 1
♾ This book is printed on acid-free paper.

Library of Congress Control Number: 2013951573

To Siva, Sneha, and Jhansi
my thanks,
such small words for so large a gift

*There are two ways to slide easily through life;
to believe everything or to doubt everything.
Both ways save us from thinking.*
—Alfred Korzybski

CONTENTS

AGAINST DOGMATISM

Beyond Fundamentalism
and Atheism

As a student of the world's religious traditions, I have always been intrigued with the intricate ways in which doubt functions to enrich faith. And yet, while the close interplay of doubt and faith is so manifestly found in the writings of the most enlightening religious thinkers and in different traditions around the world, far too many of today's most vocal discussions of religion rely on flat portrayals of faith that seem threatened by any significant account of doubt or skepticism. Faith is often restricted to simple belief statements or creeds. Many consider the strength and merits of faith to lie in an individual's unshakable certitude. Doubt is often depicted as an enemy to faith altogether, or at best an uncomfortable hiccup along the glorious journey to faith, a purifying fire that functions to distill true faith. If we were to listen only to the loudest voices, we might mistakenly believe that the entire world had descended into partisan camps of religious fundamentalists and dogmatic secular atheists. It is certainly possible to articulate either atheism or religious faith without being dogmatic. Doing so requires one to remain open and questioning, to admit humbly that one does not possess all the answers.

By definition, religion places us in tension between the ordinary finite reality we see and experience clearly and the infinite and ultimate reality that presumably lies outside our concrete experience, between what Mircea Eliade termed the profane (ordinary life) and the sacred (meaningful underpinnings of ultimacy). Religion deals explicitly with the infinite, what Immanuel Kant called the *noumenal* realm that lies beyond the boundaries of ordinary knowledge, what is thus called the supernatural. Of course, religious views have also taken this ultimate to be more truly real than what we can see and experience in the world, and have affirmed its transcendence of ordinary knowledge. The *Daodejing* teaches that the Dao that can be known or named is not the eternal Dao, even while it can be experienced. In his recent book *Without Buddha I Could Not Be a Christian*, Paul Knitter poses the troubling yet unavoidable question of "whether there really is a Something More, whether it is truly worthwhile to struggle for love and justice, whether there is anything beyond the portals of death."[1] Knitter's question echoes the nagging doubt and persistent desire to know what is true, a desire many of us experience. Is there something more beyond the life we can see? As the coming chapters show, faith does not resolve and end this question so much as exercise the questioning itself. Knitter's own response suggests the open-ended nature of the questioning that also builds a posture of faith. "The results of these struggles are always inconclusive. So, I trust. So I let go. So I believe. . . . I know in trust what I cannot know in reason."[2] Such a juxtaposition of faith as trust alongside a persistent struggle with not knowing marks a rich space of faith and doubt that rejects the easy answers of what the fundamentalists insist we need to accept on faith or what the New Atheists demand we deny because of a lack of proof.

This book navigates, faithfully but nonconfessionally, the space that is possible by abandoning certitude and dogmatic skepticism, where faith and doubt are interwoven in dynamic ways of being attentive to the depth and height of spiritual reflection and speculation. Through three distinct sections that discuss faith, doubt, and hope, I trace a nondogmatic faith that responds creatively and responsibly to living in the everyday world as limited, imaginative, and questioning creatures. Part 1 uses expressions from several religious traditions to illustrate the experiences and commitments of faith. Part 2 uses a tradition-specific approach to discuss various dimensions of doubt as protest against or transcendence of worldly understanding in Protestant Christianity and Hinduism. Building on the groundwork laid in the first two parts, part 3 focuses on skeptical and mystical unknowing or self-correction and how it can contribute to a contemporary nondogmatic Christian hope that incorporates a mutual dynamic of faith and doubt. This book addresses those in society who earnestly reject dogmatic extremes, and it invites them into a conversation with our world's religious traditions, which are full of persistent and eloquent voices of faith, doubt, and hope. These voices of spirituality humbly yet boldly speak to us in the twenty-first century of the depth of a spiritual life that resists dogmatism. These voices rise from very different times and places, and they articulate very different doctrinal views and theological commitments. What they share is a commitment to struggle deeply with the content of faith and doubt rather than take the easy road of unquestioning faith or unrelenting skepticism.

Some of the guiding questions for this book include the following: What are some historical interpretations of faith that are relevant for our contemporary discourse? If faith is not primarily about certitude, then what is it? If religious faith does not consist primarily of assent to a set of belief propositions, then what is it? How are faith and doubt related? In what ways can doubt help strengthen or challenge faith, and keep in check our unrelenting yet understandable desires for security and certainty? In what helpful and constructive ways have different religious thinkers and traditions of interpretation formulated the relationship between faith and doubt?

My discussion actively resists two varieties of loud insistence on having all the answers. On the one hand, this book addresses the so-called New Atheist critics of religion and faith who simply dismiss religion as superstitious and irrational nonsense.[3] As political satirist Bill Maher is quite fond of saying on his HBO show, *Real Time*, it is irrational to believe in the "talking snake," referring to the colorful stories in the biblical Old Testament Book of Genesis. Maher and the New Atheists dismiss faith altogether on the basis that it requires one to accept unequivocally the literal meaning of odd claims made in scripture. In this line of thinking, if one is to be a Jew or a Christian, she or he must by necessity believe that an actual snake spoke to Eve in the Garden of Eden and convinced her to disobey God's commands and eat the fruit of the tree of knowledge. Maher and others effectively reduce all religious faith to belief in the literal truth of scriptural statements, and reduce the biblical narrative, prophecy, and myth to flat propositions of nothing but factual value. In *The God Delusion*, Richard Dawkins makes a threefold argument challenging the validity of religious belief: he attacks as baseless the straightforward attempts within the scope of religion to explain the origin of the world; he illustrates the many ways in which we do not need religion to justify morality or meaning in life; he demonstrates the vast amount of evidence that religious dogmatism has contributed to violence.[4] However, Dawkins's reading of religious faith is altogether reductionist. Insofar as he targets the claims of religious dogmatism to explain and regulate human life, he is correct. However, he fails to address any more sophisticated and messy expressions of living, nondogmatic faith. Admittedly, this is not his concern, but by attacking all of religious faith as if it were only unqualified belief, he effectively makes his discussion irrelevant regarding the life of faith. Christopher Hitchens, perhaps the most eloquent of the dogmatic New Atheists, repeatedly indicted religion both for the violence that has resulted in its name and for the propensity it allows to believe without proof. A tagline of the website "Daily Hitchens" proclaimed, "what can be asserted without proof can be dismissed without proof."[5] This is a bit like applying the "eye for an eye" form of justice to the field of personal conviction. Hitchens provides excellent criticisms of the validity of religious belief statements, and he is certainly correct in criticizing the reliance on any uncritical literalist interpretation of scripture. He poses important challenges to exercise critical reason. However, insofar as he reduces all of the religious life to such uncritical literalist claims and dismisses all possible conversation about religious faith on this basis, he falls short in contributing to a serious and thoughtful conversation about how richly humanity can express what we do not know and can respond creatively to such experience. There is a legitimate dimension to the question of the validity of religious belief or the investigation into what qualifies as evidence for religious belief. However, to those who reduce the religious life to a simple certitude about a religious creed that asks people to believe in the unbelievable, thereby reducing the religious life to a belief in the "talking snake," I want to say, "No, religion is *not* about a talking snake." Those atheist critics of religion may respond by saying that this reductionist view of faith is not theirs, but what the fundamentalists in fact advocate. They may be correct in this, but it is simply irresponsible to allow only the most dogmatic and uncritical among us to define the conversation we all *can have* and *should have* about religious faith and questions of ultimacy.

On the other hand, this book speaks also to religious fundamentalists who defend their interpretations of reality on their particular "literal" reading of scripture and insist on the certain and absolute truth of those particular faith propositions about God and human destiny. Any so-called literal reading of scripture depends on multiple interpretive decisions, including how to translate words and ideas from ancient languages into modern languages, which verses to prioritize over others, how to understand the "original" meaning intended by those ancient writers or translators for their particular audience, and how to extrapolate from the particular circumstances addressed at the time to our very different circumstances. Claims to understand what holy scripture literally and "clearly says" impose several levels of interpretation on the words of scripture, and any denials of the role of interpretive decision-making are simply false. Such fundamentalists need to be reminded just as much as the dogmatic atheists that faith is not about a talking snake. So I find myself resisting dogmatism in religious belief in both directions. Both fundamentalist defenders of the literal meaning of scripture and atheist critics of religious faith miss vital points about the rich and dynamic character of spiritual questioning and answering. Both camps mistakenly see the power of faith to lie in the dogmatic reception of scripture as straightforward propositional statements that describe reality in the flattest and most uninspired way possible. Within the hallowed halls of academic philosophy of religion, this is described as an onto-theological problem, meaning that whereas religious faith purports to deal with what is *ultimate* reality, beyond the visible world of things we can understand and manipulate, both fundamentalist defense of faith as certitude and atheist dismissal of faith as irrationality effectively reduce the ultimate and transcendent subject of religion, or the sacred, to the finite world of things. In other words, they confuse what is finite with the infinite, and they collapse transcendence into immanence. The passion on both sides reflects a deep anxiety and insecurity with the religious value of mystery (not to be confused with blind acceptance of whatever one does not understand). In the twenty-first century we are moving through a time of rapid cultural changes. Many experience these changes as frightening threats to security and respond with a strident trenchancy in matters of faith and reason. Therefore, many retreat to positions that are more comfortable, due to their clarity and simplicity, if untenable for contemporary culture.

Even a brief list of the real dangers of dogmatic fundamentalism presents a bleak picture. The hostility toward any scientific study that challenges biblical accounts of divine creation and providence has led many conservative Christian Americans to confuse the scientific method with the results; it influences educational policy and the engineering of our science textbooks, ranging from the addition of stickers announcing that "evolution is just a theory" to more activist creationism impacting the science curriculum.[6] A handful of biblical verses are used out of context to legitimate moral judgment and legal discrimination of homosexuality, without considering anything more than the narrow literal meaning today of a text that emerged in a very different cultural setting and that can, like any sacred text, be read in a number of ways. Enforcement of the *hudud* laws by Muslim fundamentalists subject contemporaries to the moral norms arrived at by an altogether human and narrow interpretation of a sacred text compiled in language most appropriate for a seventh-century Arabian society. Claims to rely only on the literal meaning of scripture without any human interpretation are faulty and insidious: faulty because even the decision to rely on literal meanings of words across different settings is an interpretive choice; and insidious because they effectively provide a divine stamp of approval on those human interpretations. Behind all of these is a claim to absolutism on the part of particular narrow interpretations. Absolutism often helps legitimate violence for a "higher cause" or "higher law" that claims supremacy and resists critical examination because it is by definition purportedly of nonhuman origin.

Examples abound of violence justified on the grounds that God demands it of the faithful. Of course, such judgments are usually the interpretations of religious leaders who claim to deliver the unquestionable intentions of God. Perhaps the most egregious and most publicized case in recent history is Osama bin Laden's 1996 call for jihad against Americans. Despite repeated condemnation by Islamic legal authorities of bin Laden's abuse of the Islamic principle of jihad, a dangerous minority continued to appeal to this so-called higher law for divine justice. Of course, violent suppression of freedom of thought is not exclusively the result of religious absolutism. Totalitarian governments have employed atheism to dethrone any transcendent divine judge as a source of a higher law and seize for themselves an absolute authority. The dangers of absolutism are clear in the big picture. In the particular conversation taken up here, the problem is the closure and narrowness of reflection that results from dogmatic thinking, whether in defense of religious faith or against it.

Atheism and agnosticism are more tolerated today than in times past. There is greater acknowledgment today that there is room in the traditional religions for serious doubt. I find this contemporary tolerance of diverse views and capacity for serious doubt most promising, but the fact is doubt is by no means the exclusive property of contemporary critical thought. The very old and longstanding religious traditions themselves have addressed serious and pervasive doubt for thousands of years. Doubt is neither a modern loss of faith that is to be lamented as part of some unfortunate postmodern decline (likely to be blamed on the 1960s hippie movements) nor an innovation we supposedly enlightened moderns can impose on the traditions to improve and reform them. What we find when we examine how the traditions have addressed religious faith is that faith is not unshakable certitude, and doubt is not a gutless lack of nerve or an intellectual skepticism. What today's dogmatists on either side miss is the tremendous capacity within the longstanding global religious traditions for self-criticism, self-correction, and self-transcendence. Against the charge that religion itself is dogmatic by nature, the religions contain numerous important resources that actively resist dogmatism. Rather than lead us away from the organized religious traditions of our heritage, the deeper middle way necessary today between certitude and skepticism guides us back into these internally diverse and elastic traditions to plumb the resources fostered there for battling dogmatism in the interest of spiritual depth.

This middle way values religiosity without denying rational, scientific, historical, or psychological knowledge, one that can articulate the deeply interwoven dimensions of faith and doubt without a simplistic reduction to one or the other. This middle way should not be confused with the popular call for "religious moderates" to speak out against extremism. That interpretation mistakenly implies that any serious commitment to religious faith must naturally be extremist. The "moderate" stance can easily represent a vague and noncommitted religious faith. In contrast, the middle way that is desperately needed today articulates a robustly committed spirituality that refuses to rest with easy creedal statements or with a dogmatic insistence on having all the answers.

James P. Carse, in *The Religious Case Against Belief*, distinguishes religions from belief systems, and the religious from believers.[7] Beliefs, on his reading, depend on straightforward propositions that seek to describe the world while religion involves poetic response to the unknown depth or source of the world. Believers articulate belief statements explicitly to refute other opposing beliefs. The religious articulate a depth of experience that does not define itself by opposing some other experience. Where believers seek to end their ignorance and claim to know something with great certainty (a certainty that even critical knowledge does not possess), the religious respond to a reality that they clearly experience yet cannot positively describe. Carse describes a "higher ignorance" or a "learned ignorance" at the heart of religion that we witness especially among the great mystics. It resembles the mystical project of unknowing to be examined in chapter 5 of this book. John Caputo, in *On Religion*, discussed in chapter 6, suggests likewise that we do not know what it is we love when we love God, and that this not knowing is precisely *who we are* as religious human beings.[8] Against this backdrop of the value of a higher ignorance, Carse diagnoses what he calls a second Age of Faith, in which religions are becoming too closely aligned with belief systems. The growing fundamentalism in the contemporary age is evidence of such an unholy marriage of religion (which should be, according to Carse and Caputo, an abiding engagement with ignorance or the lack of knowledge) with belief (which, for Carse, seeks to end ignorance by claiming descriptive knowledge). Religion is being overtaken by ideology, but nevertheless, Carse closes his book by observing that the poets will continue to emerge and evoke our wonder at the sacred depth of our experience. Greater and deeper wonder is what he calls for in the contemporary world, but it can emerge only by developing and nurturing such a learned ignorance.

This book echoes Carse's valuation of a learned ignorance, and while the distinction he draws between religion and belief is important, I am reluctant to draw it quite so sharply as to dismiss the role belief plays in religion. Belief statements seek explicitly to describe the world we inhabit, prescribe how we should inhabit it, and articulate our proper relationship with ourselves, with the sacred, and with others. They are therefore a central component in religion and faith. I would not divorce them as clearly as Carse seems willing to do. The danger is that we are left with a religious consciousness without definable content, a poetic feeling of wonder or appreciation for the sacred dimension of our existence without any definable object, or a "spiritual not religious" identification that is simply overused by many who are attracted to that convenient lack of definition. In resisting the dogmatist articulations of faith or doubt, we must also be on guard against a convenient and casual spiritual eclecticism that allows one to dabble with various beliefs that one finds attractive without allowing oneself to be challenged and changed by them. The spiritual life ought not only to be about seeking and discovering one's love(s), but must also be about the commitment and hard work of *lov-ing* that changes who one is. Therefore, my intention in this book is to call attention to components of religious faith that are not swallowed up by straightforward belief propositions. Religious faith certainly includes beliefs that describe our place in the world in which we discover ourselves. However, an assent to such belief statements does not constitute faith. Faith lies in the response of wonder that Carse describes, and evokes a journey described in the pages that follow as a posture of trust, active commitment and responsibility, faithful protest and doubt or unknowing, and active hope. It is a journey that does not quickly arrive at a secure destination. Rather, because religious faith has principally to do with what Paul Tillich calls an Infinite Concern, what the mystics have considered an abyss or a ground-less ground, what Karl Barth terms revelation that breaks in on our own learning and thinking, or what Carse terms a learned ignorance because a revealed or revealing God does not, in the act of revelation, lose the char-acter of mystery, religious faith always remains our human response to the unknown around us and the unknowability that defines us. Faith cannot be the elimination of doubt or the journey beyond doubt. Faith might better be described as a dynamic journey of believing, doubting, and trusting that constitutes one's humanity and one's nature as spirit. Faith and doubt are not simple polar opposites in this vision, but may reflect something like a binary star, that is, a pair of stars that orbit around a common center of mass. They feed off each other, orbiting around the unfathomable depth experience of religion, which both attracts us and terrifies us, comforts us and calls us to account for our comforts and our very presence. This book looks at substantial articulations of such doubting and trusting that are often overshadowed by the loud reductions of faith to dogmatic belief seen among both the atheistic dismissals of religious faith and the fundamentalist avowals of creedal statements.

In the interest of challenging our conceptions about the experience of faith, I want to cite briefly the example of the late Mother Teresa of Calcutta, whose reflections are recorded in her private letters published in 2007 under the title, *Mother Teresa: Come Be My Light.*[9] This woman's humility, generosity of spirit, and impossible saintliness are very well known around the world. The publication of her private correspondence revealed to the world the achingly painful suffering she experienced in terms of her own faith. Her words echo "the dark night of the soul" described by many mystics, most notably, the sixteenth-century St. John of the Cross. Commentators have noted the remarkable length (lasting many years without relief) and depth of Mother Teresa's experience of darkness, and her words articulate the immense suffering she experienced. "The place of God in my soul is blank.—There is no God in me.—When the pain of longing is so great—I just long & long for God—and then it is that I feel—He does not want me—He is not there."[10] Mother Teresa expresses an utter lack of the vital and sustaining connection to God that she so desperately craved. It introduces a complicated dimension to her faith, which, despite the lack of experiential assurance, led her to continue relentlessly her work to love and care for the souls abandoned by the rest of the world. She asks God in another letter, "Where is my faith?—even deep down, right in, there is nothing but emptiness & darkness.—My God, how painful is this unknown pain. . . . I am told God loves me—and yet the reality of darkness & coldness & emptiness is so great that nothing touches my soul."[11] Her words display a faith that does not rely on evidence or the assurances of inner experience, and yet this is not a simple expression of doubts about the gospel or God's intentions or God's work to be fulfilled in the world.

Brian Kolodiejchuk calls attention to the sharp contrast between the pain Mother Teresa was experiencing and the way she chose to act, guided by pure faith. "Paradoxically, the more she felt stripped of faith, the more her reverence and love for God grew."[12] This is truly a leap of faith that does not rely on confident belief, especially in the experience of darkness where she did not enjoy assurance of God's presence. Connected in her experience are the pain caused by God's absence, extreme longing for God's presence, and love and reverence as her response to this experience. After corresponding with her confessor regarding this continual pain of God's absence, she comes to regard the darkness itself with love because it links her with Jesus' own suffering. Her confessor teaches her that her longing for God is itself a gift from God that links her to God most intimately and thoroughly. "Thirst is more than absence of water. It is not experienced by stones, but only by living beings that depend on water. Who knows more about living water, the person who opens the water tap daily without much thinking, or the thirst tortured traveler in the desert in search for a spring?"[13] The thirst and longing for God are themselves faith experiences because they are not possible without the soul's unequivocal orientation toward God. They confirm the nature of the soul in solidarity with God. Mother Teresa's self-described experience raises a complicated and challenging expression of faith. It challenges us because the depth of suffering encountered is so extreme and longstanding because it exhibits a true leap of faith without assurance, a commitment to God's work in the world without the assurance of experiencing God's presence in the soul, and because it defies our categories of faith and doubt, including the ones I employ in this book. As such, I cite it only as a testament to the complicated and transcendent relationship inherent in the religious life that does not simply oppose faith and doubt and as a testament to the radical power of doubt and the experience of darkness to confirm the ultimacy of a faith perspective. As Carse describes, where belief seeks to end ignorance by settling on a presumed knowledge, religion (or faith in my reading) must embrace a higher ignorance. Faith must find a way to make itself at home with the unknown, to dwell in the discomfort of not knowing, or as we see in Mother Teresa's account, in the pain and suffering of darkness and utter absence of God. Dimensions of sustained ignorance, unknowing, doubt, or skepticism all are necessary to prevent reducing faith in the transcendent and ultimate sacred to an idolization of what is finite and our own.[14]

The approach taken in this book may strike many as unconventional, as it traverses several different religious traditions and communities, without privileging any particular one. I am led to this work as a student of religion. This work is not confessional, but it is certainly influenced by perspectivalism and ideological commitments that affect all philosophical, historical, and confessional approaches. I have not attempted a comprehensive study of the treatment of faith and doubt in the world's religious traditions, although that would be a rewarding and much-needed project. My goals here are far less ambitious, though perhaps no less bold in their premise that setting aside questions of what the religions agree and disagree on, we nevertheless can learn much from one another. The first lesson may likely be that we know a little less than we believed and have much to learn. Therefore, this is not a properly comparative study of faith, but a humble foray into what may be termed parallel study of the world's religious traditions and teachings. Today, we can discern in the religious climate two broad trends of concern.

One is that despite our greater interaction with people of different religious traditions and commitments and the greater access we have to information about the variety of religious ideas and practices, we have a great deal of work to do in learning about other people's commitments. In addition, we find fervent episodes of interreligious dialogue occurring everywhere among liberals and skeptics across different traditions. What we desperately need, however, is greater genuine dialogue among the religiously conservative and committed. The collective conversation would benefit from the insights and concerns of those deeply entrenched commitments. They in turn need to become more familiar with the variety of interpretations and approaches that stretch the boundaries of their own broader religious traditions. The intention throughout this book is to locate religious resources of faith that can inhabit the uncomfortable yet deeply nourishing space that spiritual seekers of different traditions have described beyond certitude, without reducing the mystery of the sacred to idols that can be manipulated.

The case against dogmatism is laid out progressively through six chapters, organized into three distinct parts. The first part of the book addresses components of faith that rely not on creedal statements, but on characteristic experiences of trust and commitments to a mode of human responsibility. Chapter 1 examines faith understood as a posture of trust, a feeling of absolute dependence, humility, and connection to a larger world. This chapter highlights, for example, the value ascribed to humility in Christian mysticism and Muslim piety, nineteenth-century Christian theologian Friedrich Schleiermacher's discussion of faith as a feeling of absolute dependence, and Hindu *puja*, or ritual worship, as an enactment of cosmic belonging. Chapter 2 examines faith understood as action, commitment, and responsibility. This chapter discusses Hindu teachings on *dharma*, or sacred duty, C. S. Lewis's treatment of Christian responsibility in the fictional world of Narnia, Islamic constructions of religion as human responsibility in the world, and Jewish depictions of faith as covenantal responsibility to struggle in a worthy relationship with God.

While part 1 draws into conversation particular examples from among the different world traditions, the second part of the book uses a tradition-specific approach to investigate doubt as protest against or transcendence of worldly norms. Chapter 3 examines how the Protestant Principle is reflected in three figures who heavily influenced twentieth-century Christian theology, Søren Kierkegaard, Karl Barth, and Paul Tillich, and exhibits the integral relationship between Christian faith, doubt, protest, and the paradox that constitutes human religiosity at the juncture between the finite and the infinite. Chapter 4 examines how dimensions of doubt inform Hindu philosophy and epic and mythological narrative to enact spiritual transcendence. This chapter looks at the ways in which the Upanishadic value of intuition, the *Bhagavad Gita*'s teaching of *bhakti*, the doctrine of *maya*, and the divine juxtaposition of contradictions in the divine figure of Shiva embody spiritual transcendence of conventional human understanding.

Building on the argument laid out through the multifaceted descriptive analysis of the faith posture and commitment of part 1 and the targeted treatment of doubt in modern Protestant Christian thought and Hindu philosophical and narrative traditions of part 2, part 3 roughly outlines possible components of a nondogmatic faith. Chapter 5 examines how self-doubt or skepticism can function as a needed check on dogmatism by tearing down the idols we inevitably construct. This chapter looks at some atheist criticisms of dogmatism as well as the mystical paths of unknowing as taught by theistic Christian mystics and in nontheistic Buddhist traditions of emptiness. Chapter 6 examines Jürgen Moltmann's theology of hope, Raimon Panikkar's pluralism, and John Caputo's analysis of religion as love for the impossible as three constructive contemporary proposals for formulating a more tenable relationship between faith and doubt, one that exercises an expectant hope tempered by contemporary realism.

PART ONE

Re-examining Faith in Action

CHAPTER ONE

POSTURES OF TRUST

Medieval Christian theologians drew a telling distinction between *fides qua*, the act of faith or trust in God, and *fides quae*, the specific content of belief statements. The former refers to the experience of having faith, of trusting in God, of recognizing the world as God's world. The latter refers to what one believes about that world, themselves, and God. At first glance, this distinction may look like one between a vague sort of feeling and a clearly articulated faith, but the way the medievals responded to these two forms of faith is interesting. They referred to the former as implicit faith and to the latter as explicit faith. Those with implicit faith participate in the life of church tradition in obedience without a clear and explicit understanding of the doctrines of the church. Explicit faith refers to the ability to articulate what one believes and why. Interestingly, the medievals held that implicit faith, on its own, was enough for a person's salvation, but explicit faith alone was not. Knowing the doctrines of the church and articulating them clearly was not viewed as sufficient to guarantee salvation. Trust, obedience, and participation in the tradition were required. On the one hand, this suggests a pragmatic concern with the uniformity of external practice over the intellectual deliberation on doctrine, and allows a simpler, minimalist sort of faith for the general uneducated medieval public that was distinct from the deliberate learning and doctrinal interpretation that was part of monastic study. On the other hand, the link between trust, obedience, and participation, or *fides qua*, and their practical superiority to the explicitly stated faith of *fides quae*, suggests that the act of trusting God was considered far more integral to the value of faith than one's clear understanding of God. Thomas Aquinas, while distinguishing faith from knowledge, still suggested that faith does yield proper knowledge of God because it is rooted in the act of assent to divinely revealed propositions of faith as directed by

God's grace. The act of assent or trust that takes places in faith enacts a proper relationship to God's grace.

It is this priority of trusting God over creedal propositions that informs this first chapter. In many ways this runs counter to the need often articulated in today's very self-conscious society, that one should understand exactly why one believes something for it to be valuable and strong. I do not intend in this book to trace the development of the modern emphasis on what one believes, but we can certainly point to the Enlightenment, the Protestant Reformation, and the rising values of individualism, reason, and autonomy to identify the multilayered influences of this pattern of thinking. In one sense, modern people have appropriated the Socratic intuition that "a life unexamined is not worth living" to criticize faith that is unarticulated as perhaps only immature and inferior. We even refer to it in a derogatory manner as "blind faith." While that is very often a valid criticism of those who unreflectively cling to their views, it may also be a mistake to privilege the intellectual and logical exposition of doctrine over the emotional act described by the religious as trust. Although faith certainly includes the articulation of certain positive beliefs, its exclusive focus can overstate the role of individual autonomy in the spiritual life and fail to recognize the degree to which trust embodies an acceptance or acquiescence to being moved by something deeper, larger, or more sovereign.

Part 1 of this book comprises a descriptive approach to faith. If faith is not primarily about certitude or creedal statements, what is it? This first chapter explores several articulations of faith as the consciousness of humility or dependence, on the one hand, and belonging to a world of meaning, on the other hand. These two forms of experience together identify some defining sense of trust in the sacred. Treating them in turn allows me to better identify the relationship between humility and belonging, or between consciousness of dependence and spiritual confidence. I begin with a discussion of humility, as treated by several Christian mystics and ritually enacted by Muslims in the five pillars of faith. Humility functions somewhat differently in Christian reflection and Muslim reflection, given the unique Christian espousal of the doctrine of original sin. Next, I consider nineteenth-century Christian theologian Friedrich Schleiermacher's treatment of religious experience and Christian God-consciousness. Described in Christian terms, this consciousness of absolute dependence suggests two distinct moments: the consciousness of one's finite limitations and estrangement from God, and the consciousness of the reconciliation promised in God. The experience of reconciliation, whether as promise or as realized, then takes us to the third section of the chapter, which considers in detail a South Indian Hindu puja, the *Satyanarayana vrata*, as a ritual and mythic enactment of belonging to a larger world. These postures of humility, absolute dependence, and belonging are not mutually exclusive, but rather, together express the components of two complementary elements of religious consciousness: finitude and infinite possibility, or finitude and transcendence. The posture of religious faith both confronts one's human finitude and trusts in God's plan or in the transcendence anticipated in one's relation to sacred reality.

Humility as the Door to Faith

The Power of Humility for the Christian Mystics

Mysticism refers to the pursuit of immediate connection or communion with God or sacred reality, and it employs various spiritual techniques and training to bring about such direct experience.[1] The Sufi tradition in Islam describes the mystic as one who is impatient for God. While others may hope to unite with God in the afterlife, the mystic craves this contemplative union right here, right now, in the midst of life. The writings of the mystics of different traditions are often filled with expressions of aching hunger or desperate thirst for the divine object of devotion.

Among several common elements in the writings of the Christian mystics is the articulated need for discipline and structure in the practice of contemplative prayer. Teresa of Avila, a sixteenth-century Spanish Carmelite nun, wrote *The Interior Castle* as a manual on contemplative prayer for her fellow nuns. In it, she describes the soul as a castle composed of many mansions, and prayer as the door by which one enters this interior castle. The thirteenth-century Italian theologian Bonaventure likewise explains in *The Journey of the Mind to God* that the journey to seeing God more clearly begins with prayer. He writes that prayer is the "mother and origin of every upward striving of the soul." By praying, he says, "we are given light to discern the steps of the soul's ascent to God. For we are so created that the material universe itself is a ladder by which we may ascend to God."[2] There are many spiritual fruits that are born out of the disciplined life of prayer for mystics, but the one that is most applicable for the present discussion is the lesson of humility.

In Christian teaching, believers must recognize their own sinful nature and their dependence on God. Teresa writes, "It is God's will that His elect should be conscious of their misery and so He withdraws His help from them a little—and no more than that is needed to make us recognize our limitations very quickly."[3] Recognizing one's own limitations enables an individual to see clearly what she lacks and needs and what she receives only from God. This requires a surrender of the will to God's will that is achieved only as the result of great spiritual training and discipline to overcome and subdue the individual will. She writes, "what matters is not whether or not we wear a religious habit; it is whether we try to practice the virtues, and make a complete surrender of our wills to God and order our lives as His majesty ordains."[4] What such a commitment requires above all is a humble and thorough surrender to God's will. Teresa says it is the lack of humility that prevents progress in the spiritual life and through the interior castle that is the soul. She urges her readers to renounce self-love and self-will in a particularly eloquent image of a silkworm, which she likens to the soul that truly comes to life when it surrenders its will and receives the Holy Spirit and nourishes itself with church teaching, meditations, and sermons. "Let the silkworm die—let it die, as in fact it does when it has completed the work which it was created to do. Then we shall see God and shall ourselves be as completely hidden in His greatness as is this little worm in its cocoon."[5] Teresa even identifies becoming spiritual with becoming "slaves of God."

Many readers note with interest a paradoxical use of humility in Teresa's work. While she urges humility and claims weakness, her actions argue otherwise, as she boldly seeks to teach others based on her spiritual experience. It seems her humility is only with respect to God and not to the male priest confessors whose judgments she depended on. Carol Slade presents a feminist analysis of Teresa's strategic use of humility to establish her authority to teach the word of God in a climate where a woman independently interpreting scripture would have faced excommunication.[6] Slade points out the strange position in which Teresa found herself. She was at the mercy of male priests to evaluate her spiritual experience, yet most of those confessors did not have the range or intensity of spiritual experience she did, so she needed to supplement her accounts of experience with the criteria for measuring them; therefore, she advises confessors to use correspondence with scripture as the test of truth. Slade argues that Teresa's feminist interpretive principle consists of a dual hermeneutic of humility and enjoyment. With the former, she denies any capacity to understand scripture by active means of analysis. However, this very inability enables women to receive understanding by direct communication with God, from the enjoyment of spiritual union.[7] Teresa uses an admission of weakness to assert the strength of her authority to teach the word of God. It is a cunning and powerful sort of authority, as she denies any individual power as a woman and instead claims only a passive reception of God's direct communication, which she claims women are better able to receive because they are not inhibited by the masculine skills of rational analysis. Teresa's clever citations within her prayer manual of the male superiors who would undoubtedly read and correct her own poor attempts at communication are themselves a strategic cautionary defense against any potential charges of heresy. Beyond such strategic claims of weakness on her part as a mere woman, Teresa's use of humility in the service of self-discipline to help prepare the soul to approach God echoes themes raised by other Christian mystics.

Perhaps fourteenth-century English nun Julian of Norwich expresses the theological purpose of suffering and humility in the most powerful and imaginative way. Like Teresa, she suggests that God intends people to learn humility, to become conscious of their limitations in order to become open to God's help and grace. Julian uses the rich metaphor of a mother whose tender yet tough love will lead her child to learning its limitations.

> Often when our falling and our wretchedness are shown to us, we are so much afraid and so greatly ashamed of ourselves that we scarcely know where we can put ourselves. But then our courteous Mother does not wish us to flee away, for nothing would be less pleasing to him; but he then wants us to behave like a child. For when it is distressed and frightened, it runs quickly to its mother; and if it can do no more, it calls to the mother for help with all its might. So he wants us to act as a meek child, saying: My kind Mother, my gracious Mother, my beloved Mother, have mercy on me. I have made myself filthy and unlike you, and I may not and cannot make it right except with your help and grace.[8]

In Julian's description, shame is not the best response to the clear understanding of our wretchedness because it can be paralyzing. The related but distinct posture of humility, however, is the first step toward genuine prayer because it means both admitting a need for help and requesting that help.

Humility can serve as a first step in prayer or proper relationship to God, by admitting need and vulnerability because it enables openness and receptivity to the other. Just as we become open to another person when we ask a genuine question and then listen because we do not already know the answer, humility, by admitting a need for something beyond our own production capability, enables receptivity to God. Prayer as a faithful address to God reflects a posture that is very different from a creedal assent to certain propositions about God. Rather than describe God in the detached way in which we talk about mere things (a very presumptive stance, in any religious circle), prayer hopes to engage God in a plaintive relationship and therefore respects the distance and transcendence of the sacred over the world of things that we can understand, manipulate, and discuss.

Julian explains that only by seeing our weaknesses clearly can we come to enjoy spiritual rest in grace. Humility is necessary to open the heart from its own self-sufficiency, to make it open to what can only be given it by God in grace. "Though we may be lifted up high into contemplation by the special gift of our Lord, still, together with this, we must necessarily have knowledge and sight of our sin and of our feebleness; for without this knowledge we may not have true meekness, and without this we cannot be safe."[9] Meekness or humility is a necessary spiritual virtue because without it, we are unable to be receptive to God's entering into us and working on us. Here Julian connects the value of humility with a traditional Christian interpretation of grace, in which God's salvation is given to individuals as a gift, a free gift that cannot be earned or deserved or repaid. Given the Christian concept of God's grace, humility is needed for salvation. An individual must acknowledge her weakness in order to become open enough to receive this unearned gift. In fact, Christian theologians like twentieth-century British author C. S. Lewis discuss the spiritual value of trying to earn salvation, of working hard to better oneself, even while supporting the doctrines of original sin and divine grace and acknowledging that we cannot perfect ourselves. Aiming for self-perfection is ultimately doomed, but it may be a necessary preliminary step because this failure to perfect oneself prepares one to become open to God's grace through genuine humility.[10]

Having discussed the prominent Christian mystical acknowledgment of the need for humility, I turn now to some ritual manifestations of humility in Islamic tradition. Whereas the Christian mystical concern is with adequately preparing to become open to the need for God's grace, in Islam, the virtue of humility helps express the absolute and unique sovereignty of God.

The Exercise of Humility and Islamic Faith

The five pillars of Islamic faith embody the value of humility in the spiritual life, and they help illustrate the experience of faith as a posture of trust in God rather than a set of beliefs.[11] Chapter 2 expands on this discussion with a look at an Islamic treatment of the integral human responsibility as God's deputies on earth. This section focuses on the theme of humility as it is exercised in the five pillars of faith, that is, the five ritual observances required for Muslim identity: the *shahadah*, or witness to faith; *salat*, or daily prayer; *zakat*, or almsgiving; Ramadan, a month-long fast; and the Hajj, or pilgrimage.

The shahadah is simply the witness to Muslim faith, and it consists of reciting the words, "There is no God but God, and Muhammad is His messenger." The first part of the shahadah articulates divine unity, absoluteness, and uniqueness, while the second part specifies the revelation given to Muhammad and recorded in the Qur'an as authoritative. The shahadah is recited at the beginning of every salat, or daily prayer; it is whispered into the ears of newborn infants, and its solemn and sincere repetition before witnesses is the only requirement for conversion into Islamic faith. The uniqueness of God suggested in the first part of the shahadah is central to Islamic theology, and requires the proper human posture of humility. There is no one like God. "God is One," encapsulated in the Islamic principle of *tawhid*, or divine unity, means not only number, but also absoluteness. Unity or oneness is a powerful way in the monotheistic traditions of speaking about power, transcendence, and absoluteness.[12] For Muslims, more than perhaps for Christians who interpret the incarnation as a revelation of God as Immanuel, or God with us, God is unique or uniquely absolute. No one can be compared to God.[13] Consider the stark difference between the Islamic view of God as unlike any other and the Christian view of God as Father.

While some see the Christian idea of God's fatherhood as purely metaphorical, there is likewise a strong tradition in Christian theology of affirming this as a substantive part of God's revelation. For Christians, the doctrine of the incarnation (that God has become incarnate in Jesus Christ) and the doctrine of the Trinity (that God has revealed His nature to be triune as Father, Son, and Spirit) stipulate that these are not mere metaphors to further human understanding, but revelation of God's nature. For Christians, God has revealed in Jesus God's nature to be Father to a Son and to be among and with humanity. Jesus reveals that God is to be related to as a father, as best seen in the prayer he teaches his disciples, "Our Father who art in heaven." While this does not exclude the sense that God's fatherhood is metaphorical, it does intensify the appropriateness of relating to God in such concrete and intimate ways. In a Christian view of the incarnation, by becoming flesh, God has explicitly rejected any sense of remoteness or unapproachability and instead become quite directly present as "one of us," encountered through our own human relationships.[14]

In Islamic theology, God is quite explicitly *not* "one of us." God is unique. This does not mean, however, that Muslims emphasize God's remoteness from human life. In fact, the very opposite ensues: because God is unique of *every* particular thing, God is intimately among *all* things. Muslims caution against identifying God with any particular thing because what so often happens as a result is the confusion of that particular thing with the divine and the idolization of something that is not divine. Hence, Muslims view the Christian worship of Jesus as idolatry. Theologically, to say that God has a son compromises divine uniqueness. This should serve to remind us that what makes theo-*logical* sense in Christian tradition does not make theo-*logical* sense in Islamic tradition. This is because, while they are not completely systematic and closed wholes, religious traditions are dynamic webs of interrelated concepts and worldviews that help define the broad parameters of their theologies. Each tradition has its own cohesive web of interpretive parameters. For Christians, the incarnation and the Trinity are central, and they suggest the intimacy with which God miraculously and graciously becomes directly present among people. For Muslims, the uniqueness of God is central to emphasizing God's absoluteness. The shahadah's articulation of "no God but God" is not just a declaration of the number of actual deities in the universe, but a declaration of the singularity of proper worship. Proclaiming "all the world belongs to God," Muslims emphasize that all human worship is to be accorded to God, and not to any other, not to anything finite, not to the pursuit of wealth, fame, or status, not to a particular person or thing, whatever it may be. The proper recognition of God as absolute and unique plays a significant role in the religious posture of humility, as only God is worthy of worship.

Salat, the second of the pillars of Islamic faith, is the practice of daily prayer. Muslims may pray spontaneously and personally at any time, but *salat* refers to the five required "appointments" Muslims have with God each day.[15] The practice of daily prayer reveals at least three particular ways of exercising humility in ritual life.

First, it demands the discipline to structure one's day around these fixed times for prayer. Just as the shahadah expresses God's sovereignty over all other concerns, the requirement of daily prayer establishes its value above all the other pressing matters each day may bring. This does not imply ritual exactitude, as exceptions are allowed and accommodations made when the specific times of daily prayer cannot be honored. However, devout Muslims are also taught that any prayer that is missed for a good reason must be completed when the time allows.

Second, the repeated gesture of prostrating oneself on a prayer rug during salat ritually enacts the exercise of humility. Any religious ritual, by definition, requires some physical act, some bodily gesture. An effective ritual, methodologically speaking, connects closely the physical action or gesture with the emotional and spiritual value that is being exercised. Prostrating oneself, kneeling, and then touching the forehead to the ground is a dramatic physical gesture and both requires humility and recalls the need for humility. It is a telling lesson for a new convert to discover how much discomfort and resistance she or he feels in performing prostration, whether in Islamic prayer, Hindu puja, or Buddhist meditation.

Third, the effect of humility is expressed in the uniformity of ritual prayer. The Qur'an teaches that everyone is equal before God. At each daily prayer, individuals line up side by side, participating in the same ritual at the same time, facing in the same direction of Mecca, worldwide.[16] Remarkably, the uniformity of the ritual has been preserved over centuries and throughout diverse cultures. More than an explicit expression of humility, this uniformity evokes the sense that one is a small part of something much larger and wider than oneself, a small part of an infinite yet united whole that is the Islamic community, or *ummah*.

Zakat, the third pillar of faith, is an obligatory tax paid to support established charitable causes. Tradition requires that one donate 2.5 percent of one's total accumulated wealth as well as 10 percent of one's annual income. In premodern cultures this money was used to fund community support for widows and orphans (the most vulnerable members of society), and to build mosques, dams, and other institutions deemed necessary for the community. Ideally, according to Qur'anic teaching, wealth should not be accumulated and hoarded by a few individuals or families, but should circulate equitably for the benefit of all. This practice expresses humility to the extent that it recognizes all wealth as a gift from God that is to be used and shared by all. Those who have more are not intended to value its accumulation, but are made responsible (by virtue of God's generosity to them) for the welfare of the rest of the community.

The Ramadan fast and the Hajj are the remaining two pillars of Islam. Even Muslims who do not rigorously practice daily prayer participate in the Ramadan fast. For one month, Muslims around the world abstain from food and drink, including water, from daybreak to sunset. The mood during the month varies between being solemn, as pious individuals sacrifice their comfort and ease, and being quite festive and jovial, as Muslims gather at sundown to break the fast together with a special meal called iftar. The month of Ramadan represents in many ways an especially spiritually charged time. Tradition holds that it was during the month of Ramadan that Muhammad first began to receive revelations from God, and in fact, that all earlier revelation as well—for example, the Torah—was received during the month of Ramadan. Ramadan expresses the value of humility in the experience of hunger, as participants in the fast are reminded of their dependence on their bodies and their physical weaknesses. Once again, as a ritual, it is particularly effective as it closely correlates the physical sensations of weakness, hunger, and dependence with the spiritual lesson of the smallness and vulnerability of human life in dependence on God's mercy.

The Hajj, or pilgrimage to Mecca, is a requirement for every Muslim who is able to complete it. Much like the experience evoked during daily prayer of being a small part of a much larger whole community, the Hajj also induces incredible awe, as one joins more than two million other Muslims from around the world to circumambulate the Kaaba, all in ritual uniformity. Upon arriving in Mecca to begin the Hajj, Muslims enter a state of *ihram*, or ritual sanctity. For men, this state of ritual sanctity is also represented in the simple, two-piece, shroud-like white cloth that one wraps oneself in. The resemblance to a burial shroud echoes the symbolism of death and re-birth in the Hajj. To prepare to embark on the Hajj, individuals must settle their financial affairs, write a will, and seek forgiveness from any they have wronged. Once they enter the state of ihram, believers must be perfectly mindful of thoughts and actions, guarding against any impurity. During the days of ihram, sexual intercourse is forbidden, as are anger, jealousy, and other flaws of human emotion. At the end of the Hajj rituals, men shave their heads and women cut a small section of their hair to represent their new, cleansed status as Hajjis.

One particular component of the Hajj, "Standing at Arafat," evokes a sense of humility most sharply. It is in fact the central rite of the Hajj, so that some even remark, "Arafat *is* Hajj." Men and women gather on the hill where Muhammad is said to have given his final sermon; they stand all day long (during what are often extraordinarily dry and hot days in the desert) and pray to God for forgiveness. "Standing at Arafat" is an intensely personal experience in which the believer stands before God, emotionally naked, prepared to embrace God's judgment and seek forgiveness. The ritual is said to foreshadow the future Day of Judgment when all shall be called before God to account for their actions. Many believers break down into tears as they plead for forgiveness from the God they love. This emotional nakedness that is required evokes humility perhaps more deeply than any other element of Muslim ritual practice.

The theme of Muslims belonging to a larger, global community of believers has been raised in this first section on humility. Hindu devotional practice (the focus of the third section) focuses on belonging to a sacred universe. Humility and belonging together articulate ways of thinking about faith in terms of a consciousness of human finitude and its relationship to what infinitely transcends it. Having treated the religious theme of humility, I turn now to how religion has been articulated similarly by Christian theologian Friedrich Schleiermacher in terms of absolute dependence.

Friedrich Schleiermacher: Religious Consciousness of Absolute Dependence

Friedrich Schleiermacher, in the early nineteenth century, in a "modern turn to the human subject," approached religion from the lens of human experi-ence. He demonstrated that one could both theorize about religion from within the realm of human experience and be theologically committed to

Christian dogmatics. In *On Religion: Speeches to Its Cultured Despisers*, Schleiermacher sought, without appeal to any supernatural or divine a priori, to locate the essence of religion not in thinking or acting, but in intuition and feeling. "It wishes to intuit the universe, wishes devoutly to overhear the universe's own manifestations and actions, longs to be grasped and filled by the universe's immediate influences in childlike passivity."[17] Religion, for Schleiermacher, is the intuition of the larger universe of which one plays a tiny part. Religious consciousness intuits everything individual and limited as part of this larger organic whole.

Schleiermacher echoes the descriptions of religious consciousness found in many traditions, that is, seeing the true unity behind all things. A religious mind recognizes all things and all events as the actions of God. Albert Einstein reportedly said, "There are only two ways to live your life. One is as though nothing is a miracle. The other is as though everything is a miracle." A religious person looks at the world and sees the miracle of God's work in the world. Muslims express a similar sentiment when they say that all the world belongs to God, or that all the worldly gifts we enjoy like our very lives, our health, and our wealth, as well as the painful experiences we endure, come only from God. Rabia al-Basri, an eighth-century Sufi poet, said that loving God left her no time to hate the devil. Schleiermacher repeats the words used by mystics in different traditions about seeing everything in life as intrinsically good because it is from God. "To a pious mind religion makes everything holy and valuable, even unholiness and commonness itself, everything it comprehends and does not comprehend."[18] He goes on to say that religion is the enemy of all one-sidedness. While one-sidedness elevates one viewpoint over others as the only legitimate view, religious consciousness recognizes things as interconnected parts of one whole universe.

Schleiermacher published *On Religion: Speeches to Its Cultured Despisers* in 1799, on the eve of the nineteenth century. He was a virtual unknown at the time, but he came to exert immense influence on modern liberal Christianity in particular and on modern philosophy of religion in general. He brought to the study of religion his own early influences of Moravian Pietism and German Romanticism. By articulating religion in feeling and intuition, he was appealing to the culture of German Romanticism that simply did not see religion as an adequate avenue for the highest expression of humanity. The German Romantics turned to art, literature, and poetry as the best ways to express what it meant to be human. In *On Religion*, Schleiermacher sought to counteract the Enlightenment suspicion of religion as a superstitious relic of dogmatism that was alien to the new, modern sensibilities that privileged reason above all, and he did this by appealing to the value of human subjective experience that was so highly valued by the Romantics. He consistently resisted any appeal to the supernatural in explaining the phenomenon of religion, seeing it instead as a universal human capacity, even if it varied in degree of development among people. On Andrew Dole's reading, this allowed Schleiermacher to combine a naturalist or scientific study of religion with an engagement of Christian dogmatics. In the first edition of *On Religion*, which Dole favors over the second edition, which contains revisions that reflect the pressure Schleiermacher faced to defend his work against charges of pantheism, Schleiermacher does not appeal to the divine as the source of religious feeling. The object of religious apprehension is the relationship of everything finite to the universe. Any appeals to God or the gods are claims made within the determinate religious traditions; they are not themselves the content of religious feeling, which lies simply in the connection of everything finite to the infinite universe.[19]

In his later treatise of systematic theology, *The Christian Faith*, Schleiermacher describes Christian religion as the feeling of absolute dependence. He writes, "to feel oneself absolutely dependent and to be conscious of being in relation with God are one and the same thing; and the reason is that absolute dependence is the fundamental relation which must include all others in itself."[20] What exactly does absolute dependence mean? Rooted in the intuition of the universe as an organic infinite whole, it articulates the feeling that we are not self-creating or self-sustaining beings, the "consciousness that the whole of our spontaneous activity comes from a source outside of us."[21] The degree to which Schleiermacher considers the feeling of absolute dependence to be the truth of Christian religious consciousness is expressed in his admiration of the historical Jesus. Instead of admiring the purity of his ethical teaching or the uniqueness of his character, which are all merely human things, Schleiermacher esteems Jesus' clarity about the connection of everything finite to the divine. He finds most noble Jesus' constant reference to God as his "Father who art in heaven," his recognition of the need for God's will to help finite human beings connect with God. While it reiterates his definition of religion as intuition of the unity and infinity of the universal world Spirit, this formulation also emphasizes our recognized need as finite human beings for the infinite world Spirit's assistance. In Christian terms, whatever is most true and real in humans depends on God. Our recognition of our need for God's help (the Christian dependence on grace) to connect us with God is a particular Christian expression of religious consciousness as a feeling of absolute dependence. Beyond being absolutely dependent, we must *affirm* this dependence on God in order to connect with God. Affirming dependence on God enacts both humility before God and belonging to

God for our spiritual destiny. We both recognize our own limitations and failures and affirm the possibilities of divine promise. Just as people often say it is necessary to identify the problem before one can begin to solve it, Christians express the need to confess sinfulness and the need for God's help as a preliminary step to embracing that help, or grace.

From his earlier to his later writing, we can distill from Schleiermacher a sense that religious consciousness consists of a twofold intuition, one outward and one inward. Religious consciousness sees the infinite whole and views oneself as a small part of this whole. Schleiermacher clearly considers the outward aspect of intuiting the infinite and the inward aspect of self-reflection as inextricably linked. God-consciousness is a pious self-consciousness. "In each and every situation, we ought to be conscious of, and sympathetically experience, absolute dependence on God just as we conceive each and every thing as completely conditioned by the interdependence of nature."[22] It is not to say that we find God inside ourselves, but rather that we experience both freedom and dependence in our relationship with the infinite that constitutes human self-identity.

Schleiermacher expresses this twofold consciousness of human finitude and the infinite divine as part of the intuition of Christianity. "The corruptibility of all that is great and divine in human and finite things is one half of the original intuition of Christianity."[23] The other half, he says, is "that certain brilliant and divine points are the source of every betterment of this corruption and of every new and closer union of the finite with the divine."[24] Religion, for Schleiermacher, is the intuition of the infinite, the universe, the whole interconnectedness of life. Christianity in particular intuits the corruptibility of humanity and the divine potential for betterment, and it intuits these two things together. The human experience of estrangement and the divine promise of reconciliation imply each other. This twofold consciousness of one's own human finitude and the capacity to participate in the infinite fullness of God's being is expressed in Christian doctrinal terms as *sin* and *grace*.

The Christian doctrine of original sin expresses the innately limited character of human being and human action. The doctrine of original sin is unique to Christian tradition in the way in which it imputes a hereditary sinfulness on human beings. This doctrine has its roots in the theological outlooks of the first-century apostle Paul and the fourth-century theologian Augustine of Hippo. According to Paul and Augustine, original sin represented the "bad news" of human capability. The depth of this bad news of what humans are capable of improving and perfecting in their nature points to the "good news," the Christian gospel of Jesus and what God has done for human beings in him. The Christian doctrine of grace emphasizes the character of a freely given gift by God, an immeasurable and unequaled gift that cannot be earned or repaid. Schleiermacher's articulation of absolute dependence suggests such a sense of an immeasurable and absolute gift, unlike any other feelings of dependence.[25]

The terms *sin* and *grace* are used so casually among Christians that too many fail to reflect on the very bold claims being made in these Christian doctrines. The doctrine of divine grace as free gift stands out against ordinary human values and ethics that favor fairness and equity in relationships. Most adults interpret "gift" in a very different sense than the Christian doctrine of grace demands. Consider the difference between the absolute gift, as represented in the doctrine of divine grace, and the gift exchange in which we often participate among friends. Most of us, in our ordinary and responsible relationships with others, see gift-giving as an exchange, as the give-and-take balance of good relationships. We try not to simply receive a gift as a free gift. Instead, in the ways we interpret it and respond to it, we very often turn it into an obligation in our minds that must be repaid. A classic example of how we turn gifts into exchanges occurs at weddings. A newly married couple, or their parents, may keep a record of gifts received along with a clear sense of the value of each gift from each sender. Why do we do this? In the short term, it is to provide a record useful for writing thank you notes. In the long term, however, it is so that one day when our friends or our friends' grown children get married, we can reciprocate with a gift of at least the same value. We work very hard not to be in debt to anyone. We strive to keep the give and take of our friendships equitable, taking turns picking up the tab or splitting the check, because we are not comfortable being in debt to those we love. We effectively rob the gift of its free character as gift and replace it with an economical exchange, where we balance out any gift-debts with reciprocal gifts and consider ourselves free from obligation to anyone. The Christian doctrine of divine grace rejects precisely this sort of balance sheet in ultimate human destiny. Unlike the gifts we exchange with one another, divine justification, in the Christian teaching of grace, remains a gift that we cannot earn or repay in kind. Together, the Christian doctrines of sin and grace express the religious consciousness Schleiermacher articulates as absolute dependence and God-consciousness.

In this section, I have examined Schleiermacher's definition of religion as the intuition of the infinite and the posture of absolute dependence, which provides some of the intellectual content of the posture of humility discussed in the first section. Absolute dependence echoes the sense articulated in many traditions of interdependence or connection of everything particular to a larger, single sacred reality. Now that I have dealt with the intellectual content of religious humility and absolute dependence, I can turn to a particular Hindu ritual and narrative expression of belonging to a larger, sacred order. Together, these three sections consider faith as an experience located in a certain posture of existential trust, following the medieval expression of *fides qua*, that may be articulated in terms of humility, absolute dependence, or belonging to a larger world.

Hindu Puja: Belonging to a Protected World

Hindu devotional worship, or puja, reflects these two dimensions of religious response to the Supreme Reality, that is, humility or smallness on the one hand, and connection to an infinite sacred on the other hand. The ritual components of puja embody a sense of transcending one's individual isolated self and participating in a larger world that is God's world.[26] Modern-day puja can be loosely traced to the ancient *yajna*, or Vedic fire sacrifice, performed to ensure social and cosmic harmony, but there are crucial differences between the two. While the yajna required the correct pronunciation of mantras and ritual purity, and therefore had a role in the development of a professional priest class, or Brahmins or *brahmanas*, the rise of group puja reflects part of a radical transformation that occurred between Vedic Brahmanic religion and medieval Hinduism. Key elements of the growing prominence of puja include a focus on bhakti, a path of devotion accessible to all across caste and gender lines; *vrata*, vows taken in exchange for divine blessings; *dana*, gifts given to ensure these divine blessings; and *katha*, stories that explain the mythological roots of the pujas, consequences of human deeds, and divine intervention. The combination of puja and katha in particular helps reinforce moral conduct and promise spiritual merit for ordinary people who express their devotion as recommended. According to Vijay Nath, the recommendation of dana, or gift-giving for spiritual merit, even to members of lower *varnas*, or castes, multiplied the occasions for vratas, thus ensuring the continued essential place of the Brahmins through this radical economic and political transformation that threatened their place of privilege.[27]

In the course of a puja, the worshiper takes necessary steps to purify herself and prepare for an encounter with the deity, and then calls the deity to become present in the image, icon, or idol being used. A worshiper performing a puja to Lakshmi, for example, invites the goddess into the printed image or stone or metal idol and then regards the image or idol as manifesting Lakshmi's presence. She offers food, water, milk, flowers, and clothing—all the good things that one has available to offer as well as praise and devotion—to the deity who is considered temporarily present in the idol. Just as one would welcome a guest into one's home and treat that person with great honor, the worshiper offers obeisance to the deity. After singing devotional songs or mantras and making all the intended offerings, the worshiper then releases Lakshmi from the idol and bids farewell, again as one would bid a fond farewell to an honored guest at the conclusion of a visit. A key consummation of puja is that the special food that was offered first to the deity is distributed and eaten by all the worshipers. This food is *prasad*, which is considered a gift of God's grace. By eating this, the worshipers all take into themselves the divine blessings procured by means of the puja.

The recognition of the many gods and goddesses as symbolic representations of one Supreme Reality, or Brahman, follows in most pujas as well. It is very common, for example, in the course of a puja to honor not one, but several different deities. In preparing for her life as a wife, a new bride may perform a puja to Lakshmi, goddess of household prosperity; she also performs elements of that puja to Ganesha to remove any obstacles from the puja, for example, and to Vishnu to ensure that a loving God will intervene as necessary with a watchful eye over her new family's household.[28] While Schleiermacher's concept of God-consciousness incorporated a sense of one's own smallness and dependence on God's grace, which defined and consecrated one's self in relation to God, Hindu puja articulates one's small but sacred place in a larger world in which human beings are vulnerable to suffering. While puja is a devotional practice, it also plays a role in the dharma (sacred duty) of a Hindu householder. Just as the ancient Vedic fire sacrifices were undertaken to ensure family and social harmony and divine blessings, modern pujas are undertaken with sacramental importance. Even those who are not particularly devout see value in participating in the celebration of various holy days or the pujas that accompany various life-stage transitions like birth, naming, initiation, marriage, and death.

One of the most common pujas performed today in the South Indian state of Andhra Pradesh is the Satyanarayana vrata, which is offered to the god Vishnu in the form of Satyanarayana Swami for the sake of good fortune in one's family life.[29] This puja is described in the *Skanda Purana*. Like many pujas, it involves the ritual narration of a katha, or story, which explains the origin of the puja, the procedure, and its importance. According to the katha, the Satyanarayana puja is a simple but powerful way to obtain both spiritual merit and worldly fulfillment. The story explains that during the time of the Kali Yuga, the last of four stages of the world and a time of moral depravity and strife, the Lord Narayana, witnessing the degree of human suffering, promises by divine grace to ease suffering and fulfill the small and large wishes of his devotees. According to the katha, whoever performs the puja and listens to the story will obtain riches and happiness now and salvation after death. Even those who only observe others performing the puja or listen only to the end of the story and take prasad will see all their sins destroyed by the grace of God.[30] In the course of this puja, the worshiper makes offerings symbolic of one's inner devotion to the nine planets of the cosmos, to Ganesha, to Lakshmi, and to others because all of these represent expressions of how finite human beings address the transcendent Supreme Reality. This puja in particular illustrates the posture of faith as an affirmation of one's place in a larger reality that is within the protective fold of God. It is undertaken most often on the occasions of marriage, housewarming, or prayers for children, but it can be performed at any time, especially when a family feels a need for blessings or the comfort of divine grace. At important life stages like marriage, the individual worshipers are committing to their particular place in a larger family and affirming their role in a larger, interconnected world.

The Satyanarayana puja is an elaborate ritual requiring special foods, incense, betel leaves, betel nuts, coconuts, almonds, a platform on which to place the deity's image, tulsi leaves, copper jars, sandal paste, flower garlands, a conch shell, pieces of cloth, rice grains, ghee, and oil lamps. Like other pujas, it may be performed alone or with the guidance of a trained *pujari*, or priest. According to the katha, the performance of the puja is a promise to God in thanks for the gifts of divine blessings or whatever one desires (children, security, health, or prosperity, for example). Within the story, several characters fail to complete the puja in its entirety and to fulfill their promises to God. One character, Kalavati, has eagerly prayed for her husband's safe return, but on hearing reports of his return, she forgets her promise and fails to eat the prasad, which symbolizes one's grateful acceptance of divine blessings. As a result, she suffers. A lesson that is ritually recited in the puja is that one must be thankful to God and never ignore or forget the gifts one receives from God.

The attitude evoked in puja, described above as welcoming God as a guest who graciously becomes present among the worshipers for a brief visit, reflects a twofold understanding of God as both perfectly transcendent and perfectly immanent. Perfect transcendence enables a thorough immanence, in Hindu theology. In other words, it is only because God or the Absolute transcends *every* particular thing that God can become present in *any* particular thing. Clearly, a loving personal God is addressed in the pujas described above, but while there are irreducible elements of personality in all the deities, what is equally abiding is a sense of the Absolute that is utterly beyond the limitations of any particular personality. Also, within the devotional attitude of the puja, the personalities of God are multiplied because even though each divine personality can embody the full revelation of the Absolute, at the same time, no single particular representation can exhaust the Absolute. The resulting theology is not of a personal figure who has a personal relationship with particular persons or communities, but rather an absolute and ineffable Reality that is nevertheless directly available to worshipers who approach with open hearts of humble devotion. The elements of personality in Hindu theism have at times been dismissed as the lower-order popular religion of the unsophisticated masses bearing little relationship to the higher-order speculative mysticism of the Upanishads. This may be a side effect of a modern suspicion toward ritual, devotion, and emotion that unfairly privileges intellectual and rational formulations of religion. However, when taken seriously on its own account, puja incorporates a unique posture of humble entreating of the deity who is personally manifest to the devout, and an experience of belonging to a much larger cosmic reality in which one has a small but divinely protected place.

The discussion here of preserving the sacred's transcendence of every particular symbolic representation of it is especially relevant to chapter 5, which looks at doubt as a resistance to dogmatism and as a vigilance against idolatry. The relevant point for this first chapter is the sense of holistic belonging to a world affirmed to be permeated by and protected by the sacred. In puja, Hindus ritually enact or re-engender this sacred world of which they are a part and affirm through the act of bhakti, or devotion, their gratitude for the divine grace that is so needed in this world of tremendous suffering. The sheer act of venerating the physical elements of the cosmos and the planets affirms their sacred and life-sustaining dimension. Religious skeptics and theologians alike have said that we humans fashion our own gods.[31] In the language of twentieth-century Christian theologian Paul Tillich, we each have an ultimate concern, in that we each value something ultimately, but the only truly ultimate concern is that which does in fact transcend our symbolic representations and what is described best in religious language as the sacred depth and dimension of life.

The Satyanarayana puja is a good example of the ways in which Hindu ritual worship embodies a sense of belonging to a larger world. First, puja itself is a ritual of personally connecting to a transcendent deity. Second, such devotional rituals incorporate different deities for different purposes and wishes and powers in the world, articulating the sense of connecting concretely to this larger world. Third, the attitude of welcoming deities like

honored guests and relating to them personally in devotion expresses humility and something akin to what Schleiermacher calls God-consciousness.
Fourth, by eating prasad, the worshipers take directly into themselves divine
blessings. Fifth, in the course of the elaborate Satyanarayana puja, the nine
planets are honored as minor nature deities, incorporating the sense of
sharing a small space of the larger world. Sixth, the Satyanarayana katha
especially embodies the idea that all that we enjoy are divine gifts that must
be remembered in gratitude. Seventh, the common teaching that children
and family prosperity will result from the devout performance of this puja
is also a kind of self-enlargement, or belonging to a life that is larger than
oneself. Together, these details reinforce the sense that we humans are neither independent masters of the universe nor isolated atomistic beings, but
fortunate members of a larger, interconnected world. In the Kali Yuga, we
are terribly vulnerable creatures and therefore especially dependent on God's
good graces, which, according to the Satyanarayana katha, are overwhelm-
ingly generous.

Conclusion

This chapter represents an opening into examining faith as an experience
variously described as trust, humility, absolute dependence, or belonging to
a larger whole, whether that larger reality is the religious community, the
universe, or God. I have discussed descriptions of the experience of faith
from three different traditions here, not because they represent varieties of
a single uniform experience, but because placing them side by side allows us
to discern something more about how each of these communities and traditions articulates faith as a posture of active trust. These descriptions reflect
the common concern of maintaining the transcendence of sacred reality even
while affirming meaningful experience of it here and now. For example, while
humility is a religious posture of recognizing one's limits and even failures, it
goes hand in hand with the recognition in Islamic teaching of God's unique
sovereignty; likewise, practicing humility is a key exercise in locating one's
proper place in a larger reality. Christian mystics like Julian of Norwich
and Teresa of Avila claimed that humility was the first step in the religious
life because it helped prepare the soul to become receptive to that which
lay beyond its understanding and control. The individual in faith is able to
affirm her dependence on God and trust in God's grace-filled restoration of
the world, articulated by Schleiermacher as a feeling of absolute dependence
that enables God-consciousness. The Hindu puja facilitates the intimacy of
devotional worship while enabling a humble sense of participating gratefully

in a larger sacred world. In puja, worshipers can welcome their chosen deity into their lives, interact with him or her intimately, and affirm their gratitude regarding such an intimate relationship with an ultimately transcendent divine who is both absolutely powerful and generous in protecting devotees in what is acknowledged to be a vulnerable human role in a world full of suffering and tumult. In a sense, the self-limitation of the posture of humility enables the self-expansive movement of belonging to the larger whole. I turn now to various treatments of human responsibility in and for the world, which develop out of this experience of participating in a sacred world.

CHAPTER TWO

What Is Our Sacred Responsibility in the World?

This second chapter examines four particular ways in which faith has been expressed as a commitment to one's responsibilities vis-à-vis one's community and God. It extends the discussion of the first chapter, as the commitment to a certain path or a sense of religious responsibility emerges from the experience of trust in the sacred, dependence on God, or belonging to a world of meaning and value. Here as elsewhere in this book, my choice is guided not by an intention to be comprehensive or even equitable in the attention given to each tradition, but rather, by what I find to be thematically most relevant. That said, this chapter discusses Hindu epic illustrations of dharma, or sacred duty; an allegorical extrapolation of Christian responsibility in C. S. Lewis's Narnia series as well as his discussion of the relationship between faith and works;[1] Islamic understanding of human beings as God's caliphs (*khalifa*) and the responsibility for jihad; and Jewish articulations of human responsibility in a covenantal relationship with God. These examples concern a specific interface of religious ethics and the commitment to faith, by which one embraces a tremendous sense of responsibility for the very fate of the human world.

Hindu Dharma

Dharma can be translated as natural law, sacred duty, responsibility, or even religion. In common parlance, it represents an ideal way of life that promises happiness and well-being. Many religious commentators depict dharma as the center of Hindu religion. Hindu tradition and texts teach that every person has a set of duties, or *svadharma*, uniquely his or her own, determined traditionally by one's caste, gender, age, opportunities, and web of relationships with other people. These are not merely practical obligations, but sacred duties that weave individuals together to constitute a society. The centrality of dharma and its content (what are one's duties) are most powerfully illustrated in the great epics, the *Ramayana* and the *Mahabharata*, and conceptually justified in Dharmasastras like the *Laws of Manu*. Dharma is less a legal code than a moral ideal that has been enforced by cultural custom and, in earlier times, by royal ordinance.[2] The *Laws of Manu* derives dharma from revealed and traditional scripture as well as from social custom and even what is pleasing to oneself.[3]

Dharma is one of the four central goals of human life, according to Hindu teaching. The others are *artha*, or economic prosperity and well-being; *kama*, or sensual pleasure; and *moksha*, or liberation from the cycle of rebirth. While moksha is the ultimate goal of human life, Hindus believe it requires a sophisticated level of spiritual development that may occupy hundreds or thousands of lifetimes. Dharma, artha, and kama, by contrast, are the goals pursued at every stage of spiritual development within a current birth. Seen together, they demonstrate a Hindu value of balance in life's pursuits, and a sense that there is an appropriate time and place for all the good things in life. J. A. B. van Buitenen suggests that artha, kama, and dharma are all essentially dharma, insofar as they uphold the established order, while moksha abandons it for a higher self-realization that is not possible in the realm of *samsara* (the cycle of rebirth).[4] Dharma cultivates norms for action in this world of samsara. Because a person's dharma is determined by her particular life circumstances and relationships to others, it defines personal identity in relation to others. Who am I? I am specifically a daughter, a sister, a wife, a mother, a friend, and a teacher. My individuality emerges from this particular web of relationships and obligations that comprise my dharma. My very identity as this unique person and not somebody else is constituted by my dharmic relationships. As Arti Dhand notes, Hindu formulation of dharma offers a relational constitution of self and rejects the notion, proffered in some Western ethics, of a universal person, with general and universal duties. There is a universal notion of selfhood (located at the level of *atman*, or soul), but a person is always particularized. One is never a generic human, but a woman or a man of a particular ethnicity and other such particularities.[5]

The root *dhr* means to support or maintain, so dharma also means the right, the good, or the natural or moral order, which all living beings follow. These various levels of dharmic duty are interwoven, so that an individual's performance of dharmic duty ensures her own well-being and the well-being of her family. If families follow the rules of dharma, they and the societies around them reap the benefits; if entire societies or nations follow dharma, the entire human world flourishes and the whole cosmos runs harmoniously. Therefore, despite the relative incommensurability of dharma and moksha, as one refers to an external penultimate good for the society here and now and the other refers to an internal and ultimate good for the soul in the end, the interpretation of continuity between the two also stands. Because the performance of duty helps foster worldly harmony and well-being, dharma can embody the spiritual freedom of moksha within the earthly realm of samsara.[6] An individual's particular set of social duties implicates him in a sacred relationship of responsibility to family and society, on which his own well-being depends. This interrelationship echoes a concern manifest in the Buddhist idea of interdependence and in recent Christian articulations of relational ontology. Both reject an atomistic view of personhood and instead interpret the being of a person or a thing as dynamically and richly constituted by its relationships with others.

Among the mythological characters of the epics can be found models of perfect dharma as well as those who utterly fail to live up to dharmic ideals and then suffer the consequences. Every epic revolves around a great challenge or problem, and in the *Ramayana*, as in the *Mahabharata*, this challenge includes the question of rightful succession to a throne. Rama is depicted as the ideal son, husband, and ruler.[7] He follows his duty as a son to uphold an oath made by his father even though it means exile from the kingdom; he rescues his kidnapped wife Sita, but as a ruler, he puts public welfare ahead of their marital happiness. Sita likewise exhibits the dharma of a woman, wife, and mother. Lakshmana exhibits the dharmic ideals of brotherhood, and Hanuman serves as a model friend, loyal and selfless.

Hindus grow up hearing these stories and formulate an elaborate system of ethical mores based on the particular illustrations in these epics of what is dharmic and what is not. Contemporary scholars often question whether dharma, properly speaking, qualifies as ethics. It certainly provides a roadmap for right action and a normative way to live. However, insofar as it relies far more on particularized duties (svadharma) than a universalizable law (as in Kantian ethics) and is imbued with social conservatism or maintaining the status quo of society, it challenges some common Western philosophical notions of ethics. While it is explicitly about duty, Hindu dharma reflects a form of virtue ethics, by which one actively cultivates one's self by living according to these norms. In addition, as Arti Dhand notes, dharma also has a universal component in addition to the particularized duties one acquires by one's relationships with others. Dhand identifies a universal care for others that actively transcends one's obligations to one's closest relations. Care for others, or indiscriminate friendliness with strangers, even makes normative the ideal of sacrificing oneself and one's closest kin in order to provide for the welfare of distant unrelated strangers.[8]

The *Mahabharata* is an especially long epic that serves as a fascinating sourcebook of dharma, with hundreds of characters coming and going and interacting in ethically challenging ways. Unlike the *Ramayana*, which revolves around the heroic exploits of Rama, an ideal son, husband, king, and incarnation of the divine Vishnu, the *Mahabharata* traces the interactions of countless individuals, many who are righteous and many who are obviously flawed, and presents dharma as a more complex set of conflicting ideals. Distinguishing between the idealized characters of the *Ramayana* and the flawed characters of the *Mahabharata*, David Shulman identifies a "poetics of perfection" in the former and a "poetics of dilemma" in the latter.[9] In the situations encountered by righteous individuals, the challenges of following dharma become clear. Shubha Pathak develops the contrasts in how Yudhishthira, the unfairly displaced king of the *Mahabharata*, and Rama, the unfairly displaced king of the *Ramayana*, experience dharma. While Rama is presented as morally impeccable (despite engaging in dubious actions) and comes to rule a kingdom that is prosperous for the entire society, Yudhishthira experiences doubts, personal imperfections, and moral struggles.[10] We see embodied in the life challenges of Yudhishthira and other characters in the *Mahabharata* the realization that there are things we can control (our own behavior and responses) and many things we cannot control but to which we must nevertheless respond in a dharmic, or responsible and dutiful, manner, whatever the outcome we face.

The basic plotline of the *Mahabharata* follows two sides of one royal family, each struggling to control the kingdom and each with a legitimate claim to the throne. The epic follows the struggles of these two sets of cousins, the five righteous Pandavas (sons of Pandu) who exhibit dharmic ideals at nearly every turn (in fact, the eldest Yudhishthira is also known as *Dharmaraj*, or king of dharma) and the hundred Kauravas led by the eldest, Duryodhana, who repeatedly exhibits jealousy, conspiracy, hatred, greed, and an overall lack of virtue, or dharma. As we follow these characters through years and years of this struggle, we witness repeatedly the clear righteousness of the Pandavas and the obvious wickedness of the Kauravas. When the plot turns to an inevitable epic war between these cousins, we the audience have clearly taken sides, convinced not only that the Pandavas best deserve to rule, but also that their rule would be best for the kingdom as a whole. The Hindu epics generally teach that when a king rules according to dharma, the entire society flourishes, so here the kingdom desperately needs the Pandavas to fight and win this war. It is at this point in the larger epic of the *Mahabharata* that we come to the *Bhagavad Gita*, which presents the profound spiritual conversation that takes place between Arjuna, one of the five Pandavas, and Krishna, his charioteer and friend, whom we also discover to be God incarnate, an avatar of Vishnu.

While it is a part of the *Mahabharata*, the *Bhagavad Gita* stands alone as one of the world's great spiritual texts. The basic plot is as follows: Immediately before the battle is to begin, Arjuna, an archer, asks Krishna to drive him out to survey the battlefield. Arjuna looks around. He sees his cousins with whom he was raised, as well as his beloved uncles and teachers who trained them all, and he recoils at the horrors of the impending death and destruction of a war among family. He says he would rather die than lift his bow to kill his kinsmen, and so he refuses to fight. At this point, Krishna proceeds to counsel him through this spiritual crisis. Krishna's basic argument is quite simple. As a prince, Arjuna has a responsibility to ensure the kingdom's safety and well-being. Krishna explains that following one's own dharma imperfectly is far superior to following another's dharma perfectly. Arjuna must support his brother's fight to gain the throne for the good of the entire society. In some ways, this is the only direct response given in the text to the issue at hand—it is his duty to fight, and he must not shirk his duty.

Krishna's fairly simple teaching of the centrality of dharma is supplemented and developed in the context of his conversation with Arjuna. Krishna explains, for example, the nature of *karma*, the natural moral law that all actions have consequences that attach to a person's soul and determine the circumstances of one's future births. Even the failure to act will have profound consequences for the individual soul and the world. In Arjuna's case, refusal to fight could lead to his family's defeat and contribute to the political and moral decline of the entire society, which depends on righteous governance in order to flourish. Turning from the matter of *what* Arjuna must do to *how* he must do it, Krishna explains that it is not the action itself that accrues karma and ties one to this endless cycle of rebirth, but rather the desire or intention of action that accrues karmic residue. A person can gain spiritual freedom, Krishna teaches, by doing one's ordained duty without clinging to the fruits of that action. This means in essence that an action is truly free only when one acts according to the rules of duty alone, impartial to success or failure, impartial to reward or punishment. This echoes the fairly universal teaching that one should do the right thing, no matter what. Obviously, this all depends on discerning what the right thing to do is, but in this case, the long narrative throughout the *Mahabharata* illustrating the Kauravas' unrighteousness makes clear what is needed for the greater good. Krishna is teaching that living according to the rules of dharma is not only right and practical for an individual's well-being and a family's and a society's prosperity, but also that the correct attitude toward this duty can result in the ultimate spiritual freedom of moksha. At the heart of all spiritual imprisonment is karmic residue, which accrues from the desire or fear that motivates any of our actions. One who can discipline herself into a purity of intention can experience the profound freedom of enlightenment or liberation, which is the stated goal of the religious life, and truly, of life itself.

Complicating this picture of social harmony built on the realization of dharma are the actual conditions at the end of this mythic battle of the *Mahabharata*. Once Arjuna resolves to fight, the battle proceeds for eighteen days with epic fighting all around. At the end, all but twelve warriors lie dead, and the ultimate victory of the Pandavas occurs only by means of deceit by the god Krishna himself, who explains that the outnumbered Pandavas could never win in a fair fight. Echoing Shubha Pathak's discussion of the *Mahabharata* as interrogating the struggles of righteous behavior and of Yudhisthira's own doubts, flaws, and complicated experience of victory, Gurcharan Das notes in *The Difficulty of Being Good* that both these reflections cast a disturbing light on the ethics of dharma.[11]

In addition, the teaching of dharma obviously has the impact of legitimating the current status quo—by teaching that everyone has their particular sets of duties to fulfill, Hindu rules of dharma help reinforce one's given station in life, provoking criticism on ethical grounds.[12] The content of dharma and its very justification reinforce the centrality of caste in one's identity and one's responsibilities. It is necessary to re-examine dharma itself to accommodate the rapid social changes that have been occurring in Indian society during the past half century. Austin Creel identifies the contemporary problem as follows: on the one hand, because dharma is rooted in custom rather than metaphysical principles, it is subject to change; on the other hand, if dharma is rooted in social stability, it certainly will need a modern reconstruction independent of caste-based formulation of identity.[13] Because it has functioned more as an ideal whose content emerges from custom, dharma can continue to provide normative guidance for behavior that is not tied to caste in one's dynamic nexus of relationships. This profound ethical system not only supports one's duties to others, but even defines an individual's fundamental identity and purpose in life in the context of his or her relationships with other people. The *Bhagavad Gita* goes beyond this reinforcement of people's duties by promising spiritual freedom through the disciplined and impartial performance of one's particular duties.

The *Bhagavad Gita*'s teaching of freedom through impartial dutiful action likely appeals especially to contemporary Hindus who cannot justify the continued norms of caste but seek to reconcile the centrality of duty with the value of social mobility. In a 2008 article in *Tikkun*, Arvind Sharma comments on the need for a reformulation of the relationship between karma and dharma, from a backward-looking explanation and justification for a current state of affairs into a forward-looking ethic of action and self-determination.[14] This would reverse the directional momentum of proceeding from presumed actions of the past (karma) to justify the current duties one receives virtually as a birthright (dharma). Because of the expanded range of moral choices, Sharma argues, the flow from karma to dharma can be reformulated into a flow from dharma to karma, beginning with one's web of relationships and duties and moving from there to the wide range of self-determinative actions possible today.

In the teachings of dharma, human action has tremendous value and significance, perhaps even more clearly today because our possible avenues for action are not nearly as circumscribed and predetermined as in generations past. The microcosm of the individual and family directly and powerfully impacts the macrocosm of society and world. This can take the form of reinforcing current norms of society as it is, or it can allow change of customs and norms. Disciplined dutiful action can also lead to personal spiritual freedom. If we articulate a common goal of religious life to be salvation from a life of suffering and ignorance, the Hindu view of dharma demonstrates that dutiful action can *save* the individual and the world in a multitude of ways. Dharma transcends beliefs about God and creeds altogether by placing people into relationships of obligation that are prior to any personal reflection on what one believes about the sacred.

What Can Mere Humans Do in Narnia?

This section explores an example of a Christian worldview that emphasizes the tremendous value of human action and interprets the relationship often discussed in Christian theology between faith and works. Twentieth-century theologian and writer C. S. Lewis wrote a series of books set in Narnia as children's fiction in order to provide allegorical models for Christian virtue.[15] I do not intend here to discuss the full Christian symbolism of the Narnia books, but only to call attention to the power of human dutiful action to help "save" the world, as it is presented in Lewis's fictional vision. It is telling that it is children who are faced with this enormous challenge in Narnia to help save that world for its citizens. These children could very well leave the creatures of Narnia to their own misfortunes at the mercy of the White Witch who has taken over Narnia. However, they are presented with a responsibility to help these creatures who are no more than friendly strangers. As soon as the four children begin to respond with a sense of responsibility for this community, there emerge signs of hope in Narnia. The winter that has been going on forever, that is, a winter without Christmas,[16] now looks like it may give way to springtime renewal. Signs of hope appear everywhere that Aslan, the Prince of Narnia, may return.

In a scene that is particularly striking in the Hollywood film version, the children are surprised with presents from Santa.[17] These presents are not the frivolous toys most children enjoy collecting, of course; they are tools, even weapons, to help them in the vital work that lies ahead. These children are not simply play-acting as grownups, but indeed are faced with serious challenges and serious work. Watching them embrace their responsibilities in Narnia, we realize that life is not a game. It is a matter of life or death, freedom or slavery. The battle that ensues has tremendous repercussions for all the creature-citizens of Narnia. They have been suffering under the oppressive rule of the White Witch, and they desperately need help. These creature-citizens appear along the way to assist and guide the four children in wonderful friendship and loyalty, but they are also the ones who will suffer the worst for the children's failures to defeat the White Witch. In Lewis's Christian allegory, each of us, despite our limitations, has gifts and duties; our failure will result in tremendous suffering for everyone. While life is not a game, and the duties each of us faces are quite serious, we also come across remarkable friendships in one another; we practice Christian virtue in these relationships of loyalty and sacrifice. The greatest sacrifice in *The Lion, the Witch, and the Wardrobe* is presented in the actions of the Christ-like Aslan, who ransoms himself in exchange for the freedom of Edmund, the little boy who acted out of his own greed, jealousy, and foolishness to create the disastrous situation in the first place. As a result of this gift and the gift of forgiveness from the rest of his family, however, Edmund is not imprisoned by shame, but instead learns his errors, repents, and comes to learn Christian virtue as well. In this allegorical vision, the world is a serious place with serious problems. It is broken or ruptured in all kinds of ways, but nevertheless witnesses hope in the courage and selflessness of the young, in the capacity for rehabilitation, and in the friendships and generous love that can transform the world for the better and restore it to its potential goodness.

The value given to human action in this Christian allegory raises the theological question of the relationship between faith and works, which must be considered in light of the Christian doctrines of original sin and divine grace. According to these elements of orthodox Christian thought, humans are fundamentally broken and corrupt, and they cannot repair themselves.

They require divine redemption, which is given to humanity as a free gift. The illustration of grace as a gift is a telling reminder because a gift is not an even exchange of items of like value. Instead, redemption is a one-sided, unidirectional gift from God that is considered unearned by humanity and even undeserved, according to many interpretations. In the discussion about the relative value of faith and works, the Catholic standpoint basically agrees with the Protestant view first articulated in the sixteenth century: justification happens by faith and this is accomplished as a matter of divine grace, a freely given gift from God to humans. The Catholic standpoint, however, rejects the Protestant exclusion of the merit of works. The Catholic Church rejected the "only" or the "sola" element of "sola fide" and "sola gratia" proclaimed by the Protestant Reformers, in order to make room for the real value of good works and for the real merit of some human action, that of the saints, for example.

What Martin Luther meant by "justification by faith alone" is quite different from the view taken later by many Protestants that sinners are justified by their acceptance of the creed that Jesus Christ was the divine Son of God, died for human sin, and rose from the dead to proclaim victory over death itself. Luther was especially tormented with anxiety that his acts of piety were not good enough. Against what he interpreted as the medieval church's condoning of a spiritual uncertainty regarding one's eternal destiny, an anxiety that could be alleviated only by more and more works of merit (purchasing indulgences, relics, and Masses for the dead, for example), Luther expressed the need for confidence that one was indeed justified. This led him finally to focus not on what humans could do, but on what God has already done in grace. Following Paul in the New Testament Book of Romans, Luther determines that we can be set right with God not by doing anything adequately, but only by trusting God. We can enjoy spiritual confidence because our eternal destiny depends not on how piously we live, but on the gracious transformation God has brought about for us. In response to some sophisticated theological debate, Luther expressed the heart of his concern by saying that all he cared to know was that Christ had redeemed him. Karl Barth a few centuries later would respond likewise. When asked to summarize his complicated theological system, Barth replied playfully but honestly, "Jesus loves me; this I know, for the Bible tells me so."[18] This suggests the difference for Luther between the law and the gospel. Both were the word of God, or God's revelation, but while the law proclaimed clearly what human beings ought to do, the gospel, according to Luther, proclaimed the good news of what Christ has done for humanity. As Robin Lovin explains in his guide to Christian ethics, law and judgment do play a role in Christian ethics. Judgment is not something we can prepare for through the moral life; instead, judgment has already happened. However, "because that judgment is covered by grace, we are free to reorient our moral lives toward the future rather than continually reviewing the failures of the past."[19] Echoing Arvind Sharma's suggestion that the karmic looking back to the past be replaced with the forward-looking expectation and responsibility of dharma, Luther's teaching of justification and faith suggests that God's grace liberates the faithful from endless self-recrimination and frees them to consider the needs of others.

Many Christians commonly misunderstand the Jewish interpretation of the law because it means something so different to Christians and to Jews. Given the Christian doctrines of original sin and the work of salvation that is accomplished in Christ, the law to Christians represents commands that *must* be followed and yet *cannot* be followed adequately. A distinctly Jewish interpretation of the law, however, does not lead to such a preoccupation with doomed failure. Instead, the law represents God's gift of a dynamic relationship. Observing the law through the commandments is seen by observant Jews as a way to participate actively in the covenant and the comprehensive experience of God's presence in all aspects of life here and now. In a Christian worldview (with the doctrine of original sin) humans cannot ever live up to God's commands. In fact, this is the direction that Lewis takes in his famous apologetic text *Mere Christianity*. In discussing the relationship between faith and works he says works are necessary, not to merit salvation or God's good graces, but rather to illustrate concretely for individuals the impossibility of independently living up to God's intentions for humanity. Lewis says that one must apply oneself, work very hard, and try to practice the Christian virtues; by failing to live up to these high standards, one realizes her own imperfection. As Lewis writes, "no man knows how bad he is till he has tried very hard to be good."[20] This newly found humility is key to one's becoming open to the transformation of divine grace. He describes a common theological error when one "has the idea of an exam, or of a bargain in his mind. . . . One of the very things Christianity was designed to do was to blow this idea to bits. God has been waiting for the moment at which you discover that there is no question of earning a pass mark in this exam. Or putting Him in your debt."[21] Instead, Lewis explains, God is the source of every human capability. In the Protestant Christian view, one cannot earn redemption or pay it back. Lewis ridicules the suggestion that one could give something back to God in return for the tremendous gift of redemption by saying, "it is like a small child going to its father and saying, 'Daddy, give me sixpence to buy you a birthday present.'

. . . It is all very nice and proper, but only an idiot would think that the father is sixpence to the good on the transaction."[22]

We can see in Lewis's theological explanation as well as in his allegorical fiction his sense of the complicated relationship between faith and works. Faith is an act of trusting God and it is itself God's gift. The way that some contemporary people talk about faith as deliberately assenting to a set of factual propositions seems a misguided attempt to turn faith into a human work, thus defeating the meaning of the Protestant teaching of justification by faith alone. The central point of the Protestant emphasis and of Paul's theology was that justification happened by God's grace alone, and not by any human act of change. Human faith, then, is not primarily intellectual assent, but trust in God's promise and commitment to live according to the responsibilities entailed by that promise. Lewis demonstrates a clear value for good works, or Christian virtue and responsible action, even while he refutes the possibility that these can in any way earn a person salvation. Speaking of the correct orientation to the virtue of charity, he writes, "Do not waste time bothering whether you 'love' your neighbour; act as if you did. As soon as we do this we find one of the great secrets. When you are behaving as if you loved someone, you will presently come to love him."[23] Perhaps then, the focus on the creedal or intellectual content of faith is not entirely misguided, but only simplistic. Perhaps one believes a creed or believes God's promise as articulated and witnessed in the Gospels as an initial act or *work*, but faith consists in the transforming work that God accomplishes in people while they patiently work at such belief. The power of virtuous action seems not to be that it will effect one's salvation, but that it transforms a person. Lewis is clear that it is God acting through us and that it is a silly question to ask what God does and what we do. In fact, he says, God is acting through all of us at all times. Human actions are the location for God's transformative and redemptive work.

We can also see the extent to which Lewis echoes Luther's views: first, that faith is trusting God's love; second, that one cannot adequately come to this genuine faith without first trying with all of one's efforts to live the Christian virtues. So one must first try one's hardest, fail to live up to these ideals, and realize humility. Only then can one sincerely stop trying and trust entirely in Christ. Lewis still notes that there is a responsibility to keep trying to obey God, not in order to earn one's way, but rather as an active commitment to trust God enough to obey Him purely without any other agenda. "Thus if you have really handed yourself over to Him, it must follow that you are trying to obey Him. But trying in a new way, a less worried way. Not doing these things in order to be saved, but because

He has begun to save you already. Not hoping to get to Heaven as a reward for your actions, but inevitably wanting to act in a certain way because a first faint gleam of Heaven is already inside you."[24] Lewis's description of obedience pure of self-interest echoes the Hindu teaching of dutiful action that relinquishes the fruits of action, discussed in the earlier section on Hindu dharma. Ultimately, what Lewis emphasizes in his discussion of faith and works is that God works through people. If we apply this to the allegorical world of Narnia, we get the sense that human action does matter tremendously, and that people have responsibilities to one another, but that people are best able to fulfill these responsibilities with and through the help of others. We see young Edmund become healed from his bitterness and jealousy in his own experience of humility and forgiveness. People are better able to fulfill their responsibilities when they themselves experience the gifts of friendship and generosity. While in the previous Hindu model of dharma, human dutiful action contributes to society's well-being, in Narnia it seems that dutiful action provides the necessary structure of relationships through which Christian forgiveness and generosity, which are themselves extensions of divine grace, can radically transform the troubled world.

God's Caliph on Earth

A discussion of human responsibility in Islamic teaching must begin with a basic Islamic structure of the relationship between God and the world. Islam upholds God's absolute sovereignty over the world and its creatures, and the Qur'an consists of God's revealed intentions for humanity. It therefore provides guidance in morality and religion, which are remarkably intertwined. Religion, as the human response to God's revelation, suggests a debt to be repaid to God for the gift of creation. The three monotheistic traditions, Judaism, Christianity, and Islam, all share a strong sense of a human relationship with a personal God in which religion is a response (in responsibility) to God's actions of creation, revelation, and redemption. The first section of this chapter developed the operation of dharma in interpersonal responsibility, while the second section gave an example of how this relationship is portrayed in Christian tradition; this section focuses on Islam's perspective; the fourth section discusses the relationship (covenant) in Jewish theology.

The most central teaching in Islam is that all the world belongs to God. Muslims call out in prayer, *Allahu Akbar*, or God is greater, that is, greater than any particular thing. Religion then is, by definition, the normative human responsibility, first, to acknowledge that all the world belongs to

God and, second, to continuously strive to live this basic insight of Islam by surrendering one's will to God's will. To understand how Islamic tradition treats human responsibility I examine the concepts of khalifa (caliph or God's representative on earth), Shari'ah (the narrow path of God), and jihad (striving in the way of Islam).

While the word *caliph* has historically referred to a political ruler over an Islamic community, the Qur'anic use of the word refers to the authority and responsibility granted to all of humanity to be God's vice-regent on earth (Qur'an 2:30). As God's representatives on earth, humans are endowed with the powerful responsibility to inhabit the earth, cultivate it, and govern it according to God's rule. Qur'an 2:30, while granting human leadership, casts doubts about it; the angels are skeptical about humanity's ability to resist corruption and do good, but God reassures them about some divine plan that they do not know. Another verse explains that God originally had offered such responsibility to the heavens and the earth, but only human beings, being unafraid, accepted it (Qur'an 33:73). As Abdulaziz Sachedina explains, the Qur'an appears to establish the boldness and potential capability of humans as the only creatures to accept this authority, even while also acknowledging human vulnerability to evil and temptation and the need for divine guidance.[25] Humanity's role as vice-regent is grounded in the Islamic view of the world as containing both good and evil and the need to employ all of one's moral reason to recognize and fight against evil. Humanity is capable of ascertaining the difference between good and evil, but Satan effectively damages this innate capability. God's intimate relationship with humanity and intentions for human welfare are revealed in God's guidance for humanity on how to live in the best way possible for human welfare, that is, in submission to God's will. As God's caliph on earth, humanity has both a tremendous power and authority over other creatures and a bold responsibility for human welfare. Sufis, the mystics of Islam, suggest that all the world's creatures pray constantly to God, but only humans must choose to do so.[26] In other words, only humans, who alone have free will, must choose to do what comes naturally to other creatures.

The precise hows and whats of governing according to God's rule make up the very meaning of *Islam*, or surrender to God's will. The particulars of instituting this divinely ordained moral order bring us to the concept of Shari'ah, or the straight and narrow path that God intends humans to follow. One cannot find Shari'ah explicated in a clear, numerically ordered list of commandments revealed to Muhammad and recited in the Qur'an. Rather, Shari'ah was developed during the first three centuries of Islamic history as a way to systematize the law and place the authority of individual rulers under God's authority. This ideal system of God's law must be approximated or derived by gleaning general rules, particular applications, and explicit instructions from the revealed Qur'an and the composed Hadith, and by using formal techniques of jurisprudence such as interpreting by analogy from the examples explicitly given (*qiyas*), juridical consensus (*ijma*), imitation of legal interpretations given by earlier jurists (*taqlid*), or original reasoned interpretation of the Qur'an and Hadith (*ijtihad*).[27] Islamic jurisprudence has traditionally been a very sophisticated science combined with a spiritual art of surrendering in all things to God above all. The only parts of Islamic law that have been explicitly identified as universal obligations for all times and places are the five pillars of faith discussed in chapter 1. Other matters of religious ethics require a more comprehensive look at the explicit preferences and recommendations for behavior in the Qur'an and the explicit statements and actions of Muhammad in the Hadith, followed by extensive interpretation using analogy, consensus, imitation, or independent reasoning.[28] All of this jurisprudence is to be guided by the spirit of jihad, that is, striving to overcome one's egotism to better realize God's will. It is guided by the commitment to be Muslim, to surrender to God, and to be responsible (and to respond appropriately) to God as one's singular Lord.

Humans are to continually strive to submit the selfish will to the higher order of God's will. This is the meaning of jihad—the continual striving or struggling to live faithfully according to God's will for a just society of moral order rather than one's selfish egoistic interests and worldly attachments. The responsibility of jihad is so central it is often called a "sixth pillar of faith." In another sense, however, it may be taken to be the primary religious responsibility because surrendering to God's will requires constant vigilance and effort. Once again, the Islamic view of the human world takes seriously the potential for good and the constant danger of corruption and temptation of evil. Because humanity has free will, it remains always vulnerable, and must be vigilant for the innumerable ways in which the inclinations of the lower self can rise up.[29]

Jihad has two meanings in Islamic teaching. The greater jihad is the internal struggle of conscience to always submit one's will to God's will. The lesser jihad is the external struggle to defend Muslims against any aggression that undermines God's intentions of moral order. Because of its historical use to justify military struggle, the external struggle has gained immense attention, this despite its status below the internal work of self-improvement and despite the many restrictions on its use to justify armed struggle. For example, jihad is restricted to defensive armed struggle as opposed to offensive attack and prohibits armed struggle for any material gain. In a 2004 article, Paul Heck details how the use of jihad reflects the changing needs and historical circumstances of Muslims, and how the relationship between jihad and Islamic hegemony raises questions about which parts of this historically conditioned tradition remain relevant today to Muslims and non-Muslims.[30] The Qur'anic references to jihad include a focus on the purity of one's intention and devotion to God or a divine test meant to distinguish truly committed believers from those fair-weather friends of God who can be easily swayed from God's will. Heck also notes descriptions of jihad as a spiritual exercise to purify the soul of self-concern and direct the soul away from worldly attachments and toward God. "It was thus one's own soul that was to be slain, since detachment from all save God came about only through the mortification or even annihilation of one's own evil-inclined soul."[31] Waging jihad against one's lower self is therefore a necessary component of mystical union with God, echoing the recommendation by mystics of different traditions to die to the self in order to become worthy of union with God.

The internal jihad and the external jihad are connected because the whole discussion is grounded on the Qur'anic view that human responsible living (as God's caliphs on earth) demands constant human choice between good and evil. To the degree to which jihad notes a devotion to God's cause over physical comforts and worldly concerns, it demonstrates certain parallels with the Hindu teaching of dutiful action and the relinquishment of the fruits of action. The stoicism discussed earlier in Rama's pure intention to follow the precepts of dharma in the *Ramayana* and the intention-less actions of duty demanded of Arjuna the warrior in the *Bhagavad Gita* echo what in Islamic teaching is a degree of total devotion to God that sacrifices self-interest and worldly attachments in order to facilitate a more just world. In particular, correlations with the *Bhagavad Gita*'s teachings on righteous action raise the explicit question of the justifications of armed struggle. According to Heck, the external jihad became explicitly connected with the internal jihad in the historical circumstances of Islamic expansion. The jihad of external martyrdom came to serve as the test of one's inner devotion and degree of self-sacrifice to God's will, insofar as sacrificing one's physical life was the fullest, most visible way to prove personal piety. Under Umayyad rule in particular, jihad was used to religiously motivate individual self-sacrifice and justify as righteous cause the armed struggle against non-Muslims as well as other Muslims in the interest of the Umayyad state's expansion in the eighth century.[32] Heck notes that this historical use of jihad to support political interests had lasting effects on Islamic conceptions of jihad and now poses a serious stumbling block to a contemporary definition of jihad. Whereas

Muhammad and the first four caliphs led the community politically as well as religiously, they modeled lives of austere simplicity. In contrast, the Umayyad Dynasty and the Abbasid Dynasty after they established a hereditary caliphate enjoyed worldly luxury and monarchical power. With these changes, the concept of jihad itself was redefined to support the distinctly political power of Muslim states.

Nevertheless, the link between inner piety and outer responsibility remains strong. Jihad helps provide the religious basis for morality—the purity and intensity of devotion to God that is required to realize the moral order and social harmony God has intended for humanity. It must be noted, however, that the external jihad refers not only to armed struggle or holy war, but also to any external work done to foster the moral order God intends for the world. Therefore, while the inner jihad may include the struggle to be a better person, to be more forgiving and compassionate, more hard-working and patient, or more responsible and obedient to God's will, the external jihad may take the form of working to improve society, fighting poverty and injustice, enabling greater access to education and health, or building bridges to strengthen the community and reinforce peace among nations. The teaching of jihad reinforces the tremendous responsibility given to humans as God's caliphs on earth. Endowed with the potential for perfection and the constant vulnerability to temptation and corruption, humanity faces a tremendous challenge to inhabit and govern the earth on God's behalf, instituting the moral order God has deemed the best means for human welfare.

This chapter concerns the particular and various ways in which faith is seen as a commitment to a certain way of living and acting that is grounded on a sense of sacred responsibility before God. In Islamic tradition, one further note is necessary about the explicit discussion of faith. The term for faith or belief is *iman*. Islamic tradition holds that iman is a higher stage of the spiritual life than *islam*, or the surrender to God's will. In other words, one surrenders to God's will and commits to living according to God's will and participating in the five pillars and other ethical guidelines. Only as a result of spiritual progress from living in surrender to God's will, from truly *be-ing* Muslim, can one realize iman, or true belief and faith. A still higher stage, *ihsan*, identifies a certain perfection and excellence of faith and practice. A person who realizes ihsan is said to live and breathe as though he sees God continuously before him. To summarize, one begins the religious life with a commitment to surrender to God's will and lives accordingly, and as a result, earns the gift of faith, perhaps as a confirmation of one's initial surrender to God's absolute sovereignty and providence, and only with further spiritual progress enjoys the coincidence of action and belief, of how one lives and how one believes. This Muslim ordering of islam, iman, and ihsan as progressive stages of spiritual progress further supports the profound significance of the faithful commitment to live in a particular way. The commitment does not just ensue as a result of one's belief, but it is a necessary precondition to true faith. The priority of the commitment to live according to a particular set of rules reflects the greater concern given to orthopraxy (correct observance or action) in Islam, Judaism, and even Hinduism as opposed to orthodoxy (correct teaching or doctrine). Whereas Christian tradition has demonstrated a far greater interest in clarifying and enforcing doctrine, these other traditions have traditionally focused enforcement on ritual observance as a code for normative human behavior. This is especially evident in Jewish observance of divine commandments, as I describe below.

Covenantal Responsibility, Partnership, and Struggle

In discussing various ways in which particular Jewish communities have expressed views of faith as a human responsibility to a certain way of living, I want to begin by reiterating a broader statement on the personal relationship with God that is expressed throughout Jewish tradition as well as in Islamic and Christian traditions. One aspect of it that is fairly unique in its strong expression in Jewish tradition is seeing this relationship with God as an active and dynamic covenant, one that should involve a vigorous struggle between two parties, and a relationship that relies heavily on human responsibility and participation. Especially in Jewish tradition, humans are essential partners in the divine plan. From Abraham's answering God's call to Moses' reception of the law from God, the covenant demands response and participation in covenantal partnership by the Jewish people, or Israel. My discussion of human responsibility in Jewish tradition takes up three related themes: a Jewish notion of covenant; the power of human action, especially as formulated in the concept of *tikkun olam*; and the central role of struggle in Jewish faith.

The Personal Dignity of Covenant

The covenantal relationship has a strongly contractual character even though it transcends contract as a strict give-and-take agreement. Consider what is entailed in entering into any conventional contract. First, a contract requires two "persons" in the legal sense of parties who have legitimate rights to enter into abiding legal relationships. Throughout history, particular groups were excluded from the dignity of full legal personhood—children, for example, and those deemed slaves. While the question of who is fully a person and therefore has the right to enter into contracts has been answered differently throughout history, the sense that contractual relationships imply full adult persons with the capacity for self-determination remains constant. Eugene Borowitz describes a Jewish experience of personhood derived "from a God who commands me yet also dignifies me with independent personal responsibility."[33] A Jewish understanding of God's covenant with Abraham and his descendants incorporates such a sense of personal dignity in the form of specific rights and responsibilities of the two parties involved. Abraham is by no means a passive party in this relationship; his response to God is absolutely necessary to initiate and define this covenantal relationship between God and God's people.

The covenant established with Israel transcends the legalistic sense of a contract in important ways. Whereas a contract usually refers to some sort of even exchange of goods or services, a covenant is a relationship, a binding together of persons and God. Recent interest in a "God gene" has speculated about the universal occurrence of religious rituals in early civilizations. Some cite the role of evolution and natural selection to explain the universal practice of religion, noting that those early communities that practiced religious rituals experienced strong community bonding, which may in turn have contributed to greater value given to community over individual self-interest.[34] Those groups that worked together most effectively maximized their chances of survival. A covenant echoes the centrality of relationship and mutual responsibilities that transcend the even exchange demanded of a contract. The covenant between Israel and God implies a building of something that is larger and more far-reaching than even exchange; the participants are expected to reciprocate an exchange of responsibilities in a sense of graciousness, not obligation.[35]

Three metaphors that have been used to describe the Jewish covenantal relationship are the relationships between king and subjects, husband and wife, and father and son. All three metaphors are rooted in a set of traditional societal and gender hierarchies that can be very paternalistic, but they also denote relationships of obligation. Although the first refers to a relationship of obligation that is largely outdated today, in earlier societies, a king had responsibilities (ideally) to lead and protect his people. The husband-wife relationship can be read in terms of traditional gendered power dynamics or in terms of a more equitable mutual relationship of love and accountability. The father-son relationship also reflects a clear imbalance of power that is echoed in obligation, as a father both exercises authority over a son and bears tremendous responsibility for his son's welfare. Incidentally, these three metaphors echo the Confucian model of five relationships that describe the basic responsibilities and obligations incumbent in how one might relate to any other person. In some relationships, we may occupy the place of greater power and responsibility, and in others, we may occupy the place of loyalty and obedience. In the Jewish covenant between God and Israel, we human beings occupy the dependent position of loyalty and obedience.

Throughout the history of Jewish interpretation, the concept of covenant has dwelled on the centrality of relationship between God and the people, one that has even been described in the language of chosenness. The idea of the Jews as a "chosen people" has at times been severely misinterpreted and cruelly mocked. While many Jews reject any exclusive claims of redemption and interpret God's laws as providing a universal template for ethical standards, the Jewish tradition has certainly described the relationship between God and Israel in terms of particularity and intimacy. God is not an abstract creator and ruler of the universe; the story of the exodus shows God approaching Moses by introducing Himself as the God of his ancestors. David Hartman discusses this special intimacy in terms of the rights conferred by God on those who participate in the covenant. He says that in prayer Jews "can make demands upon their Beloved. Covenantal mutuality implies that God is committed to taking seriously the requests and recommendations of His covenantal partner."[36] Being chosen by God means both a tremendous dignity of personhood by which one enters into a contractual relationship with God, and an intimacy of relationship by which one becomes partner to God's work of redemption. The language of chosenness echoes the intimacy of "love language" also found in the exclusivist stances articulated in many religious traditions.

The Power of Human Actions

Ever since receiving the law at Sinai, Jews have taken seriously the tremendous responsibility of embodying standards of ethics and serving as "a light unto the nations," guiding all to the basic norms of human behavior in the world. This is embodied in the centrality of tikkun olam (repair of the world). The concept of *tikkun* changes from the Rabbinic sense of repair in a limited legal sense to a broader mystical dimension of human partnership in the cosmic work of redemption as well as a modern this-worldly focus on personal morality, social activism, and eschatological mission.[37] Therefore, I look briefly at each of these in turn: a Rabbinic response to the law as a whole; a Kabbalistic interpretation of the responsibility of human righteousness; and a Reform Jewish interpretation of this responsibility.

Ever since the composition of the Talmud during the Rabbinic period in the second through sixth centuries, Jewish tradition has sustained the significance of the *mitzvot* (commandments). Like Islamic tradition, Judaism has been more concerned with orthopraxy (correct practice) than orthodoxy (correct doctrine). The role of the law in Judaism is often misunderstood by many Christians who see it exclusively through the eyes of New Testament writers like Paul who interprets it not as a typical first-century Jew would, but as a Jew who had become convinced that that law had been fulfilled and therefore cancelled out by Jesus' saving self-sacrifice. To Paul's Christian sensibilities, to maintain the Jewish law represented a denial of what God had done in Christ. This has led to a tremendous amount of misunderstanding of the Jewish commandments on the part of Christian interpreters and ordinary churchgoers accustomed to hearing Paul's biting criticism of the Jewish law. To a Christian, the effort to live righteously is a project ultimately doomed to failure when considered in light of the Christian doctrines of original sin and salvation by God's grace alone. To a Jew, the performance of commandments given by God constitutes obedience, of course, but the emphasis is not on the success or failure of *perfect* obedience, but on participating actively in the covenant offered by God. The Torah, or the law, is considered God's gift of instructions on how to live the best life possible in the world, and observant Jews gratefully embrace this gift of love. This echoes Christians' acceptance and enjoyment of the gift of atonement and redemption given by God's sacrifice of His only Son Jesus. In the Rabbinic view of the law, which consists originally of 613 commandments, every action is an opportunity to commit to covenantal life. Every action and every moment in daily life is imbued with human response to divine presence. This list of 613 unchanging mitzvot consists of 248 positive commandments ("Thou shalts") and 365 negative commandments ("Thou shalt nots"). According to the Talmud, the figure 248 corresponds to the number of parts of the male body, and the figure 365 corresponds to the number of days in the solar year. Therefore, observant Jews cite the ever-pervasive opportunity to live by God's law, to abide with God, with all the parts of the body and through all the days of the year.[38] The comprehensive scope of the commandments revealed in the Torah suggests to a Jew not an overwhelming burden of ideals and oughts, but rather the comprehensive and holistic relationship with God. Following Rabbinic tradition, observing the commandments constitutes an opportunity here and now in this world to discern God's presence and concern for human welfare all around us, in all the small and the big moments of daily life. Martin Buber, in the twentieth century, noted the centrality of human decision and deed in realizing

God's active presence in the world, saying that amid the human experience of God's distance or inaccessibility, "for the one who chooses, who decides [and acts] . . . God is the closest, the most familiar Being."[39] In the Rabbinic period, the observance of the law is tied to human participation in God's intentions for the world, but the concept of tikkun olam is limited to legal steps taken to improve society, capitalizing on the biblical meaning of the verb *tkn* as to straighten or repair. The Midrash expands this to refer to humanity's role in completing God's work of creation. It is this eschatological use that is expanded in the later traditions of Kabbalah and Hasidism.

According to Isaac Luria's Kabbalistic teaching about creation, God put His light into vessels that could not contain it and therefore shattered, allowing this divine light to disperse into the world of things and beings. According to traditional Lurianic mysticism, which influenced later Hasidic thought, the mission of human life is to restore the sparks of divine light to God. In fact, the purpose of Israel's diaspora is to gather these divine sparks that are embedded in the world and restore them to God. Kabbalist teaching therefore raises to prominence the central responsibility of tikkun olam, in terms of the human actions taken to repair the flaws in the universe and reunite the *Sefirot*, or God's emanations. Every human performance of a commandment takes on cosmic importance in the *Zohar*, the thirteenth-century mystical text of Kabbalah. Engaging in prayer and Torah study, and observing rituals or festivals, all help reunite the Sefirot and end the division between God and His *Shekinah*, or divine presence.

The mystical power of everyday human performance of the commandments is heightened with significance in the Hasidic Jewish tradition. In the Hasidic view, God has made room for human free response and responsibility. God has made humans partners in the world's destiny. As Buber says, "Creation is incomplete because discord still reigns within it, and peace can emerge only from the created."[40] Just as human disobedience caused an earlier rupture of the world from God, so acts of human obedience and faith can heal this rupture and help restore the world to God. With free will, humans are free to love God or to deny God. In this worldview, every moment is an opportunity for individuals to act with God or against God, to help move the world closer to God or to distance the world from God, to discern God's presence or to further obscure God's presence in the world. Every human action therefore can have cosmic consequences. Hasidic Jews believe that every righteous action, every fulfillment of a commandment, helps inch the world closer to messianic redemption. In fact, these actions are what sustain God's holy light and presence in the world and therefore sustain the world in existence. If for a moment, no one around the world were performing some *mitzvah* (even a relatively minor act like lighting Sabbath candles), the world would cease to be. A Hasidic saying notes those who turn to God in repentance (*teshuvah*) redeem not only themselves, but also redeem God.[41] This is again because in this mystical view, God Himself is divided from His Shekinah, who is in exile in the world and can be liberated only through human righteous action. The underlying ideas of human partnership with God and covenantal responsibility for the world's destiny are common to various Jewish traditions.

During the nineteenth-century period of Reform in Judaism, many Jews confronted the issue of the significance and value of the commandments, and their differing interpretations of how to treat the law led to the divisions of Reform, Conservative, and Orthodox Judaisms. One of the primary identifiers of what came to be Orthodox Judaism in contrast to the Reform or Conservative branches was the affirmation that the *halakha* (religious law) was in fact binding. It was intended neither as metaphor nor only an outdated requirement that applied only to ancient generations; it was uniformly binding on Jews who have been called by God to respond covenantally. Today as well, Orthodox Jews value the commitment to live according to the commandments; they may explain, "We are so commanded" or "it is a mitzvah," acknowledging the virtue of fulfilling any commandment given lovingly by God. Unfortunately, many misinterpret such strict adherence to the commandments as an archaic legalism that focuses on the letter of the law and misses the spirit. However, for Orthodox Jews, the Rabbinic treatment of religious law presents patterns of this-worldly holiness and patterns for living in accordance with God's revealed commandments. The commitment to follow halakha is itself a delightful gift of enjoying divine presence in every dimension of ordinary life and imbues every moment of life with sacramental significance.

While Orthodox Jews may consider equally the ritual commandments and the ethical commandments, Reform Jews distinguish between them, considering only the latter to be binding. Reform Jews nevertheless emphasize the theme of human responsibility in and for the world. Reform Jews today often interpret the repair of the world demanded by tikkun olam in terms of the responsibilities we all share for social justice, to heal the pain and suffering in the world and make it a better place for everyone. It has become especially common for young girls and boys on becoming *bat mitzvah* or *bar mitzvah* to incorporate a particular community service project into their transition into adult responsibility for their faith, or to request that any gifts be directed to charitable giving as part of the spirit of tikkun olam. This spirit of repairing and improving the world for all reiterates the

Hasidic interpretation that it is humanity's responsibility to help repair the world and perfect it. According to many Orthodox Jews, when the world is perfected under God's sovereignty, the promised Messiah will arrive.[42] For those who are more mystically minded, human covenantal work actually effects a completion or realization of God in the world, while others focus on the universal ethical imperative, as God's finite worldly partners, to love others and repair conflicts in the world. Despite their divergence on the eschatological and mystical import of tikkun olam, what is a common line of Jewish interpretation is the sense of human partnership in and responsibility for helping to carry out God's intentions of world redemption.

Israel: Wrestling with God

So far I have discussed human responsibility and human-divine partnership. This section addresses a more particular illustration of this partnership. According to the biblical account in the Book of Genesis, Israel is the name given to Jacob after a long night of wrestling with a mysterious angel who refuses to reveal his name. So Israel means, for Jews, one who wrestles with God. That the relationship with God, the partnership between divine and human, is not easy, but in fact requires active struggle and wrestling is one of the most vibrant insights of the Jewish tradition on faith. The values of humility and obedience are prominently discussed in religion. Those are not categorically excluded here, of course, but it is often jarring to non-Jews to encounter various Jewish expressions of responding to God in active struggle. Some contemporary Jews might even say that one is not required to believe in God, but one certainly must struggle with God. Such a proposition strikes many non-Jews as marginally impious if not entirely blasphemous, but part of the emphasis in such a statement is the degree to which faith demands a human choice to commit to and participate in the relationship with God. Many have described the relationship between human beings and God as a marriage, a relationship into which one enters to create something larger like a family. This requires a commitment to the relationship; in our contemporary sense of an egalitarian marriage, it requires a commitment to stick with it and fight for the marriage. In a marriage, for example, fighting is a far better sign of marital health than indifference or passive obedience. A good marriage might even be defined by the skills of the two parties in fighting well in a spirit of respect for the other.

Talmudic study provides an example of active struggle in faith as it values debate and argument. Talmudic study is the responsibility of every Jew, and it takes one through generations of commentary and argument and counterargument in which various Rabbis actively wrestle with the text and the tradition in order to learn something more about God's plan or intentions. Because the tradition of commentary on scripture, custom, and legal interpretation has something of great and lasting value, one seeks to enter into it more and more deeply to gain something valuable. What is most interesting perhaps is that the Talmud is not used to settle arguments. It is not for final answers that Jews study the Talmud, but to learn to ask and answer questions in a rich and dynamic way. Talmudic study has often been done in pairs, indicating that people learn better through the method of debate than by passive reading. Imagine a traditional yeshiva with rows and rows of long tables with pairs of students debating energetically, perhaps shouting to buttress some particular argument. Like the various systems of religious law in the world's religious traditions, Rabbinic Judaism can be quite complicated and can employ very sophisticated arguments to show how the commandments can be fulfilled in all kinds of changing circumstances. While these have at times been criticized as an overemphasis on legalism that misses the spiritual point of obedience to God's law, at their heart is not a legalistic search for loopholes, but rather a tremendous valuing of the intellectual vigor with which humans seek to understand and engage more deeply and more actively with a loving and generous God's revelation. As many Orthodox Jews today say, "where there is a Rabbinic will, there's a halakhic way," indicating the rich tradition of human response to God's revealed law. The questioning and answering, the conversation, and sacred arguing are the means by which Jews participate actively in the covenantal life.

Being committed to this relationship with God as an active participant also means holding the other party accountable. Examples abound that articulate this dimension of a relationship with God as one in which a mere human being might hold God accountable. The first example is Elie Wiesel's description of his experience in Auschwitz, and the second is the biblical Book of Job.

Elie Wiesel reflected many years on the event described below before writing a fictional revision of it in a play titled *The Trial of God*. It is not the play itself but the description of the original event one night in Auschwitz that is relevant for us here. The account below is two paragraphs of Robert McAfee Brown's eloquent description in his introduction to Wiesel's play.

> By the time he was fifteen, Elie Wiesel was in Auschwitz, a Nazi death camp. A teacher of Talmud befriended him by insisting that whenever they were together they would study Talmud—Talmud without pens or pencils, Talmud without paper, Talmud without books. It would be their act of religious defiance.

One night the teacher took Wiesel back to his own barracks, and there, with the young boy as the only witness, three great Jewish scholars—masters of Talmud, Halakhah, and Jewish jurisprudence—put God on trial, creating, in that eerie place, "a rabbinic court of law to indict the Almighty." The trial lasted several nights. Witnesses were heard, evidence was gathered, conclusions were drawn, all of which issued finally in a unanimous verdict: the Lord God Almighty, Creator of Heaven and Earth, was found guilty of crimes against creation and humankind. And then, after what Wiesel describes as an "infinity of silence," the Talmudic scholar looked at the sky and said "It's time for evening prayers," and the members of the tribunal recited Maariv, the evening service.[43]

This story strikes many people very deeply and very differently. Some are deeply offended at the presumption of a group of all-too-human individuals putting God on trial and then even, *God forbid!* judging God to be guilty. *Who are we to judge God?* It strikes some as outrageous blasphemy and arrogant self-idolization. Such a response certainly makes sense in the context of the view taken by many that humans are to relate to God as their Creator and Judge, the absolute and almighty Lord of all the world who generously metes out divine grace to a largely undeserving humanity.

On the other hand, when it is viewed within this historical context of God's responses to human suffering and within the context of Jewish covenantal views of partnership between God and humanity, the account suggests a commitment rather like that in marriage in which one party can and ought to hold the other party accountable, explicitly because of the degree of trust in the relationship. What is so telling in Wiesel's experience of the Talmudic scholars and their bold trial of God is that their legal judgment is followed by evening prayers. Their faith has absolutely nothing to do with belief in God's existence, which is perhaps the most trivial aspect of religious faith, or with being pleased with God. Instead, it is a commitment to a relationship within which they solidly find themselves. Judging God guilty and holding God accountable for their suffering does not by any means lead them to abandon this relationship. The relationship is for life, so to speak, or for eternity. The particular individuals involved are not skeptics or indifferent nonbelievers or even passively religious Jews. They are Talmudic scholars, heavily invested (with their whole lives and their whole worlds of meaningfulness) in this covenantal relationship with God. When they put God on trial, they do so from a position of deeply abiding respect for the relationship. They are active participants, not passive recipients of God's gifts and mercies and punishments. As indicated with the examples of Hasidic and Orthodox Judaism, they take seriously the real value and power of human responsibility in partnership with God.

Another example of such a bold human response to God can be found in the Book of Job. The part of the story most commonly retold, especially in Christian contexts, presents a Job who is a patient and faithful servant of God, maintaining his faith and trust in God throughout his suffering. Many people are surprised when they actually read the entire Book of Job to find that Job does not humbly proclaim that God knows best. One reason for this is that the basic story of Job as a patient servant of God predated the actual biblical book and has somehow persisted in people's religious imagination, especially in many traditional Christian contexts that value the interpretation of faith as patient suffering that will be rewarded in the end. If we take a look at the biblical text in its entirety, we see Job boldly seeking to hold God accountable for the sufferings that have befallen him in a way that echoes Jewish covenantal relationship.

In its present or final form in the biblical narrative, the Book of Job begins with a prologue in which we learn the true reason for Job's sufferings. We the audience or readers have the benefit of knowing what Job and his friends do not—namely, that the entire course of events is a test in order that God may win a wager with Satan, proving to Satan that Job's faith is true and constant. We know several things from this: In this particular case, there is nothing concrete to be gained or learned by Job through his suffering. In a more abstract sense, of course, what is to be gained is God's glorification, but that is beside the ordinary list of explanations or justifications that abound about human suffering—that suffering is beneficial for us, that it builds character, that it teaches compassion for others, that it helps one appreciate what one has, that it teaches humility, and the like. This last lesson of teaching humility is one that we will see in Job's case by the end of the story, but first, I examine Job's response.

Initially, when he loses his family, his livelihood, his wealth, and even his physical health, Job resigns himself to his suffering and accepts God's will. His friends come and sit with him, staying quiet, at least at first. After a while, they begin to speak, ostensibly to "console" him. Their consolations are of an unwanted kind, as they suggest that Job must have done something wrong to receive such punishments from God. Basically, they are articulating an ancient and commonsense wisdom—God rewards the good and punishes the guilty. They echo the common explanation of human suffering as divine punishment for human wrongs committed. It is a theological variant of the Hindu doctrine of karma, which suggests that good actions reap good consequences and bad actions reap bad consequences. This kind of explanation has been very popular in all ancient religious traditions; even today it is hurled by hateful and judgmental people on anyone whose actions they condemn.

(For example, Hurricane Katrina in 2006 was "explained" by some as God's punishment for moral abominations like homosexuality in New Orleans; the 2009 earthquake in Haiti was explained as a consequence of Haiti's earlier pact with the devil to gain independence from France.) The author of the Book of Job here is clearly not advancing that interpretation, as he has already given us the backstory in which God cites Job as a model example of faith and righteousness. What this does then, for the reader, is explicitly to place the friends and their explanation of Job's suffering in the wrong.

Job's response is perhaps the most revealing. While he initially accepted God's will and the loss of his wealth, family, and health, his friends' accusations that he had done something wrong and needs now to repent provoke his anger and frustration. He repeatedly proclaims his innocence and protests the injustice of his experience, becoming progressively angrier and more agitated. He goes from defending his own innocence, to protesting the unfairness of what is happening to him, to then demanding an explanation from God. One friend accuses him of explicitly putting God in the wrong and himself in the right, but he knows himself and is convinced of his own innocence. He is frustrated with the incongruity he sees between his own innocence and this idea that God is just. Using quite legalistic language, he demands that God appear in court with him and explain to him what he has done wrong.[44] Job clearly realizes how ridiculous a proposition this is—*as if one could haul God into court*, he laments. The core of his argument is that he himself is innocent and he wants an explanation. The popular image of Job as the patient and faithful servant is not exactly contradicted here; Job does have faith and we see his acceptance of whatever God gives and takes at the beginning. The trouble seems to emerge from the accusations of his friends, from their attempts to explain his suffering on rational grounds as the deserved divine consequence of some secret evil doings on Job's part. The entire drama turns out less to be a morality play about one person's faith in God, and more a morality play about the validity of human explanations of the suffering of others. Although Job gets angry at the unfairness of his experience, he is in the right, as we the readers know from the prologue, and his friends who try to explain and justify his suffering from within their limited imagination of what makes sense to them are in the wrong. A reversal occurs at the end with God's revelation. After Job's repeated demands that God explain to him what he has done wrong, and issue clear charges as in a criminal court, God suddenly does appear. In fact, God's appearance follows immediately upon a verse in which a friend Elihu says of God, "He will never answer. Therefore, mortals, fear Him whom even men of wisdom cannot see." Yahweh immediately answers Job from the storm, "Who dares speak darkly words with no sense?"[45] Although God accuses Job of "speaking darkly," it seems God has a sense of humor, appearing in a timely way to contradict Elihu's proclamation that God would never answer. It also seems God intends to set the record straight between Job and his friends.

Job has demanded an explanation, and Yahweh appears. He seems quite angry and unleashes unanswerable questions on Job. He begins with the question, "Where were you when I founded the earth?" He then proceeds through a long litany extolling His own greatness as Creator. Yahweh never gives Job an explicit explanation of why he has suffered so. He does not just let him in on the secret and apologize, acknowledging, "Sorry, you didn't deserve this, but I had to prove your righteousness to Satan." Job does, however, receive an answer of a different kind. The answer seems simply to be that God is God and almighty and unassailable. So while Job does not get an explanation or an answer to his particular question of why he is suffering, he does receive other tremendous gifts. First, he receives revelation directly from God. God responds and reveals Himself to him. As Job says at the end of Yahweh's long speech, "I knew you, but only by rumor; my eye has beheld You today" (42:5). We should remember this is a man of faith, so it would be a tremendous gift actually and personally to behold God and have confirmation of one's faith. Like every individual of faith, Job desired an audience with God, and he received it. Now, Job also receives another gift that helps situate the meaningfulness of the entire story in a Jewish view of a relationship with God in which each party can boldly hold the other party accountable. In the epilogue, Yahweh turns to the friends and tells them explicitly that He is very angry with them: "you have not spoken rightly about me as did my servant Job" (42:7). Given the context of God's wager with Satan and the prominence of the rational explanations and justifications of Job's suffering given by the friends, this result helps make the whole event a morality play about the validity of our explanations of human suffering. God does here defend Job publicly and assert him to be in the right all along. He is not in the right over against God, but he spoke rightly about God, while his friends did not. What is God referring to as speaking rightly? Again, the center of Job's argument all along was that he did not deserve this suffering, and that it did not make sense. Yahweh's criticism of the friends and defense of Job helps frame the entire story as a defense of three particular propositions: that people do not necessarily deserve their suffering, that suffering may not make sense, and that it is wrong for people to explain and justify the suffering of others as if they could speak for God or explain God's ways clearly. Although Yahweh criticizes Job for questioning God's ways, He does not punish him for it, and the fact that Yahweh responds at all makes His ferocious rage itself a gift of revelation. In the end, Job receives the explanation he sought, albeit not the precise form he expected. It is a confirmation of the responsibility in faith of holding God accountable to the covenantal relationship valued in Jewish tradition.

Conclusion

Putting these four religious visions of human responsibility into dialogue with each other adds something to the traditionally Christian and Protestant question of the relationship between faith and works. The Protestant Reformation is credited with creating a distance between Protestants and Roman Catholics on this issue. Protestants rally around the idea that people are justified by their faith in God's grace as revealed in the incarnation, death, and resurrection of Christ, while the Catholic Church teaches that faith must be realized in good works. Unfortunately, the Protestant emphasis on justification by faith alone is too often reduced to a sense that one is saved and redeemed by the acceptance of creeds about Jesus. (The following chapter examines three Protestant discussions of faith and doubt that avoid such a reduction.) Examining the ways in which religious responsibility is articulated replaces the simplistic dichotomy of faith and works as two opposed things, with the ways in which faith is dynamically embodied in works of human action. As we have seen, in Islam and Hinduism, a commitment to religious observance and dutiful action precedes the conviction of faith. The centrality of commitment to a particular religious ethic complicates any overly simplistic discussion of faith as what someone believes.

While this entire book begins with a premise of examining dimensions of faith other than creeds or belief statements about God's existence and intentions, this chapter has dealt with various ways in which faith is articulated as a commitment to a certain way of life, as a special human responsibility for the world. In the case of Hindu dharma, human responsibility reflects the impersonal and cosmic spiritual laws of consequence and duty according to one's particular relationships with others. Who one is and what one ought to do are defined by one's relationships and obligations to others. This idea that one's actions matter because of one's role in relationship is particularized in the Western monotheistic traditions into the personal relationship with God. Religion and faith become a distinctly human responsibility because of the special human status of relationship with God. In C. S. Lewis's Christian allegory of *Narnia*, even children are endowed with tremendous responsibility for saving the world. In Islamic teaching, humans are the only creatures created with free will. As God's chosen representatives on earth, humans must *choose* to fulfill their created responsibility to respond to God's sovereignty in appropriate ways that support submission to God's will and consequently improve the world. Jewish articulations of this covenantal relationship add a particularly heightened dimension of faith as an active struggle with God in a contentious but infinitely valuable relationship. Having explored in part 1 dimensions of faith as an experience of trust, humility, or belonging and a sacred responsibility to participate in a relationship with God, community, and the natural world, I turn now in the next two parts to dimensions of doubt, transcendence, and skepticism in the Christian and Hindu traditions as well as Christian and Buddhist mystical traditions and modern secular challenges.

PART TWO

THE CENTRALITY
OF DOUBT

CHAPTER THREE

CHRISTIAN FAITH
AND THE PROTESTANT PRINCIPLE

This chapter takes a closer look at three figures whose discussions of faith are among the most influential in twentieth-century Christian theology. Two, Paul Tillich and Karl Barth, are twentieth-century Christian theologians and one, Søren Kierkegaard, is a nineteenth-century philosopher, but all three determine directions taken by existentialist Christian theology in the late twentieth century. All three figures happen to be Protestant, not simply by denominational identification, but more importantly, each is guided by the Protestant doctrine of justification by faith alone to emphasize the priority of God's saving grace over any human works and human understanding. All three adhere to the Protestant Principle (an individual's right and responsibility to radically question and reinterpret questions of faith), albeit in different ways.

At the onset of the Reformation, Martin Luther's fundamental theological protest concerned the deep question of how human actions here and now could ever effect our eternal salvation. In Luther's view, sin was so pervasive, so inscribed on a person's soul, that it was simply too much for meager human actions to alleviate. Justification or reconciliation with God, for Luther, was simply not within the power of human action to bring about. This critical limitation on what human actions can do for human destiny poses a somewhat different outlook from chapter 2's discussion of the saving power of human action. While human action can help repair and reform the world, it cannot lead to salvation in a Christian view. The limitation posed by the Protestant Principle in this chapter foreshadows what Karl Barth says pointedly: *God is in heaven; thou art on earth*. Faith does not change the geography of human finitude. How can our meager earthly actions impact our eternal destiny? The *protest* that pertains here has to do with skepticism toward all human religious discourse. The consequence of such skeptical self-criticism of the ultimate power of human actions is not at all an uncritical search for the purely divine, but rather the emphasis that what we call God's, what we may call revelation and what we consider absolute and ultimate, comes entirely from outside human experience.

What this chapter focuses on is therefore not doubt in the existence of God or doubt about the Ultimate itself, but rather the nagging doubt or "protest" in any true faith that we may mistakenly worship our own ideas instead of God. Kierkegaard, Tillich, and Barth represent this faithful "protest" in diametrically different theological ways. Barth utterly rejected the turn taken by modern liberal theology, which Tillich embraced and Kierkegaard criticized. Where Tillich saw a symbiotic relationship between theology and culture, shaping in fact a "theology of culture," Barth emphasized the diametrical opposition of revelation over all human understanding, including religion, and Kierkegaard opposed the religious and Christian life to the complacent and reified culture of Christendom. For Tillich and Barth, faithful protest is a way of preserving the transcendence of the sacred in our religious discourse and a corrective to the inevitable idol-making of human imagination.[1] For all three, true faith incorporates an active self-criticism that orients one toward God's revelation over one's own self-certainty or rationality. For Tillich, faith must include doubt if it is truly directed at the infinite and not at something finite and human-made. For Kierkegaard, faith is entirely nonrational or even irrational and may carry one outside cultural expectations of rationality and morality. For Barth, faith is first and foremost a response to God's revelation in grace.

Søren Kierkegaard

Many of Søren Kierkegaard's writings are presented through carefully constructed pseudonyms so it can be difficult to ascertain precisely what his own views on religion were. Still, we can derive provocative insights about faith and doubt delivered through his works. Kierkegaard has been called the father of modern existentialism, especially of the Christian theistic variety. He called attention to the experience of the single individual who must confront the paradoxical claims that Christianity makes about the person of Jesus Christ. For Kierkegaard, humanity is caught in tension between the infinite and the finite, and the individual self defines itself in this active relation. Kierkegaard drew a distinction between what is objectively true and the individual's subjective relation to that truth. Criticizing the philosophers and theologians who focused on the objective content of Christian religion, he turned theological focus to the subjectivity of religion. He argued that

Christianity is not about objective proofs for the existence of God or any knowledge at all. According to Kierkegaard, one's subjective relationship to God is based on faith, not on rational knowledge or pragmatic understanding of God or morality.[2] This first section takes up three facets of his treatment of faith: the paradox and absurdity of faith beyond reason and morality; the existential commitment and the development of the self in faith; and the radical hope against hope in God's promise that entails Christian faith.

Faith on the Strength of the Absurd

Kierkegaard did not use the now ubiquitous phrase "leap of faith," but such a leap of faith is what he depicts in his revisionist meditation on the biblical Abraham's actions in his book *Fear and Trembling*. Abraham has served as a paradigm of faith in God for Jews, Christians, and Muslims in different ways that revolve around his obedience to God. Traditional Christianity too has emphasized that Abraham was so obedient, so great in his faith, that he was willing to give up his only treasured son, the son who was so hard-won, the son promised him and miraculously given him by God in his and his wife Sarah's old age. The conventional Christian interpretation of the biblical account of the sacrifice of Isaac stresses the extraordinary nature of the demand God placed on Abraham and Abraham's unquestioning obedience to serve God by sacrificing back to God precisely that which was most precious to him. In the pseudonymous text, *Fear and Trembling*, Kierkegaard renders a very different interpretation of what defines Abraham's actions as faith. To Kierkegaard, it is not his obedience to God or his willingness to give up and sacrifice to God what God has given him that constitutes the greatness of his faith. Instead, for Kierkegaard, it is Abraham's willingness to believe God's promise as it would be realized in his son Isaac, however paradoxical.

According to Kierkegaard, Abraham's faith is defined in his patient expectation that he would have a son in the first place. "It was faith that made Abraham accept the promise that all nations of the earth should be blessed in his seed. Time went by, the possibility was still there, and Abraham had faith; time went by, it became unlikely, and Abraham had faith."[3] Even as time marched on and it became physically unlikely and even impossible for Sarah to conceive, Abraham continued to abide in God's promise of descendants. Most of us watching someone pine away for children year after year, decade after decade, would advise them to give up, to resign themselves to reality, and to make peace with the fact that they will not have biological children. That would be a perfectly reasonable and prudent response. However, for Kierkegaard, Abraham's greatness of faith lies in his continued clinging to God's promise despite the growing unlikelihood and even impossibility of its realization. Kierkegaard writes, "it is great to give up one's desire, but greater to stick to it after having given it up."[4] In other words, to understand the unlikelihood or impossibility and still to trust God's promise constitutes the greatness of faith.

There are two dimensions that stand out in Kierkegaard's discussion of Abraham's greatness in faith. One is that it is entirely contrary to reason; it is not reasonable for one so advanced in age to expect to conceive a child. The second is that faith means believing something that may be absurd, while resignation is the acceptance of some state of affairs as reality. Much in what many commonly describe as faith is in fact what Kierkegaard terms resignation, or acceptance of reality, or making peace with whatever happens. He says it is a great thing and quite challenging and courageous to do, but faith is an act that requires a movement beyond human possibility altogether, into the realm of the impossible or irrational or absurd. I take up this active movement beyond human possibility more fully in the following section as an existential commitment to become a self before God.

Outwardly, the process of resignation and the process of faith look the same, as Abraham proceeds to take Isaac up the mountain and sharpen his knife as commanded by God. Inwardly, however, the act of resignation and the act of faith are entirely opposed. Resignation accepts the reality that one faces and gives up any other claims or hopes that are contradicted by that evident reality. Faith sees the evident reality and believes or hopes precisely what is entirely contrary to that evidence. "He believed on the strength of the absurd, for all human calculation had long since been suspended."[5] Kierkegaard's account of faith places us with Abraham in a very precarious position that cannot be reconciled with reason or even with morality. If Abraham is acting in resignation, he knows precisely what will follow. He knows he will lose Isaac, but he may take consolation, however strange, in the strength of his decision to obey God no matter the cost. It will likely be a terrible unhappiness, but it is nothing compared to the dangerous expectation entailed if Abraham is acting in faith. If he is acting in faith, he is raising the knife and preparing to plunge it into his son, all the while continuing to believe that he will not lose him. Imagine we did not know the end of the story when the ram miraculously appears and Abraham keeps his son. It is one thing to accept the loss of one's son. It is another thing altogether to expect to keep one's son and act in such a way to make that an impossibility. He could well be completely and tragically wrong. While most Kierkegaard scholars emphasize Kierkegaard's opposition of faith and resignation, Kevin Hoffman disagrees with those who interpret Abraham's faith as confidence that he will not in fact be asked to carry out the sacrifice. Hoffman instead calls for a focus on the degree to which Christian life is always an inner battle. In this interpretation, faith incorporates and moves past resignation by fully acknowledging our fragility while fully investing in what lies beyond our control.[6]

The risk of being wrong is a crucial part of what makes it an act of faith, and it turns on the role of paradox and absurdity in the movement of faith. If it were reasonable, there would be no true risk. Here, we can all readily imagine watching Abraham move in fear and trembling, not confidence, as he prepares to obey God and yet believe God's promise to abide by the covenant in Isaac. In another sense, of course, we cannot imagine it because it is so contrary to our understanding. As Kierkegaard says, however, the Christian gospel is to be believed, not understood, precisely through its offense to reason. Kierkegaard takes the sense of paradox and absurdity in faith so seriously, however, that it not only means it lies outside understanding, but that it moves one outside the realm of understandability altogether. In *Philosophical Fragments*, Kierkegaard's pseudonym Climacus denies that faith amounts to knowledge. Faith is not acquired by a natural act of will by the believer; instead, faith and the condition of passion by which one can believe the content of Christianity are received from God.[7] As Kierkegaard writes in the *Concluding Unscientific Postscript*, "there is here the certainty that viewed objectively, it is the absurd, and this absurdity, held fast in the passion of inwardness, is faith."[8]

Kierkegaard scholars are divided between those who emphasize an anti-intellectual element in his thought and those who see him articulating a Christian philosophy of faith. For example, David Wisdo emphasizes that faith is a miracle not to be explained for Kierkegaard, while Louis Pojman argues that faith, while a miracle of grace, still includes a decision of the will.[9] Engaging the debate among scholars over whether Kierkegaard is an irrationalist, C. S. Evans rejects the interpretation that Kierkegaard intends a logical contradiction and instead suggests a constructive tension between reason and paradox. According to Evans, the point of the incarnation, for Kierkegaard, was to challenge the assumption that we have reliable natural knowledge of God and human beings.[10] Evans points out our universal tendency to judge adequate our own ideas about God and refers to such confidence in our rational capacities as sin. Human sinfulness "not only blocks [us] from a proper understanding of God; it is the reason the paradox is to us human beings a paradox."[11] Evans concludes that Kierkegaard's paradox is both above reason and against reason: it is above reason in that we cannot understand how God

could become a human person, and it is against reason insofar as our thinking and expectations shaped by selfishness judge the incarnation as unlikely
and impossible. Even though the paradox is judged as logically impossible by
the unbeliever, it is not against reason for the believer. As Steven Emmanuel
argues, the absolute paradox is not a logical contradiction, but a sign of transcendence, whereby the absurd is transformed in faith.[12] Evans reminds us
too that Kierkegaard's central concern is not to argue for the reasonableness
or the unreasonableness of Christianity. "It is to argue the impossibility of
neutrality. When reason encounters the paradox, faith and offense are both
possible; what is not possible is indifference."[13]

Abraham's actions, described by Kierkegaard as a movement of faith
wherein he is ready to plunge the knife into his son even while believing
he will keep his son, cannot be understood by anyone else. Such an act of
faith pushes one outside the bounds of reason and morality because it is
not something we can condone or responsibly justify in any way. Faith, in
Kierkegaard's interpretation, makes an individual very alone in the world,
separated from others who cannot understand him and even from his own
sense of understanding and reason, which condemn him. Faith places an
individual in a position where his actions and beliefs are absolutely protested
by all as incomprehensible. While it is a matter of greatest consequence
for the self to realize this relation to God, it is not a matter of comfort or
an elimination of doubt or risk because we remain on the plane of finite
existence, or as Paul says, as long as we are mortals, we continue to see
through a glass darkly.[14] Instead, it is a commitment to a relationship with
God that proceeds always in fear and trembling because it takes us outside
any comfortable place of reassurance to this direct tension between the
infinite and the finite that defines human consciousness.

Existential Commitment
and the Development of the Self

What exactly is faith for Kierkegaard? In *Philosophical Fragments* and the
Concluding Unscientific Postscript, he presents it as an existential decision by
the solitary individual of how to relate to this supposed historical event two
thousand years ago, in which the eternal entered history, when God became
human and revealed Godself in such a way as to offer salvation. Faith is the
decision actively to trust in this "truth" of Christianity, despite all evidence
to the contrary. Kierkegaard saw his task as correcting the prominent view
of his time that becoming a Christian meant accepting certain objective ideas
about God and Christ. In the *Concluding Unscientific Postscript* Kierkegaard
emphasizes the difference between any objective knowledge or confession

of faith as a set of beliefs and the subjectivity and inwardness of Christian faith. Kierkegaard writes that faith exists in the contradictory combination of infinite passion and objective uncertainty. "If I am able to apprehend God objectively, I do not have faith; but because I cannot do this, I must have faith."[15] If one relied on evidence, it would be not faith, but a measured and reasonable response to what one has witnessed. It is not the "what," or content propositions of revelation, that is important, but the "how," or the way one relates to revelation or how one lives in a relationship with God.[16]

It is very important for Kierkegaard that faith not only does not require evidence, but it *cannot* rely on evidence at all. Having faith requires the absence of good evidence and the clear consciousness of this lack of evidence. Believing simplistically in the gospel without acknowledging its paradoxical nature would be credulity, not religious faith. The greatest stumbling block to faith, according to Kierkegaard, is that it is contrary to our expectations of what is reasonable and what we should and should not trust. Only a fool would be taken in and accept an unbelievable offer that he has not earned and that the giver has no good reason to give him. The Christian gospel, or good news, is simply too good to accept without reservation, and faith is, by definition, without reservation or caution. Faith embraces this inherent risk of being wrong; "without risk, no faith."[17]

In *The Sickness Unto Death*, Kierkegaard develops this existential decision that confronts the individual. As a self in tension between the infinite and the finite, the individual experiences despair. However, as consciousness of one's relationship to God grows, one experiences both an increasing closeness to God and an increasing despair. The individual has a choice to make of how to relate to the Christian gospel. One may choose to have faith and align herself with God's plan or may choose sin or disobedience. Kristen Deede notes the explicit connections between consciousness of sin, individuality, and relating to God.[18] According to Kierkegaard, the cure for despair, which is a state of sin, is faith, which paradoxically means both an increase in despair and the cure for it, as one decides to commit to this relationship with God in absolute faith that one will be forgiven one's sins.[19] The paradox here lies in the dialectical challenge of seeking forgiveness: genuinely seeking forgiveness requires both a serious acknowledgment of one's sin and the radical yet hopeful expectation that one may be forgiven. As Sylvia Walsh explains, consciousness of sin can move us to know our need for God, at which point we must perform a Christian about-face and believe that with God all things are possible.[20]

Faith is an existential decision to acknowledge sin and the impossibility to be what one is. Consciousness of sin distinguishes Christianity from any immanent religion because it acknowledges the self's innate failure and impossibility of relating properly to God by any means of its own. For Kierkegaard, the consciousness of sin makes way for faith, not virtue, indicating the degree to which the emphasis is not on what a person can do or be, but rather his or her relation to God and consciously standing before God. It is only through revelation that one can move from sin to consciousness of sin to faith. One becomes what one is meant to be only when standing before God in faith in Christ as the overcoming of the breach between God and humanity. As Kierkegaard writes, every individual "is invited to live on the most intimate terms with God!. . . God comes to the world, allows himself to be born, to suffer, to die, and this suffering God—he almost implores and beseeches this person to accept the help that is offered to him!"[21]

Bringing together Kierkegaard's absolute paradox, the necessary risk of faith, and the consciousness of sin as the avenue to proper relation to God, we see that Kierkegaard views the journey of faith as constitutive of the individual self. The self's own development requires a movement beyond rationality and understanding and into uncertainty. As Louis Pojman writes, "faith is the highest virtue and personal growth depends on uncertainty."[22] We must proceed through the offense to reason and social convention to trust in God and find ourselves beyond the realm of what we can understand and hope to control and before God. The existential commitment to be a self before God requires an act of the will to transcend the understanding. As Steven Emmanuel writes, the absolute paradox "reveals a basic tension within the concept of rationality itself" and "sets the stage for this decision by shifting the issue away from the intellectual (objectivity) to the realm of interest and passion (subjectivity)."[23] Becoming a self authentically standing before God requires the transcendence of what we expect to understand and control in our lives. While there is a move to transcend the limits of reason and convention, faith for Kierkegaard still appears to require an act of the will to be transformed in grace. The resolution, according to Emmanuel, is a decision to affirm, like William James did in "The Will to Believe," the role of the passions over logic. On Emmanuel's reading of Kierkegaard, belief in Christianity is a rational decision or resolution based on the desirability of eternal happiness.

Christian Faith as Hope Beyond Hope

The third facet of Kierkegaard's discussion of faith takes us to a story presented later in *Fear and Trembling*, taken from the biblical Old Testament Book of Tobit but retold to illustrate Christian faith and hope. Sarah is a young girl who has been wed seven times, each time to see her bridegroom killed on her wedding night by the evil demon who loves her. The situation is full of sorrow, as all the evidence of the past indicates she cannot and should not devote herself to love again, knowing with such certainty that it will surely be taken from her. Yet, when a young man named Tobias wishes to marry her, her family goes through the wedding preparations, albeit in tears. Kierkegaard points out here that a poet reading this story would emphasize the heroism of Tobias and his courageous willingness to risk his life in such a way. Kierkegaard proposes a different reading. He says that while Tobias acted chivalrously, Sarah is the true heroine of the story. Kierkegaard stresses that while "it is better to give than to receive," the greater mystery or challenge to our understanding is that "it is much harder to receive than to give."[24] While Tobias, and any real man, Kierkegaard says, may be heroic and want to sacrifice himself for the sake of love, what is truly remarkable and beyond our understanding is the courage called for to accept another's self-sacrifice. "For what love for God it takes to want to be healed when one has been crippled from the start for no fault of one's own, an unsuccessful specimen of humanity from the very beginning! What ethical maturity to take on the responsibility of allowing the loved one such an act of daring! What humility before another person! What faith in God that in the next instant she should not hate the man to whom she owed everything!"[25]What Tobias did took an act of daring, but the truly courageous act for Kierkegaard lies in Sarah's willingness to accept this extraordinary gift without then despising Tobias for giving it to her.[26] Sarah's willingness to accept such pity defines faith and hope for Kierkegaard because it is much harder to receive than to give. The Christian account of justification by faith in God's grace speaks to precisely this emotional and psychological challenge to genuinely and graciously receive and accept God's forgiveness in such a way that we do not hate God and ourselves for it, but instead truly incorporate it into our sense of who we are in our relationship with God. Reading Kierkegaard's *Works of Love* together with *Fear and Trembling*, Amy Laura Hall suggests that Sarah's willingness to accept Tobias's love in trust is to be contrasted with any mere confession of guilt. "Sarah does not look closely at Tobias to determine whether she will accept his love. . . . The hope to which we are summoned in *Fear and Trembling*, albeit by a confused and riddling poet, requires that we be mindful only of our own individual debt and redemption."[27]

This brings me back to the discussion of the gospel as something presented for Christians as "too good to be true" and therefore unbelievable. The greater the gift, the more unbelievable it becomes, psychologically speaking, and the more difficult it is to accept graciously. If we look at Kierkegaard's treatment of the biblical Abraham and the young bride Sarah, we see faith as an acceptance of a gift, a trust in God's promise without measure or caution. It would be reasonable in both cases to be cautious in one's hopes. A girl unlucky in love or a couple trying desperately to conceive a child may be advised not to get their hopes up because the chances of success are so abominably low. As time goes on and evidence grows against the possibility of success, we may advise not only cautious hope but also resignation to reality. This is where Kierkegaard sees the unique challenge of faith—to continue to believe precisely when it takes one outside rational or moral defense. As Hall suggests, Kierkegaard calls us to a love that requires "tenacious determination" to place our hope in the reality of forgiveness and "encourages our ridiculous trust in God's goodness and our beloved's willingness to forgive."[28] In Abraham's case, it was both irrational and immoral to trust God's promise to the point of plunging a knife into his son's flesh.[29] In Sarah's case, it was irrational to hope for God's mercy despite all repeated evidence, and it was immoral to allow Tobias to marry her, despite all the evidence that points to his almost inevitable death. The existential paradox of the faith encounter and its relationship to hope are thus portrayed. As Hall suggests, even while we remain existentially in the world with others, we belong not to each other, but to God. "We are not only to walk up Mount Moriah but also to descend again, with Isaac beside us. Thus, truly faithful engagements require hope as well as deferential distance."[30] Hope does not, of course, resolve the existential discomfort of faith, which persists in peril and risk, or fear and trembling; hope instead identifies a courageous way of living authentically in the world as fragile persons who acknowledge their own vulnerability and will to leave behind all their worldly understanding and proceed in a faithful relation to God.

Karl Barth

Karl Barth shares an affinity with Kierkegaard's infinite qualitative distinction between humanity and God. Barth is well known for his criticism of the liberal theology of the early twentieth century that had its roots in Schleiermacher's focus on religion as human experience as a point of entry into Christian theology. According to Barth, this tradition resorted to a certain variety of natural theology in that it allowed people to trust human rational power over revelation in interpreting experience. For Barth, it was far too anthropocentric and too willing to abandon the consciousness of the hidden God. Discussing Barth's criticism of early twentieth-century liberal theology, H. L. Stewart even called Barth's position a "reverent agnosticism" insofar as he objected to any tendency to trust human reason over revelation to interpret human experience. That is not to suggest a strand of apophatic mysticism, however, as Barth begins Christian theological discourse with God's act in grace of revelation and redemption.

For Barth, the Protestant Principle means that all religious discourse, all human imaginative construction, all theology, must be sharply distinguished from God's revelation. Theology should be a *faith-full* response to and appropriation of God's self-revelation in Christ. Barth says that "theology will deal with the word and act of the grace of God and the word and act of the human gratitude challenged, awakened, and nourished through it."[31] Barth fleshes out the Protestant Principle in the radical discontinuity he sees between all religious discourse and God's revelation of reconciliation in Christ.

The three themes I address in Karl Barth's theology are the meaning of God's revelation in Christ, the transcendence and priority of revelation (as God's act) over religion (as human search for meaning), and the countercultural responsibility of the church. Especially in the case of Barth's theology, what I am calling faith as protest or a critical faith is a warning against natural theology as much as against idolatry, against the danger of replacing God and God's revelation with our own constructed idols, ideas, doctrines, and judgments. What I find in his work supports a faithful protest premised on the real presence of the resurrected Christ, and directed inwardly at ourselves and outwardly at the public world around us.

The Meaning of Revelation

Barth does not stress merely that God transcends everything we may know of God; instead, he emphasizes God's self-revelation and freedom to act in grace to redeem humanity. What God reveals in Christ is God's choosing humanity as covenant-partner, giving of freedom to humanity, and loving-kindness and relationship with humanity. "It is when we look at Jesus Christ that we know decisively that God's deity does not exclude, but includes His humanity."[32] For Barth, Christ is Mediator and Reconciler between God and humanity, and the Revealer of both.[33] It is as such that Christ represents the covenant that God extends to humanity. In Christ, we see God revealed and God's humanity revealed, meaning God's choosing of humanity, God's love for humanity, and God's free election of humanity as covenant-partner.

His free affirmation of man, His free concern for him, His free substitution for him—this is God's humanity. We recognize it exactly at the point where we also first recognize His deity. . . . There is the father who cares for his lost son, the king who does the same for his insolvent debtor, the Samaritan who takes pity on the one who fell among robbers and in his thoroughgoing act of compassion cares for him in a fashion as unexpected as it is liberal. And this is the act of compassion to which all these parables as parables of the Kingdom of heaven refer. The very One who speaks in these parables takes to His heart the weakness and the perversity, the helplessness and the misery, of the human race surrounding Him. He does not despise men, but in an inconceivable manner esteems them highly just as they are, takes them into His heart and sets Himself in their place.[34]

For Barth, it is absolutely essential that we understand that the context of God's revelation in Jesus is an intimate human relationship. He calls this relationship the humanity of God, but the humanity of God is precisely what leads us to the divinity of God. God can do this, that is, reveal himself fully in human relationship because God is divine, that is, free. God transgresses the boundaries of nature and conditioned existence in a revolutionary act of freedom that is itself a gift of grace. By the humanity of God, Barth does not mean that God is like us in any way; that sort of direction of beginning with human nature and projecting from that to divine nature he explicitly attacks. Instead, God's humanity refers to the free act of revelation in grace by which God relates to humans in human relationship and enables humans to receive this revelation in faithful response. What God reveals in Christ is God's act of reconciliation of humanity with God, or God's turning toward humanity in promise and command. We ourselves cannot come to know or possess God in any way. For Barth, revelation itself is two-part—both the object of faith and the capacity to receive it must be given by God.[35]

The Priority of Revelation over Religion

Ludwig Feuerbach argued in the 1830s that theology was really only anthropology.[36] What he meant was that when we engage in God-talk, we are really talking about ourselves. Others after him have taken his insight to mean several related things. For example, if we study the gods of a particular culture, then we can understand the all too human desires and hopes and fears of that community. Feuerbach, it seemed, did not intend to destroy theism. He was simply tying a religious culture's belief statements about God to that culture's conceptions of humanity. Whatever we find best and biggest and most noble in the human spirit, we as a society emphasize and elevate in our views of divine spirit. As we value power and knowledge and mercy, we consider God to be omnipotent, omniscient, and all-merciful. Religion and theology are essentially human discourses and reflect human values.

Barth would agree with Feuerbach's sense that all religion is in fact entirely a human discourse, a human search for meaning and value, and a human spiritual sensibility and training. According to Barth, God does not reveal

Godself in Jesus in the fullness of time as a response to human religious searching for God. Revelation is not a response to human religious aspiration at all. Barth criticizes the direction in modern Protestant theology that approaches God from the grounds of religious experience and identifies the illusion at the heart of all religious conceptions.[37] Religion is all too human a discourse, while revelation bursts in upon us from God, in God's free grace. For Barth, revelation is the categorical judgment on any religious quest as idolatry, defined in general as the worship of anything that is not God and, more specifically, as the worship of anything humanly constructed.

For Barth, God and humanity are not on a continuum of lesser and higher spiritual essences, but are related only obliquely like a tangent striking a circle. As Barth says in the very passionate *Epistle to the Romans*, "We confound time with eternity. That is our unrighteousness. Such is our relation to God apart from and without Christ, on this side of the resurrection and before we are called to order. God himself is not acknowledged as God and what is called 'God' is in fact humanity itself. By living to ourselves we serve the 'No-God.'"[38] Barth warns that we replace God with our own notions about God, notions we can manipulate and adjust according to our own interests and agendas. Religion's greatest risk is that it may turn into idolatry. Barth continues, "Men have imprisoned and encased the truth— the righteousness of God; they have trimmed it to their own measure, and thereby robbed it both of its earnestness and of its significance."[39]

Religion therefore should not be confused with revelation. At first reading, this privileging of God's revelation in Christ over against all human religious thinking may suggest a Christian exclusivism or triumphalism as the sole possessor of religious truth. However, Barth was not discussing the superiority of historical Christianity's truth about God over the truth values of Judaism, Islam, Hinduism, or Buddhism. He was also distinguishing God's act of revelation from the human religious culture of Christianity. Barth says Jesus is the Christ, but he criticizes any restriction of God's revelation to a historical personage. The nineteenth-century quest for the historical Jesus had nothing to do with responding to God's gracious act of reconciliation, which is the content of revelation in Christ. His criticism of historical criticism is not in the defense of biblical inerrancy or a literal reading of scripture or a resistance to any new information about the man Jesus. It is rather a judgment against the ultimate theological value of such historical-critical insights for faith and for theology. Theology is to deal with the word and act of God's grace and the word and act of human gratitude and nothing else. As Kierkegaard emphasizes the existential decision of faith one must make with respect to the Christian gospel, Barth sees Christian theology as a response to and reflection on God's revelation in grace. The priority Barth gives to revelation is based on his emphasis on divine grace. What God reveals in Christ is a matter of grace; it is a gift, a freely given divine gift of human freedom, reconciliation, and relationship.

Barth's doctrine of revelation both enables human knowledge of God and restricts the avenue to this knowledge. Barth emphasizes a dialectical relationship of revealing and concealing. Garrett Green cautions that it is easy to overlook the negative side of Barth's dialectic of revelation, or God's hiddenness, and takes up Barth's sense that revelation means sacrament. Precisely in Christ, the hidden God has made Himself comprehensible and tangible—not directly, but indirectly, "not for sight, but for faith."[40] So when Barth says that we cannot know anything of God except through revelation, his point is not that the historical Jesus is the only true symbol of God or that historical Christianity alone guides people to God. To the extent to which Christianity addresses itself to this reconciliation and covenant that God has accomplished and communicated in Christ, it is guided by revelation. To the extent to which it asserts anything more than God's loving-kindness in choosing and affirming humanity, it has strayed from revelation. Everything that theology says must begin and remain within the framework of God's revelation and redemption.

For Barth, God is in heaven and humanity is on earth. He emphasizes the total otherness of God in order to emphasize that much more strongly that the only way to know God is through God's self-revelation in Christ. We can have no independent knowledge of God aside from God's revelation to us, aside from God's turning toward us and choosing us. All religious thinking is human effort to acquire "independent" or objective knowledge of God and to that extent is false and idolatrous. While Luther was concerned with how on earth human action could ever possibly be enough to atone for sin, Barth's restriction of knowledge to God's revelation applies this humility toward human action to the act of human thinking. As Green puts it, "The word we speak *is* not the word God speaks. But by the grace of God—that is, through God's act, our words *become* his Word."[41] Some have simply criticized Barth for returning to a pre-Enlightenment orthodoxy but that would be a mistaken reading. Barth was rejecting the liberal theological tradition of Schleiermacher that focused too heavily on human religious experience. According to Ingolf Dalferth's assessment of Barth's theological realism, "in theology we attempt to say something about God, not merely human experiences of God."[42] Dalferth points out that Christian faith, for Barth, makes actual truth-claims, all the while recognizing the possibility of being in error. This is the risk that Christian faith is to embrace courageously and cautiously. It is Barth's dialectical affirmation of both theological realism and its risk of error that refutes any interpretation of a precritical orthodoxy. Instead, Barth challenges theology to operate from the self-conscious tension between the religious insider's experience of faith and the critical outsider's worldly experience.[43] According to Dalferth's analysis, far from retreating from the discontinuity between worldly experience and faith, Barth makes it the crucial theological challenge. Dalferth identifies this methodological move of theology as Barth's participation in the methodology of Protestant theology. Insofar as Barth neither rejects the value of worldly experience for the sake of an isolationist or protectionist Christian faith nor allows it to set the parameters for Christian faith, he maintains the dialectical tension of protest in Christian theology.

The Countercultural Responsibility of the Church

The third theme is perhaps the most relevant for our discussion and extends the implications of the priority of divine revelation over human religious discourse. That is the responsibility Barth urges on the church to be counter-cultural, to be a countermovement to worldly values. He protests the accom-modation of theology to culture, which he sees in modern liberal theologians like Paul Tillich. At the same time, Barth is not advocating what we see very prominently today in American conservative circles of aligning religion and politics. What passes conventionally in American public discourse for "con-servative Christian political action" is highly problematic for a Barthian. Jesse Couenhoven develops what may be interpreted as a contradiction in Barth's view of the relationship between the church and the state. On the one hand, the church must resist the state and serve as a model of justice for the state. On the other hand, the church must also support the state.[44] Couenhoven suggests that Barth is clear that the creation of a "Christian political party" would be a distortion of the gospel.[45] Barth says that the church has a responsibility to be critical of culture and the government. The church's responsibility lies in training Christian individuals who then engage in political governance—not as a strategy of sending "Manchurian candidates" to work to infiltrate the state from the inside, but rather by fostering the proper reverence and humility before God and God's work that will build the necessary spiritual character for the ethical and political work of implementing worldly justice. Barth urges Christians to be patient in this in-between time, to let God be God, and to not circumvent this by instituting church law. God's law is not to be confused with church law. This responsibility of the church to be patient and self-critical emerges, again, from the priority of revelation over religion, from Barth's interpretation that

Christianity has to do with God's revelation that calls humanity to order, in a divine redemption that is inseparable from divine judgment.

In his own day, Barth criticized communism, participated in socialism early on, and attacked the Western church for not criticizing capitalism harshly enough. His lecture to the Workers Association, "Jesus Christ and the Movement For Social Justice," published in 1911, best demonstrates this responsibility of the church for social justice. He argues in this lecture that socialism embodies many of the ideals of the gospel of Jesus, especially responding to a call for the championing of the weak against the powerful. He speaks quite directly to the Christian churches, reminding them of their collective and individual responsibility to embody the gospel of Jesus. The tone is one of responsibility to God's command and examining one's own failings rather than one's spiritual accomplishments. He writes, "It is precisely Christians who ought to know that we *all* fall short when we look at what we're *doing*."[46] When Barth urges the Western church to criticize modern capitalist injustices and to advocate for workers' rights, he is calling for the church to be public and political, but the guiding criterion must remain God's revelation in the gospel and in Jesus. The church by itself, as institution, is not supposed to wield control over the government out of a self-protectionist agenda. Instead, it is always supposed to act out of inspiration from the gospel of Jesus. In this lecture, Barth seems to warn of the danger that the church may replace revelation with its own grandiose aspirations and become self-idolatrous. He says that the church can help people in their relationship with Jesus, but no more. "Of the church, therefore, I can only say to you: 'She is there in order to serve you. Do what you think is right.' The church is not Jesus and Jesus is not the church."[47] The guiding criterion must be Jesus. Barth seems to advocate a radical sort of the contemporary "What Would Jesus Do?" brand of ethics, while focusing not on the historical Jesus as much as God's loving reconciliation revealed in the person of Jesus.

In keeping the gospel as the guiding criterion for Christian responsibility, Barth prevents the church from absolutizing its own mundane institutional integrity into something divine and spiritual. When Barth reminds us that *God is in heaven, and thou art on earth*, he might have clarified that the church is also on earth; Christians are on earth, not in heaven. It is on earth that he sees Christian responsibility unfolding—to embody the kingdom of God on earth. Embodying the kingdom of God on earth does not mean that the Christian church, the worldly church, ought to rule over the rest of the earth in dominion, but rather that it should serve the faithful, inspire and support them in their relationship with God in Jesus. S. W. Sykes discusses the challenge Barth poses to the church of retaining its authority to speak God's word while recognizing the possibility of being in error. Sykes asks poignantly, "Are human beings capable of both supreme confidence in God and human modesty?"[48] Barth offers an eloquent criticism of the potential idolatry of the church and the Christian worldview:

> The same holds true of the so-called Christian world view. If you understand the connection between the person of Jesus and your socialist convictions, and if you want to arrange your life so that it corresponds to this connection, then that does not at all mean you have to "believe" or accept this, that, and the other thing. What Jesus has to bring us are not ideas, but a way of life. One can have Christian ideas about God and the world and about human redemption, and still with all that be a complete heathen. As an atheist, a materialist, and a Darwinist, one can be a genuine follower and disciple of Jesus. Jesus is not the Christian worldview and the Christian worldview is not Jesus.[49]

As Kierkegaard a century earlier criticized Christendom for replacing the radical paradox of Christian faith with merely Christian worldviews, Barth also opens up quite a lot of room for the church's critical self-judgment. The gospel and the person and behavior of Jesus are to be one's guides to critical self-judgment, not so-called Christian patterns of viewing the world and Christian ideas, doctrines, and narrative themes. As Barth says, Christians are those called to know that they have all fallen short of their responsibility. Nevertheless, Christians are called to speak in faith. The church must not retreat from its responsibility of speaking God's word because of its imperfection. Sykes suggests, with Barth, "that the Christian faith itself promotes its own internal dialectic and discord, and that the existence of an authentic teaching office is itself part of that process, and does not stand outside or above it."[50] The challenge of maintaining both supreme confidence in God and human modesty is an active dialectic that is itself the work of theology and the task for the faithful church.

To those who would argue that socialism and Jesus are diametrically opposed to each other on the basis that Jesus preached the kingdom of heaven, not of earth, and that Jesus spoke of spirit and spiritual restitution, not of bodily restitution here and now, Barth says such views are mistakenly dualistic, separating spirit and matter and overly emphasizing spirit to the exclusion of matter. Such a spiritualist and mystical reading is a problem he finds with much of the modern liberal theology of his time. Instead, he says that for Jesus, heaven and earth, or spirit and matter, are not two worlds, but the one reality of the kingdom of God. Redemption, he says, is not the separation or the liberation of spirit from matter, but the Word become flesh, not the other way around. God's love and justice come to rule over all things external and earthly. It is in this real world we see, Barth argues, that God's will is to be done.[51] It is this social spirit that marks how Jesus spoke and acted, and so Barth argues that social democracy is one with Jesus as it has taken up the conviction that social misery ought not to be. Jesus, he says, instilled people with the Spirit that transforms matter; he created new people in order to create a new world. As Barth says of social democracy, "it calls us back from the hypocritical and slothful veneration of spirit and from that useless Christianity which intends to come only 'in heaven.' It tells us that we should really believe what we pray every day. 'Thy Kingdom come!'"[52] It is with this focus on moral and social conscience in this actual human world that socialism represented to Barth the embodiment of the Christian gospel. Still he warns against uncritically adopting any state-powered socialism because of the possibility that the socialist responsibility could be corrupted by the state's own agenda of power. However, he does see the responsibility of the Christian church to lie somewhere to the political left, in its resistance to the capitalist injustices promoted by those who own the means of production over those who do not hold any such power. Unfortunately, what he writes of the church's laxity in criticizing such economic theory and the governments that support it is even more true today:

> Both church and state shroud the concept of private property with an amazing aura of sanctity and unassailability. It has been impressed upon all of us down to the marrow of our bones that what's mine must remain mine. In our penal code, property enjoys far greater protection than, for example, a good reputation or morality. What's mine is mine, and no one can change that! Not only have Christians become used to this notion, because temporarily perhaps it could not be otherwise, but they even act as if it were a divine law and have fallen into the deepest dismay regarding the intention of social democracy largely to eliminate private property and to transform private capitalism into social capitalism.[53]

Now, the relevant point for us in the twenty-first century is not the merits of socialism over against capitalism. More important than Barth's criticism of capitalism is his criticism of the uncritical adoption and justification of capitalism, such that, as he says, we now believe that the right to private property is not only favorable but is in fact deemed a divinely ordained order. Such a use of divine justification for the enjoyment of private property and the enjoyment of certain self-assuredness certainly characterizes the American Christian conservative movement, which has become strongly influential in the American political scene.[54] We should imagine Barth fuming over the church's self-idolatry in American religion and politics. The church, he says, has a responsibility to be countercultural, to be critical and help serve the Christians who are trying to embody the gospel of Jesus by calling them out of cultural complacency. This critical countercultural responsibility is rooted in what Barth sees as the priority of the Christian revelation in Jesus, scripture, and the church over any and all religion as human discourse or human searching or questing for God. We do well to keep in mind our responsibility in faith to be self-critical by remembering that God's revelation comes freely to us in grace, not as any earned prize. This is after all what "justification by faith alone" suggests. Faith is not constituted by human works or human ideas, but rather is the proper response of gratitude to God's act of revelation and grace. As a response to what God has done, faith must take on an actively critical posture with regard to what human cultures, modern economies, and governments do.

Paul Tillich

Over against Barth, Paul Tillich affirms the real human knowledge of God, saying, "erring knowledge is not utter ignorance."[55] He maintains that Barth leaves unexplained how revelation can communicate anything to humanity unless humanity possesses something to enable one to question it and move toward it in understanding.[56] To Tillich, Barth's emphasis on the distinction between divine and human sides too entirely with the supernatural. As we have seen in the previous section, Barth's criticism of twentieth-century liberal theology, of which Tillich is an important heir, is that it is too willing to abandon the supernatural for the sake of an anthropocentric valuing of reason over revelation. These two thinkers therefore represent rival approaches to twentieth-century Christian theology. Their differences display a unique consideration of faith in God's transcendence and grace over human religious thought. Robert Scharlemann suggests, however, that they have more similarities than differences. He summarizes the basic difference between Barth and Tillich as resting on their responses to the following question. Given that the word *God* can be used idolatrously, should theology take precautions against its idolatrous use? Tillich answers Yes, because the fight against idolatry is a necessary part of religion. Barth answers No, because the fear of idolatry identifies a condition for thinking about God. "It is precisely as idolater that one comes to know what is the redeeming grace of God."[57] The intrinsic connection between religion and the fight against idolatry is the subject of this section on Paul Tillich. I develop the value given to such caution against idolatry through the following four-part discussion: his use of the Protestant Principle and justification by faith; the character of true faith, the symbolic character of sacred reality, and the understanding of church as the collective body that balances its sacramentality with its finitude.

The Protestant Principle and Justification by Faith

The Protestant Principle affirms the symbolic character of religion and the self-critical posture of true faith, which takes the risk of being wrong and insists on being open to the spiritual presence of God who acts graciously in human faith and religion and to the supremacy and ultimacy of God by affirming the ambiguities of human understanding. The divine Spirit, which alone is ultimate, always witnesses to the fragmentary and ambiguous character of human religious experience. When Martin Luther raised questions about the authority of the papal hierarchy and about the efficacy of meritorious spiritual works, he appeared to have been raising questions for theological debate, not starting a revolutionary church that would then term itself *Protestant*. The Protestant Principle articulates what was taken to be a formative issue for the historical Protestant churches, that is, the radical right of the individual to question and interpret matters of doctrine. Tillich says the Protestant Principle has a fundamental place in all Christian theology, not only that of the historical Protestant churches, because it expresses the victory of the Spirit over religion as a human enterprise that always tends toward profanization and demonization, as it always risks idolatry. Tillich writes that it is Protestant insofar as it protests the self-elevation of religion and thereby liberates religion.[58] As a theological tool of religion's self-criticism, it actively guards against idolatry. Tillich explains that while self-consciousness represents human perfection, it can also tempt us to elevate the self beyond the limits of finitude and see it as the center of the world. He calls this "hubris" and categorizes it as a spiritual sin because instead of acknowledging finitude, it identifies partial truth with ultimate truth and makes idols of human cultural creation.[59] The Protestant Principle articulates that no claim to knowledge can stand with ultimate validity, and it fosters a kind of suspicion of anything that would function as a controlling and reality-masking ideology. "It should be regarded as the Protestant principle that, in relation to God, God alone can act and that no human claim, especially no religious claim, no intellectual or moral or devotional 'work,' can reunite us with him."[60] The Protestant Principle therefore is grounded on the doctrine of justification by grace through faith, which posits that we cannot do anything to justify ourselves, to make ourselves righteous, to reunite us with God. It is entirely out of human hands, outside the realm of human potentiality, and instead is entirely God's work of grace.

Tillich points out the semantic problems of the doctrine, which became corrupted into the doctrine of justification by faith alone, according to which the intellectual and emotional work of faith saves while physical and moral acts of work do not. However, as Tillich emphasizes, "Not faith but grace is the cause of justification, because God alone is the cause. Faith is the receiving act, and this act is itself a gift of grace."[61] In the debate between faith and works, works refer not only to outward, physical actions but to all human actions, including intellectual actions of belief, moral actions of self-improvement or self-sacrifice, and religious actions of devotion. Faith, as Tillich explains, is the human act of receiving that divine justification, and it is itself a gift of God's grace, not an intellectual assent to a proposition. Justification by grace denotes the Protestant Principle that only God can make humans right. By affirming an infinite distance between God and all human works, Tillich's use of the Protestant Principle maintains the ambiguous nature of all religion and frees it from becoming a frozen and fixed truth. Instead, as all religion remains a human enterprise and labors under the conditions of ambiguity that define finite categories of understanding, it is saved from becoming itself idolized. Its self-criticism helps keep it free from self-idolatry. As Tillich writes, "the Protestant weakness of continuous self-criticism is its greatness and a symptom of the Spiritual impact upon it."[62] The Protestant Principle, because of word choice, is always in danger of being fixed as simply a doctrine of the denominationally Protestant churches, when for Tillich, it is far more central to the Christian mission.

The Character of True Faith

In his popular work, *Dynamics of Faith*, first published in 1957, Tillich lays out the intricacies of his understanding of faith, three of which are relevant here: faith is the state of being ultimately concerned; true faith must incorporate passivity and receptivity to what is ultimate or holy, which always transcends human experience and maintains its independence and ultimacy; and faith therefore necessarily includes uncertainty and risk because of the independence of the holy.[63] First, Tillich is defining faith in terms of the subjective act of a human personality, not a proposition for belief. Such common statements of belief—that God intervenes in human history, for example, that Jesus rose from the dead and ascended to heaven, or that Jesus was miraculously but certainly born of a virgin—do not in themselves comprise faith. Instead, such statements of one's belief or of a community's creed express in straightforward propositional language the subjective experience of being ultimately concerned with what is ultimate. Faith as the state of being ultimately concerned is an act of the whole personality, a commitment to center one's entire life on the defining axis of that ultimate concern. Clearly, religion as it is often practiced is not taken truly as an ultimate concern, but only as a partial concern. An ultimate concern would refuse to be circumscribed absolutely by dogma.

Second, this state of being ultimately concerned is a concern with what transcends experience. Herein lies the difference between true faith and idolatrous faith. Many religious believers define idolatry as the worship of anything other than the true God. Who is the true God and who is the false god? For many people, the true God is the one described in one's own sacred texts, in one's own tradition of revelation, and by one's immediate community. The false god is simply the one worshiped by a different community. Tillich, however, considers as idolatry the worship of anything that is not truly ultimate. To the question of how we are to distinguish between what is truly ultimate and what is not, Tillich resorts again to the subjective character of faith. For Tillich, all we can access is our experience. We cannot jump out of our finite, conditioned human experience and see what is in fact "objectively" true and real. Epistemologically, therefore, Tillich can talk about only a human experience of revelation, not of God's being and God's acts independent of human experience of them. Any true religion, however, transcends ordinary subject-object dualism so that, for example, our knowledge of God is the knowledge God has of Himself. Any genuine prayer is possible only as God as Spirit prays within us. This character of faith to move beyond the ordinary subject-object experience is possible only because the ultimate is truly ultimate. In other words, God cannot be an object of our knowledge at all. God is uniquely always a subject even while being an object of experience or devotion. The faithful have always affirmed that we can know God only because God allows it or because God desires and intends it. Traditional Christian theologies have based all theology, all faithful understanding of God, on God's own self-revelation. This speaks to the ultimacy of such a God, the ultimacy of the object of our ultimate concern. "The finite which claims infinity without having it (as, e.g., a nation or success) is not able to transcend the subject-object scheme. It remains an object which the believer looks at as a subject. He can approach it with ordinary knowledge and subject it to ordinary handling."[64]

Many scholars have questioned the coherence of Tillich's articulation of the objective reality of revelation and God. If he begins from the questions raised by finite human existence, how can he justify the reality of revelation and God? It looks rather unsatisfactory to many, but in the end, he does affirm the reality of revelation, as well as our epistemological challenge to do it justice by respecting its distance. Dirk-Martin Grube argues, for example, that Tillich's early thought posits a transcendental Unconditional to ground his epistemology.[65] John Dourley suggests that Tillich's use of technical reason and symbol reverences the point of coincidence between the divine and the human.[66] I would add that Tillich's focus on justification by God's grace alone serves as a theological key for how he reconciles the possibility of human knowledge of God. We know God only because God knows Himself in us. On our own, we cannot possibly transcend our experience, but insofar as we are passive and receptive, we can discover God's revelatory action on us. True faith overcomes the unidirectional character of the subject-object dualism of ordinary experience in which I am over here and what I apprehend is over there. It embodies a certain bidirectional attitude that incorporates an important component of receptivity and maintains God's primacy in the exchange. In true faith experience, God is never exclusively an object of our experience, but is the subject, the agent who is acting within us.

Tillich maintains both the reality of revelation and its mysterious character. He writes, "Revelation always is a subjective and an objective event in strict interdependence."[67] Someone is grasped by the manifestation of the mystery and something occurs through which this mystery grasps someone. These two cannot be separated. The more God reveals, the more mystery and awe experienced by the faithful. Faith never exhausts its knowledge of God, but only grows in its receptivity to God's mystery. Here then, we have an element of the limits of human knowing in faith. Faith does not ever fully collapse the distance between human and God because "whatever is essentially mysterious cannot lose its mysteriousness even when it is revealed."[68] Even as it bridges the distance, it simply grows in awe of the infinite distance that remains of what is truly ultimate. "If ultimacy is manifest and exercises its fascinating attraction, one realizes at the same time the infinite distance of the finite from the infinite and, consequently, the negative judgment over any finite attempts to reach the infinite."[69] In other words, *true faith*, or the state of being *truly ultimately concerned* with what is *truly ultimate*, will always include a negative judgment over any attempts to fully reach and take hold of that ultimate.[70] Faith must always include uncertainty or doubt. If it does not, it is no longer true faith and may be idolatry instead.

Third, uncertainty is perhaps the most important element in Tillich's view of faith, not just for our purposes of exploring the religious and theological functions of doubt, but for Tillich's concern of defining true faith. He writes: "Faith is certain in so far as it is an experience of the holy. But faith is uncertain in so far as the infinite to which it is related is received by a finite being. This element of uncertainty in faith cannot be removed, it must be accepted."[71] The uncertainty of faith, the negative judgment that must not be eliminated, identifies an element of risk. "If faith is understood as being ultimately concerned, doubt is a necessary element in it. It is a consequence of the risk of faith."[72] In every act of faith the possibility of failure is present, as seen in Kierkegaard's depiction of Abraham's preparation to sacrifice his son Isaac. In Kierkegaard's telling, Abraham was not actually willing to lose his son, but was moving forward with the sacrifice believing all the while that God would stop him or reverse it in some way he could not understand. Consider the fear in that moment—*what if he had been wrong!* It would have been a monstrous tragedy. And yet, it is this fear of being completely wrong that defines, for Kierkegaard, Abraham's act as faith and not resignation to a particular realistic state of affairs. In faith, we must recognize that we may in fact be absolutely and totally wrong. For Tillich, this possibility of failure to know and understand the holy emerges necessarily from the character of the ultimate as ultimate and ourselves as finite. Faith does not transform us into gods or all-knowing beings. We remain mortals in faith and continue to see through a glass darkly.[73] Faith is an act of the finite human being to concern itself ultimately with that which confronts it as ultimate. We remain finite, and therefore, we could be entirely wrong.

While Tillich lists several kinds of doubt that may be found in religious doubt, the doubt that he emphasizes as implicit in every act of faith is the existential doubt that comes from taking a risk. "It does not reject every concrete truth, but it is aware of the element of insecurity in every existential truth. At the same time, the doubt that is implied in faith accepts this insecurity and takes it into itself in an act of courage. Faith includes courage. Therefore, it can include the doubt about itself."[74] Such existential doubt is not simply skepticism that suspects every truth or a preliminary doubt that opens avenues for further study, but instead it enacts a courage to accept one's experience of truth while simultaneously being aware of the insecurity of accepting these finite truths. Echoing Kierkegaard, it implies an existential commitment in the face of ultimate insecurity. John Thatanamil develops the degree to which Tillich differentiates mystical courage from the courage of faith; while the former seeks to transcend the conditions of finitude, faith confronts the existential experience of radical meaninglessness and skepticism and in the face of this experience, affirms the meaningfulness of the finite realm of particulars.[75] It is most interesting and important that Tillich chooses to call this courage. Faith does not overcome doubt in

Tillich's description, but rather, courageously proceeds even while actively acknowledging self-doubt. It is courageous, according to Tillich, insofar as it accepts the risk of being wrong and does not shirk away but instead proceeds to affirm itself in the face of possible failure and error.

Consider the following two contexts in which the word *courage* often comes up, acknowledging the risk of being wrong and moving forward through decision despite the risk. The first is in a military context—the decision to commit to a particular war strategy involves the risk of being wrong, the uncertainty about what one will find, and the possibility of complete failure in one's mission. And yet bold and decisive commitment to a strategy is necessary. Second, such a view of faith as requiring risk of failure and a courageous self-affirmation despite the evident threats may remind parents of the courage it takes to raise children. It often feels like we have the blessing/curse of knowing too much about the dangers surrounding our children and threatening all our efforts to protect them. Responsible parenting involves being fully cognizant of these risks and our own uncertainties about whether we are doing the right thing day to day and courageously affirming our values and our faith in our children's potential, and realizing their futures, even while we repeatedly re-evaluate and adjust ourselves lest we go astray and cling to the wrong priorities.

The Symbolic Character of Religion

Tillich emphasizes throughout his writings that religion is fundamentally symbolic in character and not literal. He cautions that if we take too literal a view of religion, we run the risk of flattening the depth of sacred reality into something that may be entirely of our own invention. In an essay titled "The Lost Dimension in Religion," published in a 1958 issue of the *Saturday Evening Post*, Tillich explains that what has been lost in religion is the depth of sacred reality. He suggests that the first step to what he calls nonreligion in the West was a scientific literalist defense of what should be described only symbolically. "When [religion] defended its great symbols not as symbols but as literal stories, it had already lost the battle."[76] He argues that all of the discussion of the existence or nonexistence of God is a symptom of this pervasive loss of depth. In his *Systematic Theology*, Tillich even states quite pointedly that "God does not exist," and that arguing for the existence of God is as much a denial of God as refuting it.[77] If ideas of God are transferred to the horizontal plane of human actuality, then God becomes a being among other beings, an object for our reductionist knowledge and dissection, a mere thing or idea, and no longer the transcendent ground of our being with which we are infinitely concerned.[78] Tillich's concern in separating "God" and "existence" is to maintain God's transcendence and ultimacy as what he calls Being-itself, or the power of being.

For Tillich symbols have six characteristics that make them appropriate for talking about God or the sacred.[79]

1. Symbols point beyond themselves to something else. In this respect, they are similar to signs.
2. The symbol participates in that to which it points. Whereas a sign only points beyond itself to that which it represents and then can be discarded or replaced easily, symbols share in the power for which they stand. (For example, the symbol of the flag participates in the power and dignity of the nation it represents and therefore cannot be replaced except after a historic catastrophe that changes the reality of the nation it symbolizes. An attack on the flag is considered blasphemy because of its participation in the dignity of the nation it symbolizes.)[80]
3. The symbol opens up levels of reality that otherwise are closed to us. In this, it shares the creative capacity of art to reveal elements of reality that cannot be approached scientifically or literally.
4. The symbol unlocks dimensions of one's soul that correspond to the dimensions of reality. It opens up hidden depths of one's own being.
5. Symbols cannot be produced intentionally or invented, but instead grow out of the individual or collective unconscious.
6. Like living beings, symbols grow and die as situations change and their meaningfulness changes.

These six characteristics undergird Tillich's sense of the essentially symbolic character of religion. The sacred reality—what is truly ultimate—transcends the realm of finite reality altogether, so no finite reality can express it directly. "Religiously speaking, God transcends his own name. This is why the use of his name easily becomes an abuse or a blasphemy. Whatever we say about that which concerns us ultimately, whether or not we call it God, has a symbolic meaning. It points beyond itself while participating in that to which it points. In no other way can faith express itself adequately."[81] Only symbolic language can retain the depth and transcendence of sacred reality because it gives concrete form to this sacred reality and maintains the respectful distance of ultimacy of the object of faith. It retains a certain humility, or self-doubt, with regard to that which it symbolizes and evokes, while at the same time, it enables a transparency through to what is symbolized and a participation in its reality.[82]

Medieval Christian theologian Thomas Aquinas expressed a similar sentiment when he argued that our speech about God is at best analogical. While many medieval Christian mystics suggested that only negative theological language was valid to refer to a transcendent God, that we could not say what God is but only what God is not, Aquinas was committed to positive theology and sought to defend the validity of our positive statements about God. He resolved the issue by arguing that when we say that God is good, we mean something slightly different from our ordinary statements that our friend Richard is good. Using Aquinas's example, we can see a difference in meaning among the following three statements:

> This soup is good.
> Mother Teresa was good.
> God is good.

Our use of the word *good* is different in all these cases. Aquinas took this further and suggested that it is not the meaning of the word *good* that changes from context to context, but rather the word *is* that changes in meaning. God *is* good in a different way of being than the way in which the soup *is* good. The soup's capacity for goodness is limited to the way in which it brings us pleasure or meets some expectations that qualify a satisfying meal. By sharp contrast, God is good in such a way that God establishes the conditions for goodness, defines the good, and enables goodness in transformed creatures. Over against the suggestion by negative theology that we could not say anything about what God is, Aquinas's concern was to guarantee that our use of language to speak about God was indeed meaningful.

Tillich's emphasis on the symbolic character of religious language shares this concern with the effective meaningfulness of religious language. Only symbol can transport us to a realm that is beyond us; only symbol can participate in the reality to which it points while preserving the ultimacy of that reality. Only a symbol can re-present that other reality without reducing the wholeness of that reality to the limited finite form used for the representation. Literal language about God is very troubling for Tillich because it shortchanges that ultimacy and replaces what is truly ultimate and entirely transcendent with what can be expressed in finite terms, in other words, with what is finite. Traditionally, the worship of something that is not God has been decried as idolatry, that is, the worship of some *thing* that is not ultimate but only a finite thing that can be manipulated by human activity. Symbolic language is essential for Tillich to retain the depth and transcendence of sacred reality as indeed ultimate and not finite. Following Tillich, to say that our religious language is symbolic does not reduce religion; it begins with the commitment to affirm the transcendence of the sacred and continues with the exercise of humility about human understanding. In other words, it affirms that God is always more than what we may say or understand about God and affirms our ability to speak meaningfully about God.

The Church and the Protestant Principle

The fourth broad area of Tillich's work that builds on the theological function of doubt or faithful protest is his understanding of the church. Rather than discuss his entire theology of the church, I focus on the meaning of the Protestant Principle for the church because it represents the critical function he requires the church to play in society. The first thing to recognize is that Tillich is not privileging the Protestant churches over the Catholic and Orthodox churches. Instead, he is evoking the activity and responsibility of critical protest, and he refers not merely to the actual worldly institutions of the church, but to the intellectual and social work of the church, to theology.

First, Tillich emphasizes that theology has primarily the task of mediation, a term he does not see as derogative but as necessary. "The task of theology is mediation, mediation between the eternal criterion of truth as it is manifest in the picture of Jesus as the Christ and the changing experiences of individuals and groups, their varying questions and their categories of perceiving reality."[83] His emphasis on the need for mediation between the eternal and changing human experience recalls his understanding of true faith as the state of being ultimately concerned with the holy, which maintains its infinite distance and independence of finite experience. Mediation is necessary because as Barth most eloquently said, "God is in heaven, and thou art on earth." Mediation is necessary because of the infinite distance between the sacred reality and ourselves as finite beings who attempt to perceive that sacred reality from within our own finite and changing cultural categories of experience. Tillich extends this crucial responsibility of mediation to the actual living church. "The church as a living reality must permanently mediate its eternal foundation with the demands of the historical situation."[84]

If the church is to realize and embody the life of true faith, it must affirm the continuing mystery and independence of the sacred over against our finite attempts to grasp it. Speaking in symbolic terms on a collective plane involves the church in its essential theological role of mediation, to maintain the distance between human understanding and sacred reality, confirm the negative judgment on faith, and still allow us to participate directly with the sacred. Symbolic language both maintains a respectful distance and enables participation. "When the divine Spirit is effective, a church member's claim to an exclusive possession of the truth is undercut by the witness of the divine Spirit to his fragmentary as well as ambiguous participation in the truth. The Spiritual Presence excludes fanaticism, because in the presence of God no man can boast about his grasp of God. No one can grasp that by which he is grasped—the Spiritual Presence."[85] Religion itself—the human efforts to talk about and reach God—is conquered by the divine Spirit. All claims to absoluteness that are made in the religious enterprise are kept in check by the Spirit that alone is ultimate and absolute.

This self-critical role of the church is rooted in the distance between what is ultimate, sacred reality and all finite attempts to grasp it in religion. However, for Tillich, this distance between the sacred reality and all human religion, which we have already seen exemplified in the character of true faith and the symbolic character of religion, is itself rooted in the Protestant Principle. Just as the Spiritual Presence is what determines the church vertically without being exclusively held by any of the churches, so the Protestant Principle is always at risk of being trampled by actual churches, denominationally "Protestant" and otherwise. In its simplest form, Tillich takes as the Protestant Principle the justification by grace through faith alone. This principle of justification underlies his view of religion as a human enterprise separated qualitatively from the sacred reality it seeks and his view of faith as including doubt and self-criticism in order to preclude the dangers of idolatry. He admires the principle of the fallibility of all religious institutions and sees their continuous self-criticism as evidence of the truly ultimate or Spiritual Presence determining them.[86] To be Protestant in this sense is actively to protest any complacency, any absolutism, any claims to infallibility within the church because the church is an institution of human religion and therefore should be open to self-criticism and the potential of being completely wrong. Church, like religion, should not be confused with God, or what is truly ultimate.

With Tillich, we are not looking at doubt in terms of skepticism in religious claims or skepticism about the meaning of life. Instead, we are looking at his affirmation of theology and faith precisely in the context of the existential ambiguities of concrete life. Only God can make us right, reunite us with Him, and integrate our concrete selves with our essential selves, according to Christian understanding of grace. We can pursue these spiritual goals only because God makes it possible through grace. Still, all our pursuits are done within the existential conditions of ambiguity. Concrete human life can never fully escape ambiguity. However, religious faith embodies a courageous self-affirmation precisely in the face of the threat of meaninglessness. Religious activity, language, devotion, and theology are all done precisely within the conditions of the ambiguities of human life.

Conclusion

Continuing with this book's examination of what faith comprises, apart from straightforward belief propositions or certitude, this chapter has sketched out a modern Christian articulation of faith as protest to claims to ultimacy. For Kierkegaard, Barth, and Tillich, this articulation of protest is rooted in the existential fact that we humans are finite mortals responding to what we understand to be infinite and beyond all our understanding. For Kierkegaard, trusting in God's promises involves a protest and a movement against rationality, understanding, and even morality because to be human is to live this tension between the finite and the infinite. For Barth, faith firmly acknowledges the tension of human life as a response to God's revelation. Reminding us that God is in heaven and we are on earth, Barth stresses the primacy of God's revelation, and protests any elevation of human religious discourse over God's free reconciliation of humanity. For Tillich, faith must include dimensions of doubt, risk, and uncertainty precisely because it has to do with a human creative consciousness and concern with what is ultimate. Hence, both the limitations and unique promise of the symbolic character of religious experience are important for Tillich. All three figures exemplify a dimension of faithful protest that maintains the confrontation in faith between what is part of human finite understanding and what lies outside it and challenges us to move beyond our finite understanding. The following chapter turns to this religious interface between finite and infinite in Hindu tradition, to examine the ways in which worldly understanding and values are to be transcended through faith.

CHAPTER FOUR

Faith and Transcendence
in Hindu Traditions

Virtually every text on Hinduism begins with a disclaimer that what we call "Hinduism" is not one uniform tradition, but an extremely loose yet cohesive set of widely varying beliefs and practices of the peoples traditionally of the Indian subcontinent.[1] Hinduism can be immensely challenging for a religious outsider to begin to study because it resists the comforting sense of definition that can be provided by recognized creed, institutional organization, historical founder, or theological uniformity. Numerous scholars have noted its simultaneous capacity for diversity and assimilation of many different beliefs, practices, and philosophies.[2]

Hindu traditions demonstrate a tension between affirmation of worldly action and transcendence of worldly life. This echoes a tension in religious thinking between time and eternity, and the ultimate value of temporal life that will come to an end. As Wendy Doniger O'Flaherty asks, "How can one fully savor the joys of the most trivial moments . . . while remaining aware of cosmic and metaphysical dimensions . . . which threaten to reduce such moments to insignificance?"[3] On the one hand, Hindu teachings, like those of other religious traditions, support social obligations and ethical duties here and now and promise to foster happiness and well-being in the life we know. On the other hand, they teach that these are to be transcended for a more ultimate happiness and spiritual freedom of Enlightenment, or moksha.

This tension reflects the ancient Indian concern over the best way of life—that of the householder who participates in society or that of the ascetic who renounces society. This tension is never fully resolved but continues to animate the existential questions that fill Hindu myths as well as philosophical and speculative texts. Although dharma (discussed in chapter 2), or the sum total of one's sacred duties, is determined by one's circumstances and relationships in life, and karma stipulates that all actions have their consequences, karma yoga teaches that true freedom from karmic residue results from selfless dutiful action, and bhakti yoga teaches that everyone no matter their social circumstances can pursue spiritual liberation and achieve moksha by devoting themselves fully and absolutely to their chosen deity. Much of the ambiguity and doubt that helps to constitute the Hindu spiritual journey is informed by the work of transcending worldliness in forms that can be considered centrifugal or ecstatic as they call into question conventional human understanding.

This tension can be seen especially clearly in Hindu traditions, which have maintained so much diversity of thought and practice side by side. Some of this can be explained as the coincidence or collision of competing historical cultures. What is now called Hinduism is thought to have roots in ancient Aryan culture as well as the indigenous Dravidian culture or somewhere in the ancient cultural negotiation of these two peoples, the former a nomadic people who migrated in repeated waves during the second millennium B.C.E. from central Asia into the Indian subcontinent, and the latter a settled people around the Indus River Valley. Since its ancient origins in the cultural negotiation of these two ancient cultures as well as the ethical and philosophical challenges posed by Jainism and Buddhism between 600 B.C.E. and 200 B.C.E., Hinduism has developed into a family of different but related strands of orthodox and heterodox views and practices.[4] Hinduism has been described as a laboratory of religion, in which nearly everything has been tried and not entirely rejected.

The many texts held to be sacred by Hindus also reflect the coalescence of competing ritual, philosophical, mythical, and devotional traditions. The Vedas, composed between 1500 B.C.E. and 400 B.C.E., show a transition in their understanding of the world, the divine, and how people are to relate themselves to the deities. Some deities fade in prominence, for example, reflecting a change in the society's own values as they move from being a migrant people to a settled people. The Vedas are considered *shruti*, or divine revelation, wisdom that was *heard* at the beginning of time by the *rishis*, or sages, who committed them to memory and recited them for generations.[5] While most of the Vedas consist of ritual instructions and hymns, the Upanishads, the final section of each of the four Vedas, explore the philosophical nature of reality. Composed around 100 B.C.E., they reflect a turn inward to reflect on the nature of the mind, its understanding of reality, and the apprehension of ultimate truth.

The great epics, the *Mahabharata* and the *Ramayana*, were composed between 400 B.C.E. and 400 C.E., and also reflect a turn inward, according to which inner intention and right thinking take priority over correct performance of outward sacrificial ritual. Although many rituals described in the Rg Veda continue to be used in Hindu worship to the present day, the teachings of dharma and theism found in the epics have been most prominent since the medieval period in the religious lives of most Hindus, due in part to their accessibility. Whereas the Vedas were transmitted orally within the strict boundaries of an elitist Brahmin caste, the epic poems were shared among families; performed at traveling festivals; enacted through holy days that noted the passage of sacred and agricultural time; and used to teach social rules, ethical lessons, and codes of behavior for different persons in particular situations. The epics and the later Puranas, rich with mythological details of different gods and goddesses, their origins, their biographies, their likes and dislikes, and their relationships with each other and with humans, also transmit much of the theistic teachings that influence so much ordinary folk religion.[6] The *Laws of Manu*, a legalistic text about dharma completed around 100 C.E., is the textual source of many Hindu and Indian cultural norms regarding social obligations. Composed in the context of an ancient society, the *Laws of Manu* strikes modern readers as legalistic, misogynist, and racist in its scrupulous cultivation of the social hierarchy of caste and gender. However, it is important to remember that most ancient societies (and in fact most societies until the very recent historical turn around the world to greater attention to social equality) were preoccupied with social hierarchy and with carefully preserving crystal-clear boundaries between different strands of society.

These very different textual traditions have together influenced the development of Hindu thought and practice, in such a way that today many disagreements or contradictions have been simply incorporated into a single larger system that accepts those contradictions. This kind of sublation into the whole system has characterized much of the history of Hindu philosophical thought and religious practice, which has often responded to challenges by competing thought systems (Buddhism, Jainism, or Sikhism, for example) by swallowing up their criticisms as partial or heterodox views within its own greater fold. This inclusivist-assimilationist tendency continues to characterize many modern Hindu responses to the variety of religions in the world. For example, many Hindus make sense of the Christian doctrine of the incarnation of God in the person of Jesus Christ by interpreting it as one of many incarnations of the divine, as in the Hindu avatar tradition. The tradition of maintaining competing or contradictory views side by side helps define the Hindu tradition as a unified and integrated culture of diverse practices.[7] This integration is not an institutionalized unity, which is nowhere found in Hinduism, but rather a structural unity, according to which the fragmented movements within Hinduism stem from Vedic revelation either explicitly or by implicit claims of validity. Those that support the focus on worldly life emphasize ritual performance, Vedic purity, and dharma. Those that focus on transcendence may emphasize yogic discipline, meditation, knowledge, and asceticism. Bhakti, or devotional religion, appears to cross over, by enabling those bound to a worldly, dharmic life of caste and gender responsibility to devote themselves directly to the Absolute and thereby overcome, spiritually at least, this worldly bondage. Alongside many particularist views will often be the understanding that opposing views are also possible.[8] This coexistence of different strands of ritual, mythology, philosophy, devotion, and mysticism is important in Hindu history, and it informs the basis for my discussion here of the ambiguities of faith in Hindu tradition.

This chapter explores several notes of ambiguity or self-correction in Hindu faith: the relationship between mystical certitude and discursive doubt in the Upanishads; bhakti (devotional faith) and the limitations of dharma in the epics; the questioning of assumptions about reality spurred by the doctrine of maya; and the paradoxical character of Hindu theism as reflected in the figure of Shiva. This fourfold examination illustrates ambiguities in a few of the very different strands of Hindu thought and practice. Behind all four thematic strands is a sense that beyond the worldly values of dharma teachings, the spiritual journey requires self-correction as part of the transformative experience of religious transcendence.

Mystical Experience and the Limits of Understanding in the Upanishads

The Upanishads, as the end of the Vedas, both wrap up the Vedic worldview and offer an alternative spiritual path that criticizes Vedic religion. The Upanishads do not reflect a single overarching philosophical perspective. As Joël Dubois points out, different concerns often appear side by side in the Upanishadic texts, and different positions describe the topic in different ways.[9] Whereas the Vedas guarantee worldly success through ritual sacrifice and prioritize a worldly life of balance with the natural world, the Upanishads turn inward to the nature of the Self. The *Mundaka Upanishad* suggests that knowledge of Brahman, the Ultimate Reality, is superior to sacrifice. It distinguishes two forms of knowledge. The lower knowledge that is contained in the four Vedas leads only to rebirth in this world, but the higher knowledge apprehends the Imperishable, which is "invisible, ungraspable, without family, without caste."[10] The Upanishads do not reject the Vedic worldview of the positive relationship between human life, the physical universe, and the gods, but they certainly limit its value by suggesting the superiority of an inward spiritual quest.

The *Chandogya Upanishad* lists three levels of duty in a way that ranks the religious teachings of the Vedas below those of the Upanishads and also privileges the certitude of the mystical experience.[11] The lowest level of duty is sacrifice, study of the Vedas, and almsgiving, all of which reflect the Vedic instruction on conventional religious life. The second level of duty is austerity, which is also taught in the Vedas' forest treatises for those who would pursue a more immediate spiritual satisfaction by conquering their sensual desires. The highest level of duty is studying sacred knowledge with a teacher, reflecting the meaning of the term *Upanishad*, or "sitting near a teacher." This highest duty is reflected in the meditative life that turns inward to pursue mystical experience. It is equally important that this is not an independent or solitary inward quest, at least initially. Instead, we see here the Upanishadic reverence for the authority of the mystical experience itself and of those who have achieved this insight and have become teachers.[12] Such reverence for the authority of the mystical experience suggests that the revealed wisdom represented in the Vedas must be fully appropriated and experienced by the spiritual seeker, not simply understood as objective fact or description of reality.

This turn inward and the emphasis on the certitude of the mystical experience clearly privilege the faculty of intuition over understanding and mystical experience over discursive reason. This questioning and doubt with regard to all conventional understanding is somewhat similar to the Christian faith's movement beyond the realm of understanding (discussed in the previous chapter). In the Upanishads, however, this movement is presented as intuitive experience or insight into ultimate reality. The *Katha Upanishad* teaches that the immortal self is not to be sought by outward knowledge at all but by an inward ascent. The wise know better than to seek what is stable and eternal among things that are unstable and constantly changing.[13] The inward ascent moves beyond the knowledge gained through the senses, and even further beyond the knowledge gained through the intellect, because the highest knowledge lies beyond all intellectual or physical capacities. The *Kena Upanishad* makes most explicit this opposition between the intuition of Brahman, or the Ultimate Reality, and ordinary understanding and discourse. "It is not understood by those who [say they] understand It. It is understood by those who [say they] understand It not. When known by an awakening, It is conceived of."[14] There are two issues to be noted here: one is that this intuitive insight lies entirely outside understanding; the other is that it is the result of an awakening or a transformation of the self. In other words, it must be experienced firsthand. This highest knowledge is the result of a transformative experience.

According to the *Mundaka Upanishad*, "He, verily, who knows that supreme Brahman, becomes very Brahman."[15] Knowledge of Brahman transforms the knower by uniting the self with Brahman or dissolving the individual sense of self. The *Maitri Upanishad* expresses this distinction between discursive knowledge and the unitive experience of knowing Brahman, which cannot be described. "Now, where knowledge is of a dual nature, there, indeed, one hears, sees, smells, tastes, and also touches; the self knows everything. Where knowledge is not of a dual nature, being devoid of action, cause, or effect, unspeakable, incomparable, indescribable—what is that? It is impossible to say!"[16] Discursive understanding and description are limited to dualistic or differentiated experience. The ultimate truth that is apprehended in self-realization cannot be described because it lacks this duality of separately identifiable things.

The impossibility of describing Brahman is a constant theme throughout the Upanishads, and this too marks a significant departure from the Vedic worldview, which reflects a confidence in human ability to understand and manipulate the physical and spiritual worlds for human benefit. The *Katha Upanishad* says of Brahman, "His form is not to be beheld."[17] It is unmanifest or hidden, and therefore higher than all that is manifest or sensible. It is soundless, touchless, formless, and tasteless; therefore, the student who seeks to know Brahman must move away from all that is sensible to a faculty of inward intuition. This fundamental intuition is described as "neti, . . . neti," or "not this, . . . not that." The Absolute is not any particular thing; it cannot be specified as this or as that. In fact, a better description of Brahman may be that it is nothing, or no-thing. The *Chandogya Upanishad* contains two famous teaching stories.[18] In the first, a fig is cut up to see what is inside. Dividing its inner parts farther still, the student comes to realize that inside the seed is nothing. And yet that nothing is reality—what can generate the seed and, from the seed, the fig and the great fig tree. In the second story, the student is told to put salt into a glass of water. The next day, he is told to bring back the salt, which he cannot do. However, when he tastes the water, every sip is salty. It is there even though it cannot be separated and distinguished from the water. According to the *Chandogya Upanishad*, that is reality. This comprises the teaching of "Tat tvam asi," or "That thou art." The relationship between Atman (the Self) and Brahman (Absolute Reality) is one of nonduality. The Self, or Atman, is above, below, to the west, north, east, and south; it is the whole world, but this must be *realized* in the unitive experience, not intellectually understood.

To summarize, the Upanishads teach a protest against the world-affirming sacrificial religion found in the Vedas. They teach the importance of turning away from the kind of knowledge gained through the senses or the intellect, which remains always of a limiting dual nature, wherein one is over here and the object to be known is over there. This higher knowledge takes the form of intuition, not understanding, and it must be experienced, not understood through reason. This experience, according to the different Upanishads, likewise lies beyond description, because the Absolute Brahman is beyond ordinary understanding—nameless, formless, and hidden. The Upanishads suggest a certitude that lies in the authority of the intuitive experience itself, but this certitude is possible only at the cost of abandoning all conventional understanding for the sake of an inward transcendence.

Bhakti, Transcendence, and Freedom in the *Bhagavad Gita*

This section turns to the Hindu epics to trace the ways in which teachings on bhakti both limit and define the teachings on dharma. The two great Hindu epics, the *Mahabharata* and the *Ramayana*, form the material foundation for popular, living Hinduism. While the Vedas were traditionally only in the hands of Brahmin elite and the Upanishads were accessible only to those initiated into the meditative life, the stories found in the epics are very well known by Hindus from all walks of life, regardless of differences in education or socioeconomic background. Also, unlike the Vedas, which are full of ritual instructions and hymns, and the Upanishads, which are some of the most sophisticated philosophical treatises of the world, the epics share the gritty stuff that gives richness and texture to Hindu patterns of thinking. In the *Bhagavad Gita*, Krishna, God incarnate, teaches Arjuna the complex doctrines of dharma, karma, maya, moksha, atman, and Brahman. Because of the inherent ambiguity of the text, different translations present the *Bhagavad Gita* as a mystical text aiming at union with a personal God, an elegant poem on moral crisis, a popular devotional song, an affirmation of Upanishadic wisdom, or a philosophical treatise that raises questions about human action.[19] It would be a crude mistake to reduce the epics to simply a popular translation of the truths of the Vedas. The epics add a rich situational texture to those complex ideas that helps build Hinduism into the living tradition it is. What I hope to show in this section is that as textual life-examples, the epics should not be reduced to mere sourcebooks for right behavior, although many people take them to function in just this way. As in other traditions, many people do in fact see the function of scripture in precisely this way, to show us clearly the singularly right ways to live, to give us role models, and to regulate our social and individual behavior in ways that are compelling. However, the Hindu epics demonstrate the moral struggles individuals may go through, and while they also show how these individuals choose to act and the consequences of their actions, the overwhelming message emerging from them is not a uniform set of rules for people to follow, but rather, a complex and varied meditation on how possible courses of action play out. The *Mahabharata* and the *Ramayana* stress an initial moral struggle, and they demonstrate the consequences of particular courses of response. Rather than answer the question of what to do in a particular situation, they emphasize the question itself and demonstrate the principle of karma—that actions have consequences and define who and what we are.

Now, while the teachings of dharma depend on the natural moral law of karma, or inevitable consequence, the teachings of bhakti found in the *Bhagavad Gita* exhibit a bit of an escape clause out of karmic consequence and the limitations of dharma. The plotline of the *Mahabharata* and the *Bhagavad Gita* has already been discussed in chapter 2, so I will not repeat it here. Instead, this section focuses on the ways in which the *Bhagavad Gita* introduces bhakti as an alternative to dharma and a superior avenue to spiritual liberation. If we consider that the rules of dharma embody the world-affirming values found in the Vedas, insofar as following dharma helps maintain personal well-being, family and social harmony, and political stability, what we find in the *Bhagavad Gita* is a relative opposition between the world-affirming philosophy of the Vedas and the world-transcending philosophy of the Upanishads.

In response to Arjuna's fundamental moral and spiritual crisis of how he could possibly fight and kill his own family members in the battle with which the *Bhagavad Gita* opens, Krishna's basic instruction is that as a *ksatriya*, or warrior and prince, Arjuna is obligated to fight to restore peace, stability, and righteous rule to the kingdom. However, while the rule of sacred duty serves as the basic answer to Arjuna's moral crisis itself, Krishna's teachings then turn to the question of what makes any action good or bad, and the greater question of how one can attain spiritual freedom and purity while acting and participating in this world of action. The problem emerges because all actions have consequences. According to Hindu teaching, these karmic consequences keep us repeatedly being reborn into the world, and yet the ultimate goal of life is not success in this world or a better rebirth, but moksha, or liberation and the self-realization presented in the Upani-shads. So, how can one continue to act in this world and pursue spiritual freedom, when all actions tie one further to the world? The question raises the issue of balance between world-affirmation and world-transcendence that represent two normative poles of Hindu spiritual life.

In his conversation with Arjuna, Krishna describes several ways to realize the freedom of the self that is taught in the Upanishads. He says the key is discipline, but it may take one of several different forms. It may take the form of jñana yoga—mental concentration, meditation, and inner visualization of the true self, of the mystical inward path taught in the Upanishads. It may employ the raja yoga techniques of self-mastery and physical discipline as taught in the forest treatises of the Vedas for those who would leave behind community life and pursue spiritual freedom through a life of physical and emotional renunciation. Jñana yoga and raja yoga are not new teachings; they represent the mystical philosophy of the Upanishads and the ascetic path of the older Vedic forest treatises. Both represent the world-denying or world-transcending values of spiritual life, over and against the world-affirming values of Vedic ritual sacrifice, caste order, and dharma, which together characterize the spiritual life of the householder who raises a family and contributes to the harmony and flourishing of society. The other two ways presented in the *Bhagavad Gita*, however, do represent novel teachings in spiritual realization: the path of selfless action (karma yoga) and the path of love and devotion (bhakti yoga).

Karma yoga depends on fulfilling one's dutiful actions while relinquishing concern for the fruits of those actions. In other words, one feeds a beggar because it is the right thing to do, not because doing so today will benefit one tomorrow by gaining admiration or securing a more comfortable rebirth. "Be intent on action, not on the fruits of action; avoid attraction to the fruits and attachment to inaction!"[20] Krishna teaches that actions accrue karma primarily because of one's desires for acting. Therefore, if one can be firm in discipline and free oneself of concern for the good or bad one receives from an action, one becomes free of that karmic consequence. "Wise men disciplined by understanding relinquish the fruit born of action; freed from these bonds of rebirth, they reach a place beyond decay."[21] Krishna empha-sizes that one should not renounce action altogether, but that one should carry on his usual life duties, or dharma, as prescribed by caste, gender, and age, but must do so with a higher attitude of detachment from what benefits or harms may result. This teaching especially corrects and balances the world-affirming value of social dharma with the world-denying values of the forest-dwelling ascetic. The *Bhagavad Gita*'s teaching of karma yoga, restated simply as "perform one's duty without clinging to the fruits of those dutiful actions," rejects the ascetic's renunciation of worldly society and responsible action. Yet it offers a way to achieve the spiritual freedom promised in the discipline of yoga even while living in worldly society and contributing to family and society. The *Bhagavad Gita* seeks to discipline the self's inner motivations because simple renunciation of action may be both unproductive for society and ineffective for spiritual liberation. Given that it may be unrealistic to demand action without any desire, Christopher Framarin identifies the criterion cited by important Hindu theologians Shankara, Ramanujan, and Vivekananda for judging which desires are justified for action: the desire for the true self or God is the only one justified.[22] This guarantees the transcendence of any particular selfish motivation.

Bhakti yoga applies this discipline and selflessness in the direction of service and devotion to God. Krishna tells Arjuna, "When devoted men sacrifice to other deities with faith, they sacrifice to me, Arjuna, however aberrant the rites."[23] The specific rituals do not matter; the choice of deity does not matter because Krishna says He, as Absolute God, is the enjoyer of all sacrifices, and it is the strength and singularity of devotion that makes it pure. "The leaf or flower or fruit or water that he offers with devotion, I take from the man of self-restraint in response to his devotion."[24] Krishna promises that one who performs action as an offering to God will be freed from the bonds of karma and achieve unity with God. "Your self liberated, you will join me. . . . Men devoted to me are in me, and I am within them."[25] What determines the purity of this devotion and links the path of bhakti with the other paths to self-realization is the discipline of selflessness and singularity of devotion. Bhakti yoga appears somewhat different from the other paths because it relies uniquely on the grace of God to accept the worshiper's devotion and sacrifice. Krishna tells Arjuna, "I grant unwavering faith to any devoted man who wants to worship any form with faith."[26] So if one exercises discipline and selflessness and wholeheartedly offers God his or her devotion, God will strengthen that faith. A stronger faith is the gift given by God in return for one's selfless devotion.[27]

In both the selfless action of karma and the selfless devotion of bhakti, the faithful self detaches from the ego and the world, and as a result, nothing remains except for the Absolute Self, according to Advaita Vedanta philosophy. This is how these paths of karma, which preserves an active and engaged social life, and bhakti, which looks very much like attached devotion to God, promise the freedom of self-realization that is described in the esoteric teachings of the Upanishads. Nevertheless, this introduction of divine grace, by which God promises to make one's faith unwavering, separates bhakti yoga from the paths of jñana, raja, and karma, all of which depend on the individual's own effort. In this, too, bhakti yoga serves as a corrective to the expectations that individual effort at discipline will achieve spiritual freedom.

Maya: That Which Is Not

Another central doctrine that pertains to the spiritual transcendence of worldly expectations in Hindu tradition is maya. Maya is translated most often as illusion or ignorance, but it is also the power of appearance or manifestation of the divine for human apprehension. Some Shaiva cosmologies see maya not as illusory, but as the material cause of our world. Maya in Hindu mythology is often personified as female and is associated with Shakti, which is either the goddess herself or the creative and manifest power of the gods. Brahman, the unmanifest, and Shakti, the visible and manifest energy of the same reality, cannot exist without each other. The relationship between the two is represented as maya, explaining how the unmanifest and absolute becomes manifest to us. The Puranas present maya as the power by which a god like Vishnu or Shiva acts in the world, to teach humans something by appearing in some particular form. Advaita Vedanta teaches that maya is the illusory character of the cosmos as a reality independent of human experience. As illusion, maya refers to reality as we see it, or as we mistakenly believe it. Etymologically, maya is *that which* (ya) *is not* (ma), indicating a fissure in our experience of reality; genuine reality is not what it appears to us to be at the moment. Advaita philosophy, grounded especially in eighth-century theologian Adi Shankara's interpretations of the Upanishads, teaches that the true reality is Brahman and spiritual freedom lies in the mystical insight that apprehends this reality in oneself. [28] Although an accurate understanding of Shankara must acknowledge Francis Clooney's caution against reducing the texts to a set of philosophical conclusions, our concern is with some of the influential ways to interpret maya, so we will rely on the most common interpretations of Shankara's commentaries on the Upanishads.[29] According to these interpretations of Shankara, Brahman is the whole of reality; the cosmos is illusion; the human soul is nothing but Brahman. Brahman's meaning emerges out of the tension of several different voices of Vedanta analysis. We humans are separated from understanding the true nature of reality by maya, whether this is interpreted as ignorance (*avidya*) or error in human judgment, or, as some Vaishnavites interpret it, a divinely generated illusion. Insofar as maya teaches that reality is not what we believe it to be, it manifests a Hindu value of transcending initial false beliefs or illusion in order to achieve a higher truth. This section examines some of the classic mythological renderings of maya and then turns to the epistemological and metaphysical implications of the doctrine, especially as developed by Shankara.

Two stories about the pious sage Narada and Vishnu help illustrate the doctrine of maya. A myth that appears in the *Matsya Purana* tells of how Narada achieves a divine boon as a result of severe asceticism and asks Vishnu to help him understand the nature of maya.[30] Vishnu tells him first to submerge himself in the nearby water. Narada enters the water and emerges as a young woman named Sushila, the daughter of a local king. Sushila returns home, eventually marries a prince of a neighboring kingdom, and enjoys all the pleasures of a life of love. She has children and watches them grow into a strong and happy family. However, years pass and her husband and her father have a disagreement that ends in a terrible war, during which Sushila's sons die in battle. As an elderly Sushila is tearfully mourning her sons' deaths, she is transformed back into Narada's body standing in the water and Vishnu once again appears, asking whom he is mourning. Vishnu explains that this is the appearance of his maya.

In another version of the story that appears in the *Devi Bhagavata Purana*, when asked to help him understand the nature of maya, Vishnu asks Narada first to fetch him some water to drink from a nearby river. While at the river, Narada encounters a beautiful woman and falls in love. He forgets about fetching the water for Vishnu and follows her home. In time, Narada and this woman marry, have children, and establish a family home. They enjoy a long and happy life, but years later, the skies turn dark and the river floods and drowns his entire family, despite all of Narada's efforts to save his children. Vishnu then pulls the weeping Narada from the water and asks him again, "Narada, where is my water?" Vishnu criticizes Narada for getting caught up in the illusion of life and forgetting about what is alone the true reality. Vishnu explains to him that all the life he had experienced was all maya, that everything comes solely from the unchangeable God.[31] Everything else is temporary and illusory. All of one's life—all its joys and tribulations, time, aging, change itself—is illusion. All of life is as a blink of an eye; it is as nothing. Maya can be considered altogether real in terms of our experience but fleeting, or it is simply that the life we live may as well be as nothing at all.

In addition to illustrating the fleeting nature of this life, these two stories about Narada and Vishnu illustrate the inscrutability of maya. Narada sought to understand the nature of maya, but Vishnu refuses to explain it, and only on Narada's insistence, agrees to allow him to experience its secrets. At the end, Vishnu tells him that not even the mighty gods can fathom the depth of maya. He asks Narada, "Why or how should *you* know this inscrutable secret?" Maya's secret is not to be known; it is impenetrable in its mysteriousness and in its power to generate the actual phenomena of our worldly existence. Upon the conclusion of the experience, Narada prays for perfect faith and devotion. Bhakti seems a most appropriate and pious response to the stupefying experience of maya and reflection on its inscrutability. Realizing one's failure rationally to grasp divine revelation, all the faithful can do, like Narada, is to move outside rationality to the commitment of intense devotion.

As far as experience is concerned, maya defines reality as we know it. It is the stuff we see, hear, touch, taste, and smell. Maya is our world, or phenomenal reality, to use a Kantian distinction. In Shaivism, maya is the actual appearance of Brahman, which is absolute, unchanging, and eternal, in the manifold form of our world. Therefore, it is the Real, but the veiled Real. To focus only on maya as illusion and as therefore false and meaningless is an oversimplification that leaves out the identity between maya and Brahman. This illusion or veil is after all based on the reality of Brahman, but it is the "power of appearance" by which the Absolute and unchanging Reality becomes manifest to us. Where Western theologies have described the world of existence as a conditioned, finite, limited place of understanding that is fundamentally imperfect in relation to the absolute, unchanging, and independent reality of God on which it depends, Hindu tradition has used the concept of maya to explain the appearance for our limited apprehension of what is unchanging and eternal truth.

Shankara offered three famous analogies to explain the function of maya. The first is a rope that at twilight may appear to us to be a snake. A second analogy is the mirage that appears in the desert at a distance. The third is a tiger perceived in a dream during sleep. In all three cases, what appears to be (the snake, the distant mirage, or the tiger) turns out to be nothing at all of what was perceived or expected. However convincing, however terrifying or promising, the snake perceived in dim light is not a snake, but only a rope, and there is nothing in the desert but never-ending sand. The dream tiger has no reality at all because as soon as one awakens the dream ends. In all three cases, the perception that turns out to be false is generated by our human fear or desire. Shankara teaches that maya is the effect of our expectations imposed on reality. These analogies express the degree to which our experience of reality feels quite convincing and real, and yet is nothing but an illusion and a false belief. What seemed like a snake in low light or a tiger during a dream turns out to be an entirely harmless rope in daylight or nothing at all when one awakens and the dream is simply over.

The doctrine of maya teaches several practical lessons on human knowledge and spiritual understanding. First, what we ordinarily consider to be true and lasting is not so. Second, what we ordinarily value is subject to change, and therefore may not be dependable. Third, all that we believe and trust is only a part of our superficial worldly imagination and is not independently real or true. Fourth, we have no understanding of what is truly real, and according to Vishnu's lesson, we *cannot* gain understanding of how this deception or appearance works. These lessons suggest that our experience and our lives as we know them are simply illusion. The teachings of maya, insisting on human ignorance and worldly illusion, spur speculation on the question of what is real and what is not. The teachings of maya and the paths of yoga support the idea that the aim of religious practice is to transcend the limits of individual ego-consciousness. Raja yoga, jñana yoga, karma yoga, and bhakti yoga all use a particular set of exercises to train the mind, achieve discipline, and overcome the individualistic selfishness of ego-consciousness. The Upanishadic teachings suggest that the real lies in the eternal unchangeable reality that is Brahman, and not in the temporary and defined world of suffering and constant change. While the operations of maya are to remain an impenetrable secret, the experience of maya, the wakeful reflection on the relative unreality of our lives and our world as we experience them, spurs the faithful to work to discipline themselves to transcend this unreality.

The Hindu doctrine of maya uniquely forces active reflection on the relationship between our experience of reality, characterized by change and defined in fear and desire, on the one hand, and Reality itself, which is unchanging, unmanifest, and Absolute. If, as according to the dominant interpretation of Advaita metaphysics, Brahman alone is real, and there is nothing but Brahman, then how are the real and the unreal related? Shankara's answer affirms both the Advaita doctrine of the oneness of ultimate Reality and maya as the vehicle of the appearance of the Real as the world we know. Scholars disagree on how to interpret Shankara's idea that the world is unreal because of persistent realist tendencies in his thought. Some see this realism as an earlier phase of his thought that he transcended, for example.[32] In addition, John Thatanamil notes the pains Shankara takes to defend theism and the duties prescribed in scripture; even though the world is ultimately unreal (following the interpretation that there is nothing but Brahman), worldly values of duty, theism, and virtuous living in householder community are not just defensible but even necessary preparation to overcome ignorance of our true nature as Brahman until we awaken to this truth.[33] A judgment against worldly values and norms does not apply until a very late and mature stage of spiritual life. Most of our lives are to be devoted to living rightly in the world.

Just as Friedrich Nietzsche's nihilism of the nineteenth century—his call for the destruction of false values—also suggested a great optimism in the creative powers of humankind and sought to pave the way for a secular humanism devoid of some other higher source of transcendence, so the doctrine that reality is only an illusion should not automatically be rendered a pessimistic destruction of meaning and value. While it is presented as a temporary and false reality that we will surpass with maturity, it is nevertheless the very stuff of human reality. Even though Narada's experience of a long and rich life turns out to be an illusion, Narada did experience a long and rich life of love and family, subjectively interpreted. Just as none of us can imagine or begin to describe living outside the categories of time or space, we cannot simply extricate ourselves from maya, except for the mystical insight, or *darsana*, by which humans can apprehend Reality directly. As the power of appearance of the gods, maya affirms the manifestation of ultimate and unchanging Reality in a manner that is accessible to us. It is the place of our human contact with the divine, the horizon of darsana. The spiritual lesson and task then address the need to see this illusion as what it is and thereby come to transcend it and achieve mystical insight into the reality of Brahman. We humans have the unique ability (or so we assume) to transcend our ignorance. As the horizon draws our eyes to the limits of our perspectival perception but simultaneously moves farther to precisely what lies beyond our view, maya both marks the limits of human experience and draws us to transcend them. Therefore, by drawing us toward the far horizon of our experience, it serves as the locus of darsana, or the mystical revelation.

Far from reflecting a commitment to the meaninglessness of human worldly experience here and now, maya functions practically as a corrective to our all-controlling, idolatrous illusions of grandeur. We do not know it all, and we cannot contain and inspect all of reality in the palm of our hand. Nevertheless, our experience does bring us to the threshold of contact with the sacred. It is as real as it can be and meaningful, even while it is not lasting or eternal. Life—transient, fleeting, and fueled by fear, desire, and ignorance—is still precious, and perhaps even more so, in the same way that childhood represents immaturity and ignorance, and yet is precious because it is a fleeting reality. Maya forces our reflection on this character of human experience; therefore, it functions as a horizon experience that pushes us toward transcendence.

The Ambiguity of Hindu Theism: Shiva

While ambiguities and paradox are abundant in the conceptions of many different Hindu deities, the persona of Shiva is especially striking in the richness of the contradictions held together in Shaivite worship.[34] Shiva is identified with asceticism, eroticism, and destruction. He wears the tiger skin reserved for the most accomplished yogi and meditates without end high atop Mount Kailasa, and yet he rewards his devotees' efforts with fierce protection and grace and is a most ardent lover and tender husband to Parvati. This final section of the chapter discusses selected ambiguities and oppositions juxtaposed in the mythological and philosophical image of Shiva by examining the ancient roots of Shiva worship, the symbolism of the linga, the paradoxical nature of Shiva's asceticism, and Shiva's function of destruction as it relates to a Shaiva Siddhanta teaching of spiritual liberation.

These juxtaposed contradictions in the views of Shiva reflect Rudolf Otto's early twentieth-century comparative analysis of the holy as the *mysterium tremendum et fascinans*, by which the holy is a mystery that both terrifies and fascinates us; it has an extremely attractive quality as well as a deeply repulsive dimension, and we are compelled to approach closer even as we are frightened to do so.[35] While some of the contradictions found in Hindu gods may be due to the convergence over time of very different regional traditions in Hindu history, there remains in Shiva's symbolism a powerful paradox of attraction and repulsion that cannot be explained simply by different sources and traditions. As the title suggests, Wendy Doniger O'Flaherty's book *Siva: The Erotic Ascetic* delineates the powerful contradictions that are juxtaposed in Shiva.[36] Sometimes he is the ideal householder as Parvati's doting husband and at other times the strange ascetic who frequents cremation grounds and carries a skull as a begging bowl. Despite the contradictions, O'Flaherty cautions against any simplistic identification of Shiva's different characters as unresolved paradox, suggesting instead that these contradictions may function as correlative oppositions of interchangeable identities that are not mutually exclusive, but instead complement each other.[37] Because of these interchangeable identities, Shiva poses a most interesting example for this chapter's discussion of world-affirmation and world-transcendence. We find in Shaivism the combination of serious asceticism (withdrawal from the world), genuine devotion (intense attachment), and a high degree of sophisticated speculation (transcendence of worldly concerns).

The paradoxical character of Hindu theism is expressed in the many ways in which the divine is seen as both transcendent and immanent. The term *lila*, or play, is used to identify the way in which the various gods are able to manifest themselves within the human world in paradoxical ways that delimit their transcendent being in order to express their manifest being in immanent ways; they appear as unknowable and mysterious even while they make themselves knowable to devotees. The lila of Krishna and Radha is illustrated as the carefree play between lovers. It contains no greater reality than the board games or role-playing games we might play for entertainment. However, even while it is *only* play, it is the play that defines creative manifestation in the phenomenal world. Lila, as play, suggests the creative activity of the divine to differentiate itself without need or necessity, and refers to the whole process by which Shiva as the absolute divine transforms himself and descends into time, particularity, and division, all of which are defining characteristics of our phenomenal world. Don Handelman and David Shulman unpack the mythological impact of Shiva's lila in a dice game that Shiva plays with his consort Parvati; the game reflects Shiva's descent out of wholeness and single undifferentiated unity into division, uncertainty, and rupture.[38] They trace moments of this dice game as phases in a process of externalization and reabsorption. Shiva begins to externalize and differentiate components of self into the division of self and other, represented by male and female (which are at first held together in the Ardhanarisvara figure of androgyny and only later separate into husband and wife, Shiva and Parvati), and then when pressed by crisis, begins to reabsorb these externalizations, or destroy these differentiated states of being, to return at the end to a state of wholeness and inward focus as a detached Yogi. Shiva's creative manifestation establishes our phenomenal world, but it occurs as a rupture within the divine and it is ultimately a lila, or a game into which Shiva enters with himself. He is both higher, or outside the game, and lower, or inside the game that he has entered.

A variety of sources and traditions coalesces in the classical worship of Shiva, including linga worship in several ancient non-Vedic traditions of southern India: Pasupati, the god of animals; Rudra, the pre-Vedic and Vedic god of darkness and stormy destruction; and Shiva the Mahayogi who practiced and preached austerity, yoga, and self-mortification. Shiva is also known as the Lord of sleep, in the sense of a rest and peace from the dynamism of life, a condition that is the supreme goal of the yogis. While humans trapped in the world of bondage mistakenly fear death, the end of death of and rebirth signifies liberation and peace. In general, Shaivism, especially its non-Puranic strands, is less influenced by Vedic orthodoxy than Vaishnavism. While Puranic Shaivism provides sources for popular worship of Shiva and supports the social orthopraxy of Brahmin householders, reflecting the norms of dharma and bhakti, non-Puranic Shaivism includes movements that break the taboos of Brahmin householder society, challenge social norms, and sometimes posed a threat to Vedic caste purity and the rules of dharma.[39]

The oldest of these images of Shiva is the ancient figure of Rudra, who appears in the Vedas but seems, by most accounts, to be pre-Vedic in origin. The Rg Veda has a few hymns to Rudra, mostly asking him to stay away and not do harm. Conceivably, this dark figure worshiped by pre-Aryan communities represented such a formidable threat to the Vedic orthodoxy that he had to be assimilated into the Vedic system (and thereby tamed). The fearful god Rudra is given the name Shiva, the auspicious one, reflecting the common ancient practice of propitiating what one fears by speaking of it only indirectly and with gentle names.[40] This absorption of Rudra into the Vedic pantheon reflects the pattern by which Hinduism has throughout history maintained its primacy in India, by absorbing competing views and allowing them a limited place within the centralized system. By the fifth or fourth centuries B.C.E., the Rudra-Shiva figure occupies a position of prominence and in the *Svetasvatara Upanishad* is identified with the supreme absolute of the cosmos.[41]

The word *linga* means sign; it is the visible manifestation of what is essentially unmanifest, unseen, and unchanging. Shiva is beyond all manifestation, beyond all duality, and so the visible linga is a sign or pointer to this undifferentiated absolute reality. Many Hindu deities, including Shiva, are worshiped in particular anthropomorphic forms. In contrast, the linga, the primary form through which Shiva is worshiped, resists anthropomorphism altogether in favor of an abstract symbol that is first and foremost a sign that points beyond manifestation to what is an unmanifest, transcendent reality. In addition to functioning as a constant indicator of the transcendence of all that is manifest, the linga united with the *yoni* represents the point of contact between transcendent undifferentiated reality and manifest nature. When they are together, the linga is the masculine and transcendent aspect and the yoni symbolizes the feminine and material aspect of reality. The linga embedded in a yoni is interpreted as the ultimate origin and source of all life on earth, beyond differentiation. The two polar opposites, masculine and feminine, are to be united both originally and for life to continue. Therefore, in the Ardhanarishvara figure, a popular subject of sculpture, the anthropomorphic images of Shiva and Shakti are combined into one single being manifesting a duality that holds together two sides without dissolving them into one. This figure speaks to the mutual dependence of feminine and masculine, and of Shakti and Shiva; it presents Shiva and Parvati as the parents whose union engenders the entire world. However, as an abstract rendition of the Absolute Divine Principle, the linga carries continued meaningfulness as it attempts to move the worshiper beyond his anthropomorphic imagination. The Absolute itself is entirely transcendent. This transcendence is what worshipers identify in the linga. This divine or absolute transcendence of all human knowledge and imagination informs the sense of ambiguity in the figure of Shiva. Remembering that the Absolute transcends all our views of God serves the function of casting doubt on all those views as, indeed, *our own views* and not God.

I turn now to the ambiguous treatment of asceticism in Shiva's mythology. From India's ancient history on, asceticism has remained a heterodox movement of some people who opt out of worldly society, both physically and psychologically. It is likely that ascetic practice of social withdrawal and restraint over the physical body predated the Vedic religion and was only gradually absorbed into the later Vedic worldview. Whereas the Vedic worldview affirms the world and supports ritual sacrifice intended to maintain the continuation of worldly harmony, the ascetic life seeks peace in the transcendence of attachment and desire and may to some extent be seen as denying or rejecting worldly life. The ascetic, who throws off family bonds and material possessions and discards his name and care for the body, and the householder, who raises a family, works for a living, and participates in the collective life of the society, represent two very different ideals in Hindu religious tradition. Society depends on the responsible lives of householders. Shiva the ascetic represents a deliberate challenge to social convention. Especially compared with Vaishnavism, which extols the concrete manifestation of the divine in the avatars, Shaivism more sharply privileges divine transcendence of all that is human, all that is conventional, all that is social, differentiated, and particular.

Shiva's personality, however, combines asceticism and eroticism. O'Flaherty notes that these components receive varying focus in different strands of Hindu tradition. The Shiva of Brahmin philosophy is an ascetic, for example, while the Shiva of Tantric philosophy is a sexual being. These two natures are to be held together, however, not kept mutually exclusive. She cites as an example Shiva's insistence that if he marries, his wife must be a female ascetic, or *yogini*, when he does yoga, and a lustful mistress when he is full of desire.[42] According to O'Flaherty, Shiva is the pillar of chastity, but this pillar is the form of an erect phallus, or linga. His chastity is the source of his erotic power, as the heat of desire and the heat of *tapas* (generated by physical austerity) are closely related. The erect phallus represents the potency or potential power generated by ascetic tapas. It is because of his ascetic powers, for example, that Shiva is able to continue to make love to Parvati without interruption, to generate and hold this potency without releasing it and ending the lovemaking. Tantric philosophy, which makes elaborate use of Shaivism and Shaktism, accepts the material reality of the world. The body is not evil or false, but is discovered to be the manifestation of Shiva and Shakti; the physical body takes part in this divine play. Just as in poison there are healing properties to be used with skillfulness (vaccinations), so also in the body lies the coiled-up energy that enables a person to reach absolute freedom. Tantric practice often involves what are otherwise considered socially illicit activities that alternatively can threaten or free the initiate from the trappings of conventional understanding. Because of this capacity of tapas to generate power, Don Handelman and David Shulman categorically reject the place of asceticism in Hinduism, suggesting that asceticism as it is understood in the West as self-denial and physical austerity is foreign to Hindu metaphysics.[43] They argue, instead, that tapas is an internal, self-heating activity that brings to fruition the latent wholeness inside a person and triggers an upward transition in levels of being or awareness by directing energy inward.

In addition, even in representing Shiva as the Mahayogi, Shiva's mythology does not teach simply that asceticism is a superior spiritual practice. A story explaining the origin of the linga that appears in the *Kurma Purana* describes an episode in which the god Shiva wants to teach a group of sages that the extreme austerities they have chosen to pursue may be useful for worldly purposes of gaining power over the senses and nature but do not lead to the highest liberation.[44] Shiva plays a trick on them, and failing to recognize him as their god, the sages condemn his disturbance of their austerities. In the end, Shiva teaches them that the path of knowledge is superior to the path of renunciation because it achieves ultimate insight into the nature of Absolute Reality, which is transformative and liberating. In the myth, the linga serves as a reminder for worshipers to transcend their limited judgments and to be attuned for the manifestation of the divine that remains invisible or hidden in a different form right before us.

Finally, we treat what may be Shiva's most famous role as god of destruction. In the Trimurti of Brahma (creator), Vishnu (preserver), and Shiva (destroyer), destruction is a necessary counterpart of creation. All of life must come to an end. Shiva as the god of destruction threatens the manifest world, reminds us continually of its pending and inevitable dissolution. Shiva may be identified with a centrifugal tendency in the sacred.[45] This is the aspect of the sacred that threatens what is unified, that tends toward dissolution and disintegration. The centripetal tendency in Hindu religion can be found, by contrast, in the monistic tendency of Hindu philosophy, the unity or identification of all the manifestations of the divine in one Absolute, the understanding of Brahman as the one Absolute Reality, or the soul's consciousness of this basic reality as its own truth as articulated in the Vedic mantra "Tat tvam asi" ("That thou art"). The transcendence discussed throughout this chapter is reflected in the centrifugal tendency, which is most explicitly articulated in Shiva's role of destruction. As a reminder of the temporary character of the manifest world, Shiva as the god of destruction and Shiva's symbolism of transcendence of all human understanding reinforce the doctrine of maya. Shiva destroys not only the physical universe, but also ignorance, which is the state of our experience of the world. In the Shiva Nataraja figure, Shiva is seen dancing triumphantly on the back of a dwarf who represents ignorance; Shiva successfully stomps it out with his right foot and promises liberation with his raised left foot. When in ritual puja, worshipers smash open a coconut and offer it at the feet of the *murti* (icon) of Shiva, it is said to symbolize the smashing and breaking open of the human ego. The dangerous darkness of Rudra, Shiva's mythic anger expressed through his third eye that burned Kama, the god of desire, and Shiva's posture as he strides forth with his trident all function to remind us repeatedly of a pending dissolution of the world we know. In the terms of Western monotheism, Shiva may be said to function in a role of suspended judgment; by confronting us with a reminder of our own ignorance, Shiva judges it to be illusion, temporary, and destined for dissolution.

The trope of destruction as a vehicle for transcendence of human understanding is related to the teachings articulated in Shaiva Siddhanta philosophy of the liberation of the individual soul. In the Shaiva Siddhanta system, all that exists can be categorized as *pati* (Lord), *pasu* (soul), or *pasa* (fetters).[46] While Siddhanta texts demand of the human worshiper a rigorous four-pronged program of study, proper conduct, yogic discipline, and ritual action, they emphasize that human agency is not adequate to loosen the soul of the fetters of ordinary human life. Human effort is absolutely essential, and it is quite demanding, but ultimately, it serves only as a necessary initiation. Only Shiva can purify the soul thus initiated by Siddhanta practice. Richard Davis cites an analogy of refining metal with fire found in the *Shiva Purana* to explain how the soul must be purified only through contact with Shiva.[47] According to Shaiva Siddhanta teachings, the soul has potentially infinite powers of knowing and acting, like Shiva, but in the ordinary human condition, these powers are constrained by the fetters of human blindness, karmic residue, and maya, or the material conditions of life.[48] Davis explains that the intrinsic powers of the soul and the external fetters that bind it constitute a state of internal struggle for each individual. However, the Siddhanta program of study, conduct, discipline, and ritual action teaches an initiate to exercise those innate powers of the soul and overcome false understanding about reality. According to Davis, increasing knowledge encourages diligence in ritual action as well as consciousness of its metaphysical foundations, and the ritual action serves as a vehicle for Shiva's grace to take effect because in the ritual actions, the initiate enacts Shiva's powers; essentially, the initiate acts as Shiva. "Saiva rituals all involve the employment of Siva's own mantra powers, and in the most important liberating ritual in the Saiva system, Siva himself intervenes through the intermediary of the initiating guru to destroy the initiate's fetters and to help recover his long-suppressed innate powers, an act of supreme grace."[49] To some extent, this emphasis on Shiva's divine grace to free the individual worshiper echoes the teachings of the bhakti traditions discussed earlier in the chapter. However, the degree to which Shaiva Siddhanta teachings reflect a far more explicit path of transcendence is reflected in the ultimate end of liberation. The liberated soul does not merge with Shiva, as is taught in some Vaishnavite traditions, but actually becomes a Shiva—equal with Shiva with all the powers and qualities of Shiva, but separate.[50]

Conclusion

In all of these ways, the figure of Shiva and his worship function to threaten the stability of our manifest world, to threaten and judge our human confidence in our rules and systems of understanding. Shiva threatens to destroy our false expectations. The worship of Shiva articulates a clear sense of ambiguity, by which worshipers are forced to actively question all that they understand in order to liberate themselves from these trappings and realize enlightenment. The coincidence in Shiva's character of the dark and dangerous Rudra, the linga as a sign of what lies beyond manifestation, the path of asceticism that seeks to transcend conventional worldly action, and the promise of destruction of the world and ignorance together represent Shiva's challenge to conventional human thinking. The Tantric model of breaking down the barriers of social convention of right and wrong by engaging in otherwise illicit activities provides a contrasting avenue to transcending human understanding to the Saiva Siddhanta program of ritual action by which one opens oneself to the operation of Shiva's overwhelming grace to loosen the fetters of the soul and empower its innate and potentially infinite powers.

In the previous chapter, we saw in the examples of Kierkegaard, Tillich, and Barth the explication of doubt or protest as an integral component of true faith because faith has necessarily to do with the divine and eternal, which we can in human life see only through a glass darkly. In this chapter, what we believe and what we do in ordinary understanding and even in religion is always held in check by the goal of spiritual transcendence. Religion as a way of maintaining harmony and well-being in the world is to be transcended. Reason, understanding, and intellect are to be transcended by the mystical intuitive insight into the nature of Reality, which is beyond name and form. The life of dharma and the rules of karma are to be transcended with the selfless action of karma yoga or the selfless devotion of bhakti yoga. The transcendence of all that we know and apprehend is especially embodied in the doctrine of maya and articulated in the powerful challenge to human convention found in the mythological image of Shiva and the devotional and philosophical traditions of Shaivism.

PART THREE

RECONCILING WAYS
OF FAITH AND DOUBT

CHAPTER FIVE

RESISTING THE REIFICATION
OF RELIGION

In *The Brothers Karamazov*, Fyodor Dostoyevsky presents a provocative situation in a section titled "The Grand Inquisitor." Christ returns and faces questioning by the Grand Inquisitor, who demands to know why he has returned. The church had been set up in Christ's absence, and now this return appearance threatens its stability. Christ explains that he came to bring freedom to humanity—in the incarnation and in his return. Dostoyevsky's criticism is leveled against the oppressive ways in which the church shuts down freedom of spiritual development, and freezes and stultifies it with its insistence on the dogmatic nature of doctrine. In Dostoyevsky's account, Christ died to atone for human sin and free humanity from its bondage to sin, but what did humanity do in response? In Dostoyevsky's view, Christians took this divine gift of spiritual freedom and built a set of virtually impenetrable walls around it, using as their brick and mortar the structure and authority of the church.

Many skeptics and humanists throughout history have leveled such a charge against their fellow human beings—that they take this gift of freedom and squander it by freely taking on bondage of different forms. A fear of freedom and the chaos it threatens lies at the heart of many fundamentalist movements that seek to turn the clock back to a supposedly simpler time when the answers to life's questions were more clear and straightforward. Today, we are haunted by a postmodern inability to know things with certainty. This lack of certainty frightens many into retreating behind straightforward formulations of faith and scripture. However, this lack of certainty is precisely the contemporary challenge to embrace the freedom of spirit that lies at the heart of many traditional religious prescriptions. The ancient biblical condemnation of idolatry does not simply criticize prayer that uses stone images; it attacks the elevation of what is human-made above God. Retreating from the abyss of nonknowing is a failure of religious nerve. Rejecting the mystery of the sacred in favor of straightforward human interpretations is idolatrous in the classical biblical sense because it limits the sacred to human manipulation.

The two previous chapters looked theologically at doubt in two of the world's traditions insofar as it is an instrumental part of spiritual transcendence. This chapter turns to the responsibility to resist dogmatism and examines doubt as an active project of the spiritual life. The first section briefly surveys some prominent modern thinkers who criticize religious dogmatism on behalf of what is a spiritual calling of humanist freedom, including Sam Harris's atheistic criticism of religious dogmatism, Friedrich Nietzsche's insight into the "death of God," Karl Marx's suspicion of religion, and John Robinson's proposal to abandon theistic Christianity. The second section examines teachings of Christian mystics regarding the explicit path of unknowing or unlearning required on the spiritual journey. The third section turns to Buddhist teachings on emptiness to see how self-transcendence requires the active limitation and undoing of self-knowledge.

Humanist Criticisms of Religious Dogmatism

Sam Harris

Sam Harris has become, along with Christopher Hitchens and Richard Dawkins, a veritable media star among today's New Atheists.[1] All three have much of value to add to the critical dialogue about the validity of certain kinds of evidence and the validity of people's certitude without legitimate sorts of evidence. They also have alienated many religious people because of their outspoken animosity for the meaningfulness and value of religion or faith. As a result, their more worthy insights often fall on deaf ears. Harris's disdain for all religion and especially his reduction of the entire Islamic religion to a particularly hateful and dogmatic fringe of outliers truly prevent any constructive conversation from ensuing out of his sometimes insightful analysis.[2] While he criticizes both fundamentalists and religious moderates for overlooking the irrationality of religious beliefs, Harris too is guilty of discussing faith exclusively in terms of propositional belief statements. There is a hint of awareness of this reductionist analysis when he writes, "It is nowhere written, however, that human beings must be irrational, or live in a perpetual state of siege, to enjoy an abiding sense of the sacred. On the contrary, I hope to show that spirituality can be—indeed, must be—deeply rational, even as it elucidates the limits of reason."[3] Harris does seem to appreciate an "abiding sense of the sacred" even while he criticizes the uncritical posture of believers. Most of the problems in Harris's treatment of religion emerge from his reduction of religious faith to the articulation of beliefs that cannot be proven scientifically. Nevertheless, he offers us several useful critical insights regarding faith and public discourse.

The most significant of these are, first, that religious beliefs, functionally speaking, are not private matters of conscience, but in fact actively affect public policy and therefore should be subject to the same critical investigation and skepticism employed toward other sorts of claims, and second, valuable for the concern of this chapter, that the problem with religion is not belief itself, but the tendency to protect religious dogmatism.[4] As Harris points out, in all other areas of life, particularly public life (which seems to be his stated concern in many radio and television interviews), we demand evidence and hurl suspicion at any kind of claim that smacks of uncritical dogmatism. We do not blindly trust claims companies make about food safety, potential harms of climate change, or even teachers' assessments of our children's learning. We demand evidence all around—fair, impartial, and *supported* evidence. However, as Harris points out, in some bizarre twist, in the area of religious beliefs and practices, we protect dogmatism. We allow people to say, think, and do what they want and reject the need to question them. We build walls of protection around our *own* religious assumptions and practices and expect others to respect them absolutely—simply because they are part of *our religion.*

Religious people need to take Harris's criticism seriously. Why do we protect religious dogmatism? Does dogmatism have a place in religion, and should it? Harris would say it does, that religion by nature fosters a dogmatic attitude, and that this is precisely the problem with it and why it needs urgently to be abandoned by any culture that claims to value critical reason. However, the mystics examined in the following section would say that authentic faith and religion strip away the dogmatism from our eyes and our certainties here and now, and tear down the idols we construct for ourselves. The worthy point perhaps to draw from Harris is an awareness of and an active resistance to the double standard by which religious communities consider their own beliefs to be rational and valid, but consider the beliefs of others to be uncritically dogmatic, or irrational "blind faith." He points out that many Christians who consider their belief in the inerrancy of the Bible to be perfectly reasonable consider Muslims utterly ridiculous in their claims that the Qur'an was revealed by God over the course of twenty-three years to Muhammad who did nothing but recite it from memory to others. Harris notes that people today generally recognize that Zeus is not real, but only "mythological," but nevertheless consider the God of the

Jewish or Christian Bible or the Qur'an to be absolutely real and true. Why the double standard in what is considered reasonable, in what is considered objective reality or human mythological imagination? In other words, we all tend to protect our own beliefs as "religion" or "faith," but we demand rational proof for the religious beliefs of others. The worthy point might be to recognize any such protectionist dogmatism as dangerous and to be cautious and modest about our religious claims.

Friedrich Nietzsche

Friedrich Nietzsche and Karl Marx are now seen as heralds of the postmodern, or the self-reflexive turn of the modern continental European ideology upon itself in the mid-nineteenth century. Their criticism of modern ideology, with its unshakeable faith in universal reason, guaranteed, as it were, by a reasonable lawgiver God, continues to speak meaningfully to us today. If we were to compile a short list of Nietzsche's philosophical proclamations, we might begin with his announcement that God is dead, and that it is we who have killed him. Of course, it is only a madman in *Thus Spoke Zarathustra* who can pronounce this truth.[5] Along with the death of God, we can extract from Nietzsche the death of all things objective, including the possibility of objectivity itself and the fiction of an absolute and singularly trustworthy human reason. All we are left with are the idols of our own making. This might be experienced as a crushing nihilism, and it will be so for most of us weak and ordinary human creatures, according to Nietzsche. However, for those few who can stand up and embrace this responsibility of idol-making, of becoming the gods (and authorities) we have ourselves created, the death of God means an evolution into a more mature and more free human being, the *Ubermensch*. Now, the particular mission that Nietzsche offers to a postmodern religious sensibility is to kill our gods/idols, and to uncover the processes of our idol-creation. It was John Calvin who suggested in a very different spiritual concern that the human mind is a factory of idols, but it was Nietzsche who targeted the particular modern manufacture of the idols of human reason and objectivity. What we gain from Nietzsche is a vigilant suspicion that what we believe we have arrived at through objective and universal and defensible reason may be in fact only the result of our particular dogmatic interpretation or idol-building.

Karl Marx

Karl Marx is sometimes described as the most religious of atheists because his critique of religious ideology is itself so spiritual; he takes the power of religion as humanity's self-consciousness most seriously. In his critique of

G. W. F. Hegel's *Philosophy of Right*, Marx famously diagnoses religion as "the opium of the people." Much like a drug, it gives a false but addictive sense of security that effectively induces complacency and even indifference to reality itself. "Religious suffering is at the same time an *expression* of real suffering and a protest against real suffering. Religion is the sigh of the oppressed creature, the heart of a heartless world and the soul of soulless conditions. It is the *opium* of the people."[6] Religious sentiment is both the cause of continued human complacency and suffering and a spiritual protest against it. Marx continues then to argue that "the abolition of religion as the *illusory* happiness of the people is the demand for their *real* happiness. To call on them to give up their illusions about their condition is to *call on them to give up a condition that requires illusions*."[7] Marx is quite explicit that religion itself must be cast aside. Religion causes an inverted world consciousness in which people put greatest value in what is unseen and promised as a reward for suffering in one's present reality. Religion is grounded in a fantastic illusion that, because of its power, is so deadly and pernicious. Marx calls for philosophy as critical thinking in the service of history to "unmask self-estrangement in its *unholy forms* once the *holy form* of human self-estrangement has been unmasked. Thus the criticism of heaven turns into the criticism of earth, the *criticism of religion* into the *criticism of law*, and the *criticism of theology* into the *criticism of politics*."[8] We can hear echoes of Marx's views in Sam Harris's criticism of dogmatism and societal protection of dogmatism in its religious incarnations. Human self-alienation is the problem Marx sees. He criticizes religious ideology because of the ways in which religion as an institution subverts human freedom and self-realization in favor of a sacred sort of slavery, by which those who are oppressed here and now by ordinary means are encouraged to accept it patiently as divinely ordained. Ethical teachings like "the meek shall inherit the earth" promise a future (and imaginary) reward for those who accept real oppression now. Doctrines like the Hindu moral law of karma help to maintain the economic and social status quo of the Hindu caste system and effectively justify human inequality by suggesting that everyone is currently reaping the consequences of their own prior actions.

Marx reduces religion to an illusion supported by and supportive of economic ideology. Sigmund Freud similarly is responsible for a reductionist explanation of religion as the illusory wish-fulfillment of an immature and insecure human psyche. While they did not succeed entirely in their existential projects of throwing off the shackles of religion and seeing religion as complete and utter illusion, both have been influential in their insights into particular motivations that can direct religious ideas. Their insights have instituted a "hermeneutics of suspicion" by which many of us today do not take things at face value, but instead vigilantly search for the agenda we suspect behind any actions or ideologies. The hermeneutics of suspicion have so pervasively informed contemporary culture that we can find them everywhere in popular culture, particularly in contemporary comedy. Comedians play an important role in making us all laugh at our respective foolishness. Comedians today effectively deliver Marxist social criticism, identifying and mocking ideologies for what they are—self-indulgent justifications for the so-called truths we idolize. Political satirists like Jon Stewart, Stephen Colbert, and Bill Maher and social satirists like the late George Carlin and Carlos Mencia have most effectively pointed out the hypocrisy, self-indulgence, and pompousness of leaders and ideologies as well as racial and ethnic prejudices and complacencies. Whether philosophy gives voice to something that has already happened, as Hegel's owl of Minerva would suggest, or trickles down from intellectual academia into popular culture, comedians today open society's eyes to its own illusions and the idols of its own imagination in a context clearly outside faith traditions. When we look at the work of these popular satirists, we see a vigilant resistance to the dogmatism of any who purport to be the final authorities and a deconstruction of the agendas and fallacies of such dogmatic truths that purport to be objective demonstrations of some obvious and undisputed Truth. John Caputo, discussed in chapter 6, suggests that the postmodern project of deconstruction decapitalizes or decapitates any Truth that purports to be from "on high," any Truth that would dare capitalize itself as *The Truth*. In these popular satirists, we witness precisely such knocking down of the privileged authority with which any dare capitalize their own take on things as in fact the single and solitary Truth from on high.

John A. T. Robinson

In his 1963 book, *Honest to God*, John A. T. Robinson proclaims the urgent need to abandon the theistic God of Christian tradition.[9] Robinson's proposal serves as a point of contact between the hermeneutics of suspicion (discussed above) that criticize the dogmatism of traditional theism and the mystical project of unlearning (to be discussed below) as a resistance to the reification of divine reality. Robinson incorporates Nietzsche's criticism of religion and displays a mindfulness of Harris's criticism of dogmatism, but he is motivated most by the theological need to liberate the Christian gospel from the reification of God he diagnoses in traditional Christian theism. His movement to abandon theism is not forced by an attempt to make Christianity less particular in its revelation or more universal, and therefore more palatable in modernity, in a manner that echoes the efforts of Friedrich Schleiermacher, John Locke, and Adolf von Harnack centuries earlier. Instead, his central argument is that classical Christian belief in God depends on a worldview and a pattern of symbolic representation that were meaningful for an earlier culture but not our own.

Robinson points out that most of us, despite all denials of anthropomorphizing God or limiting God, nevertheless imagine some variant of what he calls the "Old Man in the sky." Ancient religious imagination employed the schematic of a three-story universe, with heaven "up above," our lives here, and hell "below." According to this ancient schematic, God was considered "up there." Our more recent ancestors felt it prudent to abandon this ancient schematic and began instead to consider God "out there," beyond our physical universe rather than in a vertically higher position of our physical universe. "To have clung earlier to the God 'up there' would have made it impossible in the modern world for any but primitive peoples to believe the Gospel."[10] Just as they felt it prudent to let go of the physical location of God "up there," Robinson argues it is now time to abandon the revised schematic of a God who is "out there," beyond our world. The danger of leaving theism as it remains is that we replace God with an idol, we limit God to what we can see and manipulate, we reify the sacred and transcendent dimension of life into a figure who, I would say, looks remarkably like Santa Claus or a Hollywood inspired wizard with great and magnificent powers. Christianity and religious transcendence must be freed from this idolatrous conception of theism. Robinson affirms, "Tillich is right in saying that 'the protest of atheism against such a highest person is correct.'" He says Feuerbach and Nietzsche "saw such a supreme Person in heaven as the great enemy of man's coming of age. This was the God they must 'kill' if man was not to continue dispossessed and kept in strings."[11] Robinson's attack on theism is different from theirs, however. For Nietzsche, God's death was required for humanity's own spiritual maturing in our world, here and now, and transcendence of a slave morality wherein we obey this more powerful God-person out of fear and desire. For Robinson, it is not about humanity's growing up and letting go of silly delusions, but rather a concern for the continued meaningfulness and relevance of the Christian gospel, if it continues to rely on imagery and metaphor that accommodates an earlier culture's theological imagination that is not our own.

In Robinson's proposal, the Christian gospel must be freed of its identification with what is an outdated schematic of theism, that is, "the Old Man in the sky," and it can be, he argues. Interrogating the New Testament, he asks what Christ was and is. Whereas popular preaching says simply that Jesus was God, this is not supported by the New Testament. According to the New Testament, Jesus is the Word of God or the Son of God. It also witnesses to the apostles' conviction that "here was a window into God at work. For 'God was in Christ reconciling the world to himself.'"[12] Jesus reveals God's reconciliation of the world to Godself. Robinson suggests therefore that what is most prominent in Jesus' nature as witnessed in the New Testament is his complete lack of self, his complete living for another, by which he completely emptied himself of self, leaving only the unconditional love of God to be seen in him.[13] This is the heart of the gospel witness, according to Robinson. Not only does it not depend on the highest supreme supranatural being of traditional theism, but it actively defies it by focusing on the point that Jesus revealed the will of God and the love of God so thoroughly and transparently.

Even traditional, popular Christianity has taught that Jesus reveals God's nature not to be transcendent and remote, but to be immanent and actively in relation with humanity—Immanuel (God with us). Popular Christianity often has focused on this revelation as a historical correction of the earlier worship of a remote God who must be satisfied with performance of the law. What Robinson calls for is a further correction to a Christian clerical legalism and metaphysics that effectively idolizes another version of the Old Man in the sky. "The Church must become genuinely and increasingly lay," he writes, suggesting the tearing down of clerical laws of purity and authority.[14] He describes this as a vigilance against idolatry. "One idol is knocked down, only to be replaced by another. For the Christian gospel is in perpetual conflict with the images of God set up in the minds of men, even of Christian men."[15] Robinson says these images do serve the purpose of allowing us to get our minds around an unfathomable God. However, he cautions, "as soon as they become a substitute for God, as soon as they *become* God, *so that what is not embodied in the image is excluded or denied*, then we have a new idolatry and once more the word of judgment has to fall."[16] Consider today the tension over implementing feminine imagery or female pronouns for God. On the one hand, many traditionalists insist that all masculine God-language is only metaphorical. On the other hand, they refuse to allow feminine God-language as much metaphorical validity. Such a denial or exclusion of the feminine in God would seem to be a new idolatry, wherein the transcendent sacred is reified into a fixed static form that reinforces the veneration of what is masculine here in the world.

Robinson calls Christians to abandon the worship of a supreme person because it inevitably reifies the sacred and idolizes what we can visualize. Citing Paul's words in the Book of Romans, he writes, "To help men through to the conviction about ultimate Reality that alone finally matters we may have to discard every image of God—whether of the 'one above,' the one 'out there,' or any other. And this conviction, according to the Christian gospel, is that 'there is nothing in death or life, . . . in the world as it is or the world as it shall be, in the forces of the universe, in heights or depths—nothing in all creation that can separate us from the love of God in Christ Jesus our Lord.'"[17] Paul's words present, for Robinson, the heart of the gospel witness—not about what or where "God" is, but of this revelation that nothing can separate us from the love of God. Robinson's call to abandon theism echoes the gospel explication of Jesus as Immanuel, God with us, the gospel depiction of God as Love, and the traditional Christian Trinitarian explication of the inner relationality of God's love that boils over from the Godhead into the world. Robinson's criticism of theism therefore interprets all religious conceptions as theological tools to support the Christian gospel; when they cease to be meaningful, they must be modified or discarded. As Paul Tillich said as well, symbols die when they cease to convey the object of faith. The Christian gospel, freed of the Old Man in the sky theism, could authentically witness to these theological experiences of God and minister to modern spiritual and ethical needs by evoking Jesus' spirituality as "man for others," whose self-emptying spirit of identification with God led him to embody solidarity of love with all of those abandoned and rejected in our world. For the gospel to accomplish this theological task, however, the symbols Christians rely on must change.

The Mystical Path of Unknowing or Unlearning

The Cloud of Unknowing

The Cloud of Unknowing was written in the late fourteenth century by an anonymous English priest. It is one of the most prominent examples in Christian mysticism of the *via negativa*, or negative theology. Whereas a *via positiva* would go about describing God by way of affirmations of various attributes like goodness, knowledge, and power, a *via negativa* begins with the unknowability of God. While the former emphasizes the continuity between human nature and God, and the ways in which our virtues reflect those of God, the latter often emphasizes the absolute otherness of God. Most conventional theologies have combined the two in some sense, insisting, for example, in a Christian narrative, that humans are made in the image of God and that God has revealed God's nature, but that human sin distances us immeasurably from God, leaving no way to know God aside from revelation. *The Cloud of Unknowing* employs a *via negativa*, and its particular treatment of human knowledge of God makes it a good complement to the further discussion of Meister Eckhart's detachment and the mystical use of unknowing or unlearning that inform the development of spiritual understanding. Our discussion of *The Cloud of Unknowing* will take up three interrelated topics: longing love as the vehicle to know God; the cloud of unknowing that expresses the way of contemplation; and the cloud of forgetting that is required between oneself and all of creation.

For the *Cloud* author, it is not that God is fundamentally unknowable, but that God cannot be known by the intellect. The author explains that humans have two faculties or powers—knowing and loving. "To the first, to the intellect, God who made them is forever unknowable, but to the second, to love, he is completely knowable, and that by every separate individual."[18] Whereas intellectual knowing is a relation to some particular thing that remains independent or "over there," love is a unitive activity of participating in the object of love. "The nature of love is such that it shares everything. Love Jesus, and everything he has is yours."[19] The *Cloud* author expresses this act of love as a longing, as a naked intent of wanting that drives forward into that which one seeks. Love can reach God where knowledge cannot, *in this very life*. We cannot know God in this life because our worldly knowledge is always distorted and imperfect, but love is categorically different from knowledge. Love comes from God, it reaches out blindly toward God, and it participates in God. Love is an experience of a communion with God, an experience that is found in the act of prayer, and it is made possible by God's grace, by God's love and self-revelation in Christ.

According to the *Cloud* author, the contemplative life has three stages; the first includes works of mercy and charity, and the second involves spiritual meditations on human sin, Christ's suffering, and the joy of heaven. The third stage, and the best according to the *Cloud* author, is becoming caught in a dark cloud of unknowing.[20] According to the text, this cloud of unknowing is in fact the only way to experience God in this life here and now. "Do what you will, this darkness and this cloud remain between you and God, and stop you both from seeing him in the clear light of rational understanding, and from experiencing his loving sweetness in your affection. Reconcile yourself to wait in this darkness as long as is necessary, but still go on longing after him whom you love. For if you are to feel him or to see him in this life, it must always be in this cloud, in this darkness."[21] Darkness is not merely a preliminary obstacle, but remains the context of one's creaturely experience of God. One should beat away at this cloud of unknowing with longing love, but love will not eliminate this cloud. The cloud of unknowing is the only way and, in a sense, the best way to experience God. "No one in this life, however, pure, and however enraptured with contemplating and loving God, is ever without this intervening, high, and wonderful cloud. It was in this same cloud that Mary experienced the many secret movements of her love. Why? Because this is the highest and holiest state of contemplation we can know on earth."[22] These passages express the author's sense that unknowing is not a temporary negative state of separation from God that is to be transcended; it is rather the only proper way to see God. The author explains later, in a chapter titled "Knowing God Is Unknowing," that spiritual development rests in understanding the reason for the limitations in human understanding. One must understand that God alone is the one who limits understanding. "St. Dionysius said, 'the most godlike knowledge of God is that which is known by unknowing.'"[23] The cloud of unknowing is therefore a gift from God to help one approach God by longing love rather than by means of intellect.

The *Cloud* author urges his audience to add to this cloud of unknowing that separates humanity and God also a cloud of forgetting between ourselves and all of creation. Forgetting, or an active unlearning of ordinary worldly matters, is necessary to establish the true cloud of unknowing as a medium in which to experience God. He writes, "everything you think about, all the time you think about it, is 'above' you, between you and God. And you are that much farther from God if anything but God is in your mind."[24] The *Cloud* author suggests something analogous to meditative focus taught in different traditions to detach from ordinary worldly things. According to him, and echoing Meister Eckhart's views as well, particularized, or object-oriented thinking, in effect, separates one from uniting fully with God. Therefore, we are urged to do the hard work of "stamping out all remembrance of God's creation, and in keeping them covered by that cloud of forgetting."[25] In fact, the *Cloud* author even suggests using a single-syllable word for meditation. Whenever one is tempted to think concretely about what one is seeking, one should use this word and put that thought itself below the cloud of forgetting. The author points out that this forgetting of all things created is our human work, aided by God's grace, and that the other work of moving in love is wholly God's work. The hard work of forgetting is therefore an essential human responsibility.

The severe degree to which forgetting is to go is made clear in several passages. "See to it that there is nothing at work in your mind or will but only God."[26] The *Cloud* author urges, "Crush all knowledge and experience of all forms of created things, and of yourself above all. . . . when all other things and activities have been forgotten (even your own) there still remains between you and God the stark awareness of your own existence.

And this awareness, too, must go, before you experience contemplation in its perfection."[27] One must empty oneself of everything that is not God, to make oneself as open as possible to allow God's love to move one. The author uses the language of "nothing" and "nowhere" to express this state of emptiness where one has nothing but longing love. "'Nowhere' is where I want you!"[28] The spirit follows where the mind goes, so detaching in the mind is necessary for the spirit to become free. "I would much rather be nowhere physically, wrestling with that obscure nothing."[29] He says not to worry about not understanding this nothing because it is better felt than seen. Because the very last and most resistant thing that separates us from God is our ego, our sense of ourselves, we must go boldly into nowhere and embrace what is experienced as nothing, in order to be sure not to be placing some other thing between ourselves and God. The author also encourages his audience to lift their hearts to God alone, to "God himself, and not what you get out of him."[30] This is why he encourages us to think of nothing and being nowhere. Truly emptying ourselves of all the particular attributes of God is necessary to get beyond the anthropomorphic limits we put on God, in which we essentially reduce God to what God does for us.

The acts of forgetting, unknowing, and loving together comprise the life of contemplation. Forgetting all created things, all particular things, and our own categories and sense of self is our human responsibility. By unknowing, we are actively preventing ourselves from filling the space between humans and God with distracting obstacles. What is key here is not just the opposition supposed between the human faculties of knowledge and love, but also the opposition suggested between human work and God's work, a theme echoed in the Protestant Principle discussed in chapter 3. We can forget, unlearn, or detach from this and that particular thing, and thereby free ourselves from the things of this world. On our own, however, we can never know God. Only through the faculty of love, which according to the *Cloud*'s author is a unitive experience and a movement accomplished wholly by God, can one reach God. By applying a negative approach of forgetting to all that is human (the faculty of knowledge and understanding), one becomes open to God's gracious movement of love. Ultimately, the different passages of *The Cloud of Unknowing* together suggest that love is the faculty whereby God acts in and through people and moves them. In loving, people are not themselves acting, but God is acting in them and moving them. Loving God allows one to enjoy union with God. However, this union is possible only through the contemplative life, which according to the *Cloud* author, must always and only be in a dark cloud of unknowing that is entered by building up a thick cloud of forgetting between ourselves and worldly knowledge.

Meister Eckhart on Nothingness and Detachment

The work of fourteenth-century Christian mystic Meister Eckhart was read widely in the late Middle Ages and by the German Romantics, and it continues to fascinate contemporary students of religion, philosophy, and mysticism, especially comparative mysticism. Eckhart occupies a unique place as the only medieval theologian charged with heresy by the Inquisition. In his defense, Eckhart argued that while he may have made errors and he may very well be wrong, he *could not* be a heretic because that would involve *willful* falsification. In the end, after Eckhart's death, Pope John issued a Bull in 1329 that absolved him of heresy. He noted that Eckhart professed the Catholic faith and revoked the twenty-six articles treated as heretical "insofar as they could generate in the minds of the faithful a heretical opinion, or one erroneous and hostile to the faith."[31] Bernard McGinn points out that Eckhart thereby maintained his integrity even in the end; to our ears, his recanting sounds a bit like an unabashedly unsatisfying apology of the sort "I'm sorry that your feelings were hurt," or, in Eckhart's case, "I'm sorry my words have been misinterpreted by ignorant readers."

As to what exactly was so controversial in Eckhart's work as to provoke the charge of heresy lies in his description of the relationship between the human soul and God, and his suggestion that God's essence is one's own essence. Readers are still struck by the language of *identity* he uses between God and the human self and the intimacy with which he suggests that the human soul can come to see through God's eyes. Contemporary readers may recognize some affinity between Eckhart, the fourteenth-century German Christian, and the identity-mysticism found in the Hindu Upanishads that suggest a monistic view of Ultimate Reality. The Upanishads teach "That thou art," a philosophy of the inner identity of the true Self, or Atman, with Absolute Reality, or Brahman, or in Western terms, the inner identification of human self and God. A great deal of comparative scholarship has been devoted to the potential conversation between Eckhart's mystical unitive state and Hindu Advaita (nondualism) or Zen nothingness. Eckhart's work certainly challenges conventional categories of theism.

The monotheistic Christian tradition has never embraced a monistic worldview, but many mystics have come suspiciously close to an identity monism when they insist, like Eckhart, that God alone is Being or has independent Substance, and that our own being is entirely dependent on what God brings forth in us. The goal of Christian life is often stated, by Eckhart and others, to be the alignment of one's own will with God's will, so thoroughly as to leave nothing but God's will. Eckhart speaks of this process as the central project of human life: to return to the ground of human being, that is, to God, to get self-will out of the way in order to better recognize the truth of God's will, to recognize more sheerly and perfectly God's activity in humanity, to see and enjoy God's grace as the gift God has given. The central part of Eckhart's mystical thought that pertains to this chapter on doubt as a mode of resistance to dogmatism has to do with the program of detachment he recommends. What he means by detachment provides, within the religious orthodoxy of medieval Christianity, a contemplative faith model of resisting dogmatism. Mystical detachment involves actively undoing what we ordinarily think we know, deconstructing the ordinary categories by which we protect our faith, in order to prepare ourselves for God's gracious activity in us. While Eckhart's thought challenges conventional Christian theological categories, it would be an error to interpret his apophatic approach and discussion of detachment and nothingness as a simple rejection of Christian theism because that would ignore the centrality of Trinitarian and Christocentric theology on his discussion of the mystical journey.

Very briefly, I would like to preface Eckhart's explicit discussion of detachment with the following related theological themes: the transcendence of the Godhead beyond God, the centrality of grace, and the impact of his Christology on his view of the human soul. First, the transcendence of God beyond our categories of logic is directly related for Eckhart to the unity or Oneness of God. Everything that we ordinarily can know and manipulate is defined by particularity and multiplicity, by a sense of being one among others, and being one particular thing and not another. God alone is absolutely One without a second. What makes the Godhead unique is that it alone is "not-to-be-distinguished." Many Christian theologians have suggested that God is not a thing among other things, or that God is beyond being itself. Eckhart expresses this transcendence of all that is by saying that God is No-thing or Nothing. According to apophatic theology, or negative theology, we cannot say what God is because God transcends all that we know, at least in the sensible and intellectual ways we know everything else that we know. So in an apophatic manner, Eckhart can affirm that if the world is, God is not; if we and our world are understood as being and we purport to understand and manipulate being, God must be affirmed as Nothing.

Eckhart persistently uses language in a thoroughly dialectical way that resists a singular univocal meaning. His articulation of a Godhead beyond God and his references to nothingness therefore have stimulated profuse discussion about whether Eckhart transcends theism altogether with a more ultimate nothingness like that articulated by many Zen Buddhists. While most such comparative treatments have focused on the apophatic, nontheistic aspects of Eckhart's thought, Beverly Lanzetta explores the relationship between Eckhart's trinitarianism and nothingness. She identifies three motifs of nothingness in Eckhart's thought: epistemological, pragmatic, and Christocentric. The first declares the limits of human knowledge; the second, Lanzetta says, expresses a dynamic openness that resembles Buddhist emptiness or inter-being, discussed later in this chapter. The third is the transformation and re-formation of existence through the incarnation and death of Christ. "Christ is the deconstruction of ontology for he embodies the collapse of the transcendent-immanent distance by reenacting in history the double kenosis that occurs within the divine nature, and must therefore be mystically present in the 'now' of the world for salvation to take place."[32] Eckhart employs nothingness to affirm God's transcendence of all particularity and to articulate the movement from the created world of particularity to the indistinctness of Godhead beyond a personal God. As Lanzetta suggests, "the nothingness of consciousness yields in Eckhart's thought a liberation from metaphysical hegemony, even that directed to understanding God."[33] Charlotte Radler analyzes Eckhart's rejection of any static view of God as only One or Three, but at once dialectically One and flowing into the Trinity, flowing over into creation and overcoming a duality between Creator and creature.[34] Radler sees precisely this disruption of reification as a promising ground for affinities with Buddhist thought, but it primarily expresses a Christian mystical account of divine transcendence. Islamic tradition has, in a somewhat similar vein, taken God's oneness to coincide with God's uniqueness of all else. God is not one kind of something, and is not like anything or anyone. Eckhart's use of oneness and nothingness resists being altogether, as what Lanzetta calls "a nonsubstantializing ontology," and supports the mystical project of detachment by which one is both to "let go" and "let be."

The second component of Eckhart's theology is God's grace. Eckhart echoes Christian orthodoxy by articulating that all of humanity's relation to God, all knowledge of God, depends entirely on God's work (His free grace) and not at all on human efforts. From the act of creation to the act of the incarnation, God's grace is active. In the incarnation, God became human, took on human suffering, and made it His own, all to become more accessible to humans. Eckhart expresses the extent of God's love for humanity evident in the incarnation with a beautiful story of the love of a rich husband for his wife. The wife lost an eye and worried that her husband would love her less because of her diminished state. In Eckhart's account, the husband responds by gouging out one of his own eyes and saying to her, "Madam, to make you believe that I love you, I have made myself like you; now I too have only one eye." Eckhart notes this is what "being made flesh" is.[35] God has orchestrated all aspects of the relationship human beings have with God. In orthodox fashion, Eckhart emphasizes that there are no ways for human beings through human effort or human work alone to reach God, but that God gives humanity both the way and the means to follow it as a matter of grace, or divine gift.

Eckhart describes the ground of the soul as a spark, a guard, a light, or a free power in the spirit, and he says it escapes all names. "Whatever words we use, they are telling lies, and it is far above them. It is free of all names, it is bare of all forms, wholly empty and free, as God in himself is empty and free. It is so utterly one and simple, as God is one and simple that man cannot in any way look into it."[36] This spark in the soul is free and undifferentiated just as God is free and undifferentiated, and it too lies beyond human apprehension, even though it is deep within us. It is this free spark that makes people like God. Maintaining both the primacy of revelation and the conformity of reason and revelation, Eckhart affirms that while ordinary human understanding cannot access God, this spark within the human soul is able to comprehend God directly.[37]

The event of the incarnation discloses not only who or what God is and does, but also what it means to be human. Eckhart's anthropology (his view of human nature) is defined quite centrally by his Christology (the doctrine of who Christ is and what he did/does). Eckhart repeatedly affirms that God became man in order that man might become God.[38] Humanity's destiny is to return to its original ground of union with God. As Lanzetta describes this Christocentric motif of nothingness, the divine accomplishes a double kenosis of the divine within itself and into the human soul that frees the soul from its own particularity and finitude.[39] Because God is beyond all division and multiplicity, humanity's union with God must also take place beyond division and multiplicity. This comprehension occurs, he says, when God gives birth to the Word in the human soul. For Eckhart, therefore, the incarnation is not only a historical event that happened once upon a time, but a creative birth that happens in the individual soul and enables mystical union with God.

Eckhart's mystical program of detachment, or *Gelassenheit* (releasement), requires total passivity and deconstruction of all human claims to knowing, doing, understanding, and manipulating. He says that one must purify one's heart of all that is only created and lesser than God, that one must become "naked" of such mere clothing.[40] If we make this negative movement of consciousness and make ourselves empty, Eckhart says, empty of concepts and understanding, empty of attachments and desires, empty of religious piety and pride, God will rush in to fill our souls with nothing other than Godself. The objects of detachment are not just the things of this world, but also our conventional ways of knowing and relating to things of this world. Described variously as detachment from self, iconoclasm, forgetting and unknowing, or self-emptying, the mystical goal is to get our internal and external knowledge out of the way in order to reach silence, emptiness, and freedom, so that the Birth of the Word can be heard and felt in one's soul. They all involve detachment from the way in which we relate to ourselves or others or the world or God as things, as objects separate from ourselves. Consider the way twentieth-century Jewish philosopher Martin Buber discusses the different ways we relate to those around us. There is the *I-It* relation and the *I-Thou* relation. In the former sort of relationship, the *I* engages the *It* primarily with respect to its usefulness. It is identified by its function *for me* and *my* self-interest. In contrast, the I-Thou relation takes seriously the independence and freedom of the other. All functional object-knowledge keeps us in a consciousness of multiplicity and particularity, where everything is this or that, including God. As long as we are imposing these distorting categories on how we relate to everything we experience, including God, we are actively idolizing God, reducing God to a thing we can pretend to manipulate. Any image of God blocks the entirety of God. "Whoever is seeking God by ways is finding ways and losing God, who in ways is hidden."[41] The negative movement of consciousness in apophatic theology promises liberation from the prison of consciousness.[42] As Eckhart says, "go completely out of yourself for God's love, and God comes completely out of himself for love of you. And when these two have gone out, what remains there is a simplified One. In this One the Father brings his Son to birth in the innermost source. Then the Holy Spirit blossoms forth."[43]

The movement of relationship between the soul and God results in simple oneness, but it is a movement that has been modeled in the Christian narrative of Christ. With regard to the question of why Eckhart retains theistic metaphysics, Lanzetta concludes that the Christian theistic context serves as the necessary road to liberation in the unitive experience. "The Trinity, metaphysics, and so on are essential for *Gelassenheit* ('releasement') because it is only by following the paradigm enacted by the Son at the moment of his death, when the determinate divinity reenters the abyss, that the soul finds its true ground and understands why God is both 'One and Three.'"[44] Spirit is with like Spirit, as God relates to the soul as to Himself. "God and

I, we are one. I accept God into me in knowing; I go into God in loving."[45]
Eckhart elsewhere articulates the act of genuine prayer as that which does
not presume to talk *to God* or *at God*, but that instead which allows God
to pray within oneself. The goal of passivity and detachment from particular
things is grounded on the unique oneness of God and the free spark in the
soul that expresses this divine unity. "What is life? God's being is my life. If
my life is God's being, then God's existence must be my existence and God's
is-ness is my is-ness, neither less nor more."[46] Eckhart describes detachment
in many particular ways: letting go, cutting off, resigning, un-becoming, un-
forming, radical receptivity, passivity, silence, and breaking-through. Using
a theistic and Christian Trinitarian orientation, the spiritual journey tears
down the conceptions people have of self and God to yield a transformative
experience of freedom enabled through the union in grace with the God
who is purely and simply One.

Buddhist Teachings on Emptiness

This section of the chapter presents selective Buddhist teachings on resistance to the reification of a reality in constant flux. Like the discussion of
the mystics, it treats the spiritual discipline of unknowing or unlearning.
The Buddhist teachings on spiritual development, however, are formed in a
nontheistic tradition and are therefore quite different in terms of the meaning as well as the process of spiritual development. Nevertheless, together
with the atheistic criticism of religious dogmatism of the first section and
the mystical theistic project of unknowing of the second section, they yield
a fuller picture of the value in resisting dogmatism from different perspectives. This section will proceed through three particular discussions: the
epistemological concerns of the limits of knowledge; the Zen use of koans
to transcend conceptual thinking; and the concepts of emptiness, impermanence, and no-soul that inform Buddhist interpretations of reality.

The early Buddhist tradition indicates a general reluctance to engage in
metaphysics and a favoring of empiricism. For the Buddha, any metaphysical
assertion lies beyond the bounds of empirical experience. Questions about
what is ultimately true and real can always only be speculations, and because
they lie beyond the sphere of actual experience, they can lead to vexation and
worry. Scholars suggest that the Buddha never taught that what is commonly
understood as the soul or the self, the atman in Upanishadic tradition, does
not actually exist, but only that it cannot be apprehended. He called it an
"Undetermined Question," a flawed question because to answer yes or no
does not benefit the understanding.[47] While the theistic Christian tradition

has emphasized the transcendence of the Real beyond human understanding, the nontheistic Buddhist tradition stresses that this matter is altogether outside the bounds of empirical experience. We can say with validity neither that something is nor that something is not because this lies outside the bounds of our empirical experience.

The Buddha pointed out the limitations of all sources of knowledge, according to David Kalupahana.[48] For example, a theory based on tradition or revelation may very well be either true or false. Without any guarantee of its truth or falsehood, one must suspend judgment. Good sound reasoning also cannot be the primary criterion of truth because people can formulate consistent and sound arguments for things that do not necessarily correspond to facts. Experiential knowledge, such as the mystical intuitions of the Upanishads, may be a means to insight, but it too cannot be a valid source of knowledge of reality. Kalupahana argues, however, that emphasizing the limitations of all sources of knowledge does not reduce Buddhism to skepticism. "The emphasis on the limitations of knowledge was meant to prevent people from falling into the net of speculative theories that posited the 'nonexistent' as the 'existent.'"[49] The point in Buddhist teachings of the limits of knowledge is not to deny that we know, but to safeguard against all kinds of inevitable metaphysical speculation that assumes the nature of reality.

Recognizing these limits of conceptual knowledge, the Zen use of koans actively trains the student to transcend the habit of conceptual thinking. A koan is a paradoxical problem that cannot be solved by means of logical reason. A Zen teacher may ask a student, "What is the sound of one hand clapping?" D. T. Suzuki says the worst enemy of Zen experience is the intellect.[50] Meditating on a koan impels the student practitioner to exhaust logic and conceptual faculties and only then be able to leap beyond this way of thinking altogether; only then can one see one's true Buddha-nature, often in a sudden burst of enlightenment. David Loy lists three factors essential for Zen practice, all of which are present in the koan exercise: great faith, great determination, and great doubt.[51] These three factors speak to the degree to which Zen tradition focuses on actual practice and not on reflection on such practice. Loy highlights the degree to which Zen Buddhism and the medieval Christian text *The Cloud of Unknowing* share affinities in the value assigned to longing and intensity of practice over thought, explaining, "it is this longing that generates the mental energy necessary to cut through the deluding web of thoughts and feelings."[52] While he draws significant parallels between *The Cloud*'s method of constructing a cloud of forgetting between ourselves and worldly knowledge and the Zen method of cultivating "doubt-sensation," he also points out a significant difference. The *Cloud* author espouses the bypassing of conceptual thinking in favor of love as the proper approach to God, not for the sake of an all-encompassing questioning like Zen doubt-sensation does.[53] The Zen practice demands a pervasive doubting and questioning of all our presumptive knowledge in order to see through them all to the Buddha-nature itself or to the truth of emptiness.

Kalupahana also raises the Buddha's insight into the role of subjective prejudices in our perceptions of reality. Our likes and dislikes, our attachments, aversions, and fears, all prevent us from perceiving things as they are.[54] In today's climate of partisan politics, people often dispute the validity of findings or the wisdom of particular ideas and solutions simply because they were offered by the opposing party. Spiritual development, wisdom, or clarity of perception requires that we pay attention to these subjective prejudices; that we gradually recognize that these prejudices have far more to do with ourselves and our own interests, attachments, and fears than with the things themselves. When a teenager desperately wants an expensive pair of running shoes, what he sees in the shoes is probably not the shoes themselves, but the higher social status he expects will flow from his wearing the shoes. Spiritual development would lead said teen to discern that the shoes themselves do not produce social status, that what he really craves is status or popularity, and that the shoes are nothing more than footwear. This leads us to the discussion of emptiness and the related concepts of impermanence and no-soul that form the content of Buddhist spiritual development.

The concepts of emptiness (*sunyata*), impermanence (*anicca*), and no-soul (*anatta*) are closely interrelated and indicate the Buddhist interpretation of the way things are. Emptiness refers to the view that things are empty of any independent, substantial, and permanent essence or individuality. It does not mean that things are unreal, but that their reality does not lie in some underlying permanent essence. Things are simply what they are. From our previous example, the expensive shoes do not contain status or pride or self-confidence. Rather, the shoes are simply shoes, and nothing more inside or underneath. The doctrine of emptiness is linked with the doctrines of dependent origination and impermanence. Nothing is unconditioned or independent, but instead, is infinitely dependent on other things through cause and effect. Inquiring into the nature of a thing takes us through an endless series of causes and effects that have led to its origination. It is because things are empty, according to Buddhist teaching, that they are impermanent and can change. Therefore, impermanence, which may sound pessimistic to some ears, also enables change and growth, birth and dying.[55]

We can grow up, we can change, we can reinvent ourselves, all because of impermanence. The doctrine of anatta, or no-soul, indicates more explicitly the view that things are not composed of a hidden permanent substance. What is explicitly rejected in this view is the Hindu Upanishadic view of the ultimate reality of the atman, or the self, and the corresponding teaching that the freedom of enlightenment results from understanding that this atman is also of greatest reality. In Buddhist thought, such a concept of soul leads only to further attachment of the deepest kind, that is, attachment to the ego itself, which, as we have seen from the Christian mystics, is the greatest attachment and obstacle to spiritual freedom. The no-soul teaching may be interpreted therefore as a practical and existential teaching rather than a philosophical concept. Emphasizing the practical purpose of speech about no-self, Charlene Burns explains that learning to detach oneself from ideas of selfhood helps one practice compassion for others.[56] On the other hand, to the degree that the doctrine of no-soul or nonsubstantiality is tied to the constancy of change or impermanence, it may be a positive description of the true state of reality or the experience of emptiness, that is, constant change and impermanence. Instead of a hidden substance that defines a thing as what it is, what characterizes things is their interrelationship.[57]

Thich Nhat Hanh explains the doctrine of emptiness in terms of interrelationship, or "inter-being," in his commentary on the *Heart Sutra*. He writes that to say that a thing is empty is to say that it is empty of a *separate* self, that it cannot exist by itself alone, and that it must coexist or "inter-be" with other things.[58] Emptiness, inter-being, and fullness of being are different ways to express the intrinsic interdependence of things. To explain inter-being, he proposes we think about a sheet of paper and reflect on the process by which the paper is made from trees, which cannot grow without rain and sunshine, which themselves come from clouds and the sun. So, he says, "If the cloud is not here, the sheet of paper cannot be here either. So we can say that the cloud and the paper inter-are."[59] Hanh says that if we look more closely into the paper, we will also see the entire forest, the logger who cut it down, the wheat used to make the bread eaten by the logger, and so on. Everything coexists in that paper. Emptiness therefore implies the constitutive coexistence of all things. The paper "has to inter-be with the sunshine, the cloud, the forest, the logger, the mind, and everything else. It is empty of a separate self. But, empty of a separate self means full of everything."[60] Thich Nhat Hanh's emphasis on the need to recognize the interconnection of all things, especially between oneself and one's enemy, has fostered valuable use of the concept for matters of social justice. Alice Keefe explores the interfaces between Buddhist and feminist visions of interconnectedness. "To awaken·is to realize the truth of our inter-being with a tormented world, so giving birth to compassion."[61] Keefe extends the recognition that one's enemy also suffers to the feminist criticism of the false dualism and power hierarchies of patriarchy; interdependence demands alternative models of social relationship and spirituality based on mutuality.[62]

Thich Nhat Hanh's discussion of the fullness of this interconnected being is especially helpful in clarifying the Buddhist doctrine of emptiness, which is easily misunderstood if not explored fully. Two false interpretations of emptiness, for example, are that emptiness means nihilism, that nothing exists on any level, or that emptiness refers to some Ultimate Reality or Essence.[63] Paul Williams says the doctrine of emptiness is itself empty or an abstraction. "It is the absence of inherent existence and is seen through *prajna*, analytic understanding in its various forms."[64] Emptiness does not refer to an actual ultimate state of things, but to a constant absence of inherent existence. Williams says that the Buddha taught emptiness as an antidote to all dogmas, all views that cling to the inherent existence inside things. It is not an ultimate state, but indicates a valuable insight into the nature of things. Basically, things are not as they appear to be. They appear to have permanence or substantial being, but in fact, what they are is always interconnected with other things. Understanding emptiness implies an infinite movement of discerning the emptiness of each thing and successively of each thing that is interconnected with it. As Williams says, the function of understanding emptiness is to cease the grasping and craving that in Buddhist teaching causes human suffering.

Williams uses a popular Zen story to highlight this understanding of emptiness as itself empty. A Zen saying suggests that if one meets the Buddha on the road, one should kill him. This was intended as a teaching story for bodhisattvas who were concerned that their spiritual progress would be hindered by their past deeds, that no matter how hard they tried, they would never be able to get away from those past deeds. The instruction to kill the Buddha is intended to cut through the attachments of the bodhisattvas, to kill their attachments to the conception of Self beneath their striving.[65] Even the Buddha is empty of inherent existence. The bodhisattvas needed to understand this emptiness and thereby see their past deeds as also illusory. They needed to realize that the truth they were seeking was not outside themselves at all. Williams uses this story to discuss the doctrine of emptiness and the need to release attachment to the idea of a substantial self, but it also is helpful in understanding the value of such detachment. The account of bodhisattvas, or any of us, working to let go of the weight of past deeds is related to a Christian experience of redemption.

In conventional Christian language of original sin, grace, and forgiveness, people must acknowledge their own sins, their brokenness. By accepting this reality as it is, they become able for the first time to truly accept God's gift of forgiveness and forgive themselves. The result is the experience of freedom. In Christian language, this is freedom from the burden of original sin. The Buddhist insight into emptiness is functionally similar insofar as an honest acceptance of the way things really are fosters insight into dependent origination and the emptiness of what one formerly has been so wrapped up in and trapped by. In the Christian account, God lifts this burden and makes people right and acceptable again, and Christian faith lies in one's acceptance of being accepted again by God in this way. In the Buddhist account, gaining understanding into the way things lack inherent existence leads one then to release the fears and attachments that cause suffering. Letting go of the burden of guilt and the delusion of independent substance leads to freedom.

Conclusion

This chapter has brought together some very different ways of speaking about the unlearning that is a crucial part of the spiritual journey. The common concern throughout has been caution against fixing and reifying the sacred with conceptual scaffolding. The sacred escapes us continually, and we are always tempted to restrict the revelation of the sacred into what we can identify clearly, what we believe we know with confidence, and what we can manipulate. As we learned from Paul Tillich in chapter 3, faith is always in danger of turning into idolatry. For Tillich, true faith must include doubt in order to be sure that the object of faith is not our own restricted conceptions. The mystical teachings in this chapter exemplify the use of skeptical detachment in the journey of faith. We must unlearn or detach from our inevitable idols in order to become open to the sacred's impact on us. While the critics of religion discussed in the first part of the chapter reject the value and premise of religious faith altogether, their criticism is especially targeted at dogmatism, a close cousin to idolatry in the sense of absolutizing our own constructed ideas. The spiritual life requires and enacts a progressive detachment or active unlearning of what we believe we know in order to become open to what we do not know and what lies infinitely beyond our ken, so that it may act on us and transform us. For the Christian theist mystics, this is God acting in grace to transform the human soul and unite itself to Him. According to the nontheistic Buddhist teachings, we must exercise radical doubt about all our mental conceptions and unlearn all the false constructed ideas we cling to in order to see the true reality of things in their interdependent relationship and thereby achieve the spiritual freedom of relating to things simply as what they are rather than as tools for our own self-interest. They are by no means the same metaphysical account using different conceptual descriptions, but the process of spiritual development in both these traditional religious cases as well as the atheist case of overcoming religious dogmatism itself involves a progressive unlearning and detaching from what we think we know with certainty to facilitate a higher insight.

CHAPTER SIX

FAITH AND HOPE
FOR THE TWENTY-FIRST CENTURY

The preceding chapters of this book have drawn out more complicated models with which to think about religious faith and doubt. The weight of focus has been on fairly orthodox elements of Christian and Hindu theological traditions. Theological tradition can be understood as an ongoing conversation across the generations about how to think about and relate to what is deemed sacred. This chapter presents a fragmentary vignette of contemporary conversation in American Christian theological culture. The figures discussed in this chapter represent three rather different contemporary possibilities of how a twenty-first-century postmodern Christian faith might look.[1] What unites all three is a rejection of the simplistic oppositions between faith and doubt, and between religion and the secular, which prompted the writing of this book. They all take religion quite seriously: Jürgen Moltmann and Raimon Panikkar are prominent Christian theologians; Panikkar was a Roman Catholic priest; John Caputo is an American philosopher and theologian whose work deconstructs the boundaries between philosophy and theology. They illustrate some of the requirements that religious faith must embrace if it is to be genuinely sustainable in today's world and not languish as a nostalgic relic that stubbornly relies on certitude.

Jürgen Moltmann, Raimon Panikkar, and John Caputo demonstrate three very different theoretical ways to be religious in today's world without naïvely hiding from what we find to be unbelievable and without abandoning the possibilities of ultimate meaningfulness and mystery in life. Moltmann builds a uniquely biblical and eschatological theology that does not depend on a literal reading of scripture or echo apocalyptic fear and warnings about God's impending judgment. Instead, he demonstrates a way to stay true to the biblical narrative as a witness to and revelation of God's continuing relationship with humanity and God's intentions for this relationship. Panikkar presents a mystical and pluralistic spirituality that requires interreligious dialogue not because different communities need to get along, but because we need the claims of others to break apart the boxes we inevitably construct around divine mystery. Caputo, best known for his writings on Jacques Derrida, deconstruction, and theology, employs postmodern insights of deconstruction to investigate the components of religion most viable for contemporary Christians. He finds these in an account of love, the category of the impossible, and his proposal for an antidogmatic "religion without religion," a concept he adopts from Derrida's religiosity. This book aims to present models from theological tradition that can help move religious conversations beyond the naïve either/or opposition between faith and doubt. Thoughtful people have neither to blindly recite creeds that contradict many things they and others accept as reasonable nor to simplistically dismiss the spiritual possibilities of ultimate meaning and mystery in our lives and assume that the world is ethically ambiguous and religiously ambivalent. That represents an inauthentic choice. The three thinkers discussed here articulate models of Christian faith that are neither stubborn faith nor dismissive atheism.

Jürgen Moltmann on Eschatology

An Eschatological Theology of Hope

Moltmann introduces his short book *In The End—The Beginning* by emphasizing Christian expectation of the beginning that emerges through any end, in God's promise to make all things new. Moltmann writes, "we read the Bible as the book of God's promises and the hopes of men and women—indeed the hopes of everything created; and from the remembrances of their future we find energies for the new beginning."[2] Moltmann's doctrine of hope gives the biblical narrative primacy; it takes absolutely seriously the biblical narrative without asserting any metaphysical descriptions of God's nature; it emphasizes the biblical witness to God's promises and human hopes without applying the narrow test of creedal formulas that have defined church orthodoxy from the fourth century on. Reading the whole of the biblical narrative together as the revelation of God's promises, Moltmann relies on a firmly Trinitarian, Christological, and eschatological basis for evaluating theological proposals.

Moltmann's revival of a biblical and eschatological faith is especially interesting in its contrast with many recent popular treatments of Christian eschatology. In the late twentieth-century venues of fiction (especially the incredibly popular *Left Behind* series), film, and the spirituality of many "born-again" American Christians, we find the themes of the advent of end-times, an anti-Christ, the second coming of Jesus, and a rapture in which the faithful will be taken up by Jesus before a fiery and painful destruction of all the faithless. Many college campuses and city street corners host organized groups of "fire and brimstone" Christians who preach the need to repent before these end-times, who shout angrily of God's coming judgment on everyone who ungratefully refuses God's gift of grace. This particular line of interpretation became very popular in the twentieth century, but its roots lie more in eighteenth-century American revivalism and in a particular modern literalist interpretation of the New Testament Book of Revelation than in earlier church tradition. While church fathers believed that Christ would return at some future date, they tended to view the Book of Revelation as the apocalyptic vision it presents itself to be rather than a straightforward textbook for humanity's future.

My discussion, however, is not concerned with the superiority of metaphor and analogy in scriptural study over literalist interpretations, but with Moltmann's presentation of a biblical eschatology that is not defined finally by the apocalypticism favored by rapture preachers. For Moltmann, Christianity is by nature eschatological, in that it is future-oriented, but Christian eschatology cannot just be about the end of time. Christians live in an in-between time, a time and space that is instituted by Christ's death and resurrection and that anticipates his return. For Moltmann, Christian eschatology is experienced as the responsibility of hope in this in-between stage. "If the Christian hope is reduced to the salvation of the soul in a heaven beyond death, it loses its power to renew life and change the world, and its flame is quenched; it dies away into no more than a Gnostic yearning for redemption from this world's vale of tears."[3] It must be about how our lives are renewed. Christian hope declares, according to Moltmann, with regard to every apparent end, every cognition of *reality as it is*, that this is not the last word, but instead that Christ's resurrection transforms every end into a new beginning. *Eschaton*, he says, means eternity, not end-times and not future. The eschaton speaks to the tension between eternity and time in the past, present, and future of linear time. He writes, "When Jesus proclaims that the kingdom of God is 'at hand,' he is not looking into the future in the temporal sense; he is looking into the heaven of the present."[4] In other words, the kingdom of God is not a future heaven waiting for us to die and arrive in it; it does not come from the future into the present, but rather from heaven to earth, from eternity into time, in the model of the incarnation.

Moltmann says that in Jewish interpretation, Sabbath and Messiah belong together. Each week, observant Jews welcome in the Sabbath, which is often pictured as a beautiful temple built in time, a holy sanctuary in the structure of time rather than space. It is therefore seen as a gift to be enjoyed now and a foretaste of the messianic redemption that is promised in the future. In this sense, both Jews and Christians live in an in-between time, albeit in different ways given the Christian view of what is accomplished in Christ and yet awaits final realization and the Jewish valuation of covenantal responsibility and commitment in worldly life in addition to a future reconciliation with God. Jesus preached the advent of the kingdom of God, and so even though God has effected human reconciliation with Godself in Christ, Christians experience the continuation of history as an advent of the kingdom of God, when all will be gathered under the rule of Christ.

Moltmann's views on eschatology demonstrate some evolution. His early work in *Theology of Hope* aligns eschatology with political movements of social justice, while his later work in *The Coming of God: Christian Eschatology* demonstrates a greater pessimism about such political realization. Moltmann's mature work emphasizes the transcendence of God's reality and otherworldliness of eschatological realization.[5] Responding to the modern criticism of otherworldliness in traditional forms of Christian eschatology, Wolfhart Pannenberg defends a critical function of the otherworldliness of religious eschatology that is neither escapist nor satisfied with the purely secular. Instead, it "questions the alleged self-sufficiency of the secular world" and articulates a Christian realism to face the evils of the world without illusion. "Eschatological hope empowers the individual to carry the burden of its finite existence with all its irremovable limitations and disgraceful frustrations."[6] Moltmann's eschatology likewise enables a Christian realism and hope that takes seriously the real problems of suffering in this world and yet embraces God's promise of justice and restoration beyond anything humans alone can bring about.

Moltmann emphasizes this sense of living in an in-between time, in accordance with this promise. "The rule of Christ is as yet only the promise of the kingdom of God."[7] For Moltmann, this early Christian eschatological hope in the promise of the coming God must be retrieved out of the triumphalism of the imperial church that took over after the fourth century. The church is the place of witness to this promise, but it is as yet only experienced in Christian hope. The rule of Christ is present as advent for those who live in Christian faith, hope, and love. Christian hope implies both a living "as if," in the anticipatory experience of redemption and grace, and also a commitment to this anticipated experience. "Life out of this hope then means already acting here and today in accordance with that world of justice and righteousness and peace, contrary to appearances, and contrary to all historical chances of success."[8] Christian hope does not merely endure the present and wait patiently for a better future. Any simplistic model of faith in salvation as an attainment of a future paradise in fact represents, in Moltmann's view, a lack of faith and hope in what God has instituted. It accepts the impossibility of renewal in this world and instead only dreams of a fantasy world, ungratefully ignoring the reality that God has brought about according to biblical witness. Christian hope is instead about finding, recognizing, and enacting the new beginning, the renewal of life that lies within every apparent end. If it is not eschatological in this sense, according to Moltmann, Christian hope is reduced to a utopian fantasy that one assumes can never actually be and lives only in one's dreams.

Eschatological Interpretation of Biblical Catastrophes

Moltmann points out that the coming God is not a new and different God as Marcion claimed in the second century, but the same God who has been deepening His relationship with humanity from Adam to Noah to Abraham to Jesus.[9] The God who becomes manifest in Christ and promises to return is the God who is faithful to His creation, who has history with humanity. Moltmann cites three biblical catastrophes to illustrate this history of God's complicated yet faithful relationship with humanity.

With Noah, according to Moltmann's interpretation, God regrets having created humans and therefore allows them to perish from their own wickedness. This apocalyptic end, however, institutes a new beginning, as God establishes a new covenant with humanity and with the earth. He resolves never again to destroy it. Post-Noah, God promises to stay faithful to humanity despite humanity's betrayals and wickedness. Moltmann says that everything after this is grace. God "takes on himself the dissonance between the world's creation and its corruption, so that in spite of its corruption the world may live."[10] Much like a parent struggling with a challenging teenager, God practices patience and faithfulness with humanity, despite all of humanity's betrayals.

The second biblical catastrophe Moltmann raises in his history of God is the exile from Jerusalem following the Babylonian defeat of Israel in the sixth century B.C.E.. While this was very clearly an end in all kinds of ways, historical and theological scholarship demonstrates that the experience of the exile is a formative event in the development of Judaism. With the end of the kingdom of Israel as political entity, Judaism transforms itself from a local tribal religion to a religion of a community. It is during this time that the messianic aspirations of Judaism are formulated. The Sabbath replaces the physical temple of space with a metaphorical palace in time that foreshadows future redemption. Prayer and study become the primary and normative way to connect with God, replacing the model of animal sacrifice (even if temporarily). With the emergence of prayer and study comes also great attention to scriptural text as well as an internalization of what it means to be ethical monotheists, or those who worship their one God through a certain pattern of living. Moltmann discusses how the Shekinah came to descend on the earth and become present among the traveling community. Just as God decides to stay faithful to humanity with Noah, during the Babylonian exile, God chooses to become present among the people whenever they gather together to pray and study. God is no longer totally hidden or other, but instead becomes concretely present with His obedient people as they abide with God in the covenant.

The third biblical catastrophe Moltmann raises is Golgotha. From historical scholarship, we understand that the end for Jesus on the cross was an end to the conventional first-century Jewish view of the Messiah. On the cross, Jesus the king, religious leader, teacher, and prophet dies, as do any hopes pinned on his secular overthrow of Roman rule. For Moltmann, Jesus on the cross represents God's solidarity with human suffering and uniquely too, represents God's action not only to be with humanity, but also to take onto Himself the guilt of human sinfulness. God takes the place of sinful humanity and suffers for humanity in order to redeem humanity and *rehumanize* humanity, to raise humanity out of its corruption and into a new life. The resurrection of Christ was not a return to the life of the past, but "an eschatological event, in which God's future had acquired potency over the past."[11] This action by God demonstrates God's faithfulness and hopes for humanity that have not been forsaken despite humanity's faithlessness.

These three catastrophes demonstrate God's indefatigable faithfulness with humanity despite humanity's faithlessness. The pattern of faithfulness and victory over and conversion of human faithlessness finds its culmination in the Christ event, which definitively overcomes human failure with God's grace. The content of Christian hope has to do with God's promise of the restoration of all things, with God's promise to make all things new and bring them under the rule of Christ. For Moltmann, Christian hope trusts that the Last Judgment is not the last word in the Christian story. The last word that is borne out of God's promise in Christ is the kingdom of God, the restoration of all things. The relationship between judgment and kingdom demonstrates how Moltmann's view of Christian hope differs from any sort of humanistic utopianism or naïve optimism that things will be better someday.

Judgment and Kingdom

The most satisfying fictional stories, whether in books or films, are those that take characters through incredible conflict. The resolution that comes out of a sequence of building and culminating conflicts is greater because of these conflicts. Moltmann's theology of hope rejects any sort of naïve optimism or simple overcoming of future suffering. Instead, it develops an essential interrelationship between the Last Judgment and the restoration of all things. He points out that judgment is not the last word; it is a penultimate reality that precedes and even enables the kingdom of God and the rule of Christ. Moltmann does not deny the possible reality of hell and damnation, given the biblical evidence, but he does suggest the legitimacy of interpreting hell-fire as a purifying fire, a corrective punishment that does not last forever. While the Bible does suggest the possibility of dual outcomes of judgment—salvation and damnation—these two are asymmetrical in Moltmann's reading. Regarding the possibility of universal salvation, he clarifies that the Bible does not discuss universalism, but it does affirm the fulfillment of God's promises, listing among these, the promises to unite all things in Christ, to gather all under Christ and perfect them, and to restore all things. The last word cannot be human sin, but must be God's grace that does not simply overpower human will but calls people to faith. According to Moltmann, the last word for human destiny is God's word, "Behold, I make all things new."[12]

Moltmann locates this potent relationship between judgment and restoration in Christ. He asks first who must be our judge, and suggests that if we follow the method of providing Christological answers for eschatological questions, we must begin by looking at Christ's death on the cross. We find there, he says, the certainty of a reconciliation that is without limits, the true ground of hope for the restoration of all things, for universal salvation, and for the world to become the kingdom of God.[13] That we are judged by the one who took on flesh, and identified freely and graciously with all that was deemed low and impure and unacceptable to God tells us also about what that judgment itself consists in. He interprets Christ's descent into hell as the ground for confidence that nothing will be lost, that everything will be gathered into the kingdom of God.[14] Moltmann's emphases are on the divine intention revealed in these actions to retrieve what was lost and to do so precisely by identifying with what was lost. While the godless experience a hell they themselves have chosen, Christ disrupts their chosen loneliness and embodies solidarity with them as their companion, even in death. God overturns human choices of sin and damnation. Christ's experience of death and hell and resurrection provides two vital points for Moltmann's theology of hope: first, there is nothing too low, too mean—even hell—for God to identify with; second, all such torments are only penultimate. They do not gain the last word, and Christians are entitled to the gift of hope in the restoration of all things.

As Moltmann states, "the eschatological point of the proclamation of 'the Last Judgment' is the redeeming kingdom of God."[15] In judgment, God puts an end to everything that is turned away from God and makes the road clear to establishing the kingdom. The purification Moltmann anticipates is not the sort that some people today expect, according to which the faithful are raptured out of the way of an impending suffering that is endless for those unbelievers who remain. In Moltmann's interpretation God's judgment ultimately serves His goal and desire to restore all things. "In the divine Judgment all sinners, the wicked and the violent, the murderers and the children of Satan, the Devil and the fallen angels will be liberated and saved from their deadly perdition through transformation into their true, created being, because God remains true to himself, and does not give up what he has once created and affirmed, or allow it to be lost."[16] Moltmann's accent, then, is on God's unending faithfulness to His creation. In his reading, the Last Judgment puts things to right. Judgment is the end that contains in it the beginning of a new life. He describes judgment as "a source of endlessly consoling joy to know, not just that the murderers will finally fail to triumph over their victims, but that they cannot in eternity remain the murderers of their victims."[17]

Christian Hope and Realism

Moltmann mentions that the Indonesian word for hope means literally "to look beyond the horizon," which is a valuable analogy for a distinctly religious and Christian model of hope.[18] A horizon represents the edge or boundary of what we can see or experience. Looking beyond the horizon suggests the Christian model of faith. While by human efforts alone perfection is not possible, "with God, all things are possible."[19] When we observe with open and honest eyes our human history and potentialities of where we are now and where we are headed, the reality we see is full of unhappiness, destruction, and tragedy. History and reality as we observe them teach us that human beings are not necessarily becoming more moral or making the world and themselves a better and more just community.[20] Looking beyond the horizon in hope can mean actively moving in faith, hope, and love beyond the boundary of what is humanly possible toward the justice that is promised in God's kingdom.

Despite Moltmann's emphasis on the real tragedy and catastrophe that God promises to overcome, his vision is often criticized as overly utopian. His Trinitarian and Christological doctrines, however, offer evidence against any utopian vision. Moltmann criticizes what he calls "monotheistic monarchianism," by which the persons of the Trinity are subordinated to the monarchy of one God, and instead focuses on the God revealed in the cross. His social doctrine of the Trinity describes the relationality and community among the persons of the Trinity and then prescribes this as the nature of human community. In a 2007 article, Joy Ann McDougall provides an inventory of various criticisms of Moltmann's Trinitarian theology, for example, that it compromises the transcendence and sovereignty of God over creation and elevates the role of human action in salvation rather than grace, or that his social doctrine of Trinity anthropomorphizes the divine life and projects these as norms for human relationships. McDougall largely defends Moltmann against what she sees as these misreadings but then raises questions about his doctrine of sin, contending that Moltmann's lack of a robust doctrine of sin contributes to a certain utopianism that leaves his Trinitarianism open to charges of impracticality.[21]

Moltmann rejects the view that the Christian doctrine of hope is a naïve optimism. "No one can assure us that the worst will not happen. According to all the laws of experience: it will. We can only trust that even the end of the world hides a new beginning if we trust the God who calls into being the things that are not, and out of death creates new life."[22] For Moltmann, hope means living in expectation of God's ultimate conversion and transformation of the darkness and tragedy that pervades human existence. It is not the avoidance of death, but the promise of resurrection of the dead. This is an important difference from any triumphalist interpretation of faith guaranteeing peace and happiness.[23] He points out that resurrection does not mean simply immortality or a return to this life that goes on without end. It is instead a life after death, an entry into a life that is eternal that thereby affirms both life and death.[24] What stands out in Moltmann's discussion of Christian eschatology is the ultimate victory over death and the pain-filled reality of human experience. He cites Martin Luther's comment about how he would plant an apple tree today even if he knew the world was going to end tomorrow.[25] Hope abides in God's promise despite the very feasible defeat we witness to the contrary all around us. Dante's chosen title is perhaps most appropriate: the last word for Christians is not a tragedy, but a divine comedy that will follow any tragedy.

The point here is clear for Moltmann's justification for Christian hope. God has the last word, and that word is grace. Some contemporary American politicians have been quoted as saying with great drama that they would follow a terrorist to the gates of hell, implying their resolute commitment to completing this task, their absolute refusal to allow such terrorists to escape the reach of justice.[26] We could paraphrase Moltmann's point about God's continuing faithfulness to His creation and Christ's descent into hell along similar dramatic lines and affirm that God will relentlessly pursue us, His faithless creatures, not just to the gates of hell, but well into hell, and even suffer hell to bring us out, to rescue and restore all of His creation. God's Yes wins out over God's No, entirely because God takes this No on Godself instead of leaving it to fall on human beings, however faithlessly we may behave. Christian hope, therefore, is premised on Christ's suffering on the cross, on God's relentless pursuit of His faithless creatures through the worst hell and judgment, and on God's promise to restore all things under the rule of Christ. Moltmann's eschatological hope, therefore, incorporates both realism about the all too real tragedy inherent in human life and anticipation of God's restoration of His creation. Again, this does not mean that bad things will not happen. Moltmann says they most certainly will; however, they will not be the final word, they will not last forever, and they will be overcome.

Raimon Panikkar's Pluralistic Theology

While Moltmann and Caputo both use the language of hope as a rehabilitation of faith, Panikkar rehabilitates faith in the language of religious pluralism. In this section of the chapter, I outline briefly Panikkar's defense of Christian pluralism, by which I mean the Christian view that there exists the very real possibility of truth and salvation in many of the world's different religious traditions. Christian pluralism stands in contrast to Christian particularism (termed exclusivism by some), according to which the Christian tradition alone carries God's truth and enables human salvation, and Christian inclusivism, according to which Christians may find in other traditions partial or preliminary truth that is fulfilled in the Christian tradition of revelation. Panikkar's pluralist theology is mystically grounded and proceeds through the exercise of unknowing and deconstructing our categories and expectations. Just as Christian mystic Meister Eckhart prescribes an extensive self-emptying before God can come in and give birth to the Word, Panikkar's pluralism and mystical unknowing are premised on a mystical confidence he has to leave God to do the saving. We can and should be humble in our epistemological claims to describe God fully and yet be bold because of our capacity to know and experience truly, if not exhaustively, because God is infinitely acting on our behalf. We must be pluralistic in our religious understanding because the sacred is always more than human understanding of the sacred. The question remains, however, whether Panikkar's pluralism is still a dogmatic avowal of epistemological realism couched in a mystical orientation to divine ineffability. In other words, is he only using God's mystery to support dogmatic faith statements? I therefore examine his concepts of a cosmotheandric principle, dialogical dialogue, and pluralism insofar as they support a postmodern exercise of interreligious dialogue as a way to prevent the reification of the sacred.

The Cosmotheandric Principle

Panikkar's pluralist theology is mystical in orientation and based on what he calls the cosmotheandric principle, a mystical intuition of the three irreducible dimensions of the sacred: cosmos, God, and human. Panikkar proposes that this triadic intuition exists both in consciousness and in reality. Their interrelationship defines every moment of the real. Frank Podgorski refers to interrelatedness as "the hermeneutical key to understand and 'stand under' the mythos which both reveals and yet conceals reality."[27] No one element can subsist or be understood in isolation. Reality is defined as the *perichoresis* of the three together. They are not one, but all three dimensions characterize every moment of reality and experience.

The cosmotheandric principle elucidates that every being has a transcendent dimension and an immanent dimension, by which it both escapes us and is experienced by us. The divine dimension is characterized by its mystery or endless openness. The human dimension of every being lies in its knowability and its life in our creative interpretations and appropriations. The earthly dimension is the secular or worldly that bounds all human experience. Panikkar also describes cosmotheandrism as the interrelationship among an I, a Thou, and an It, in which "I" refers to the divine experience, "Thou" to the human experience of being addressed by God, and "It" to the cosmos as the context of this sacred relationship.[28] The three, thought together as irreducible but interdependent dimensions, describe the nature of reality that constitutes the identity of any being. Reality is not a passive, unconscious object waiting for us to acquire it in our sights but a living network of relationships. For Panikkar, the Ultimate Mystery does not exist "in itself" beyond human experience, but within the diversity of humanity and world. He explains that the particular names ascribed to this mystery by different religious communities are not just labels attached to this mystery, but that "each authentic name enriches and qualifies that Mystery which is neither purely transcendent nor purely immanent."[29] Despite Panikkar's rejection of a metaphysical system, the cosmotheandric intuition sets up a metaphysical foundation for his practical program of pluralism and interreligious dialogue, but one that is not at all a static reality but a dynamic perichoresis.

By using a relational ontology in what is basically a mystical intuition, Panikkar reframes one of the prominent questions of faith and doubt: how can we know anything confidently about the sacred, which is purported to transcend human understanding? The concern of how to know what is beyond knowledge is replaced with the concern of how to describe and correct the relationship between humanity, God, and cosmos. Because Panikkar implicates us in a relational ontology, we can and do know the sacred; even if we define it through intuition rather than critical reason to be beyond ordinary empirical experience, we already participate in a relationship with it that constitutes both it and us. Panikkar's use of relational ontology incorporates postmodern concerns about the dynamic web of relationships that establish identity as a hybrid and constantly shifting reality, but the cosmotheandric vision maintains a metaphysics of ineffable reality. Paul Williams expresses concern about this model as a useful basis for interreligious dialogue. Panikkar's contention "that Reality transcends the intelligible, the appropriate response to which is 'cosmic confidence,' which impels us to trust even what we do not understand or approve of looks to the outsider like the old claim that what Christians call God infinitely transcends all our systems and rational categories, . . . and can only be approached through faith."[30] Williams suggests therefore that most Buddhists would not accept the metaphysical presuppositions of Panikkar's ineffable sacred reality.

Dialogical Dialogue

In his short book, *The Intrareligious Dialogue*, Panikkar outlines the rules of encounter with those of other religious traditions. What Panikkar means by *intrareligious* dialogue is that before any of us engage in dialogue with people of another religious tradition, we must first have our own internal dialogue between our own system of commitments and that other tradition. Panikkar contrasts two different approaches to dialogue. Whereas *dialectical dialogue* trusts an all-powerful Reason that ensures the reasonableness of the other and of the whole process, *dialogical dialogue* trusts in the other as a mutual subject and places the other in a position not simply of equality but even of priority. Dialogue with those of other religious traditions therefore becomes a religious exercise of humility and unknowing, as one allows one's presuppositions to be inspected and challenged by the other.

For Panikkar, religious dialogue requires that one be fully prepared and even willing to be converted by the other's position.

The justification of the dialogical dialogue, Panikkar explains, lies "in the very nature of the real, namely in the fact that reality is not wholly objectifiable, ultimately because I myself, a subject, am also a part of it, am in it, and cannot extricate myself from it. The dialogical dialogue assumes a radical dynamism of reality, namely that reality is not given once and for all, but is real precisely in the fact that it is continually creating itself."[31] Instead of presuming the existence of a "thing in itself" or an atomism in which human beings are each independent monads, dialogical dialogue assumes "that we all share in a reality that does not exist independently and outside our own sharing in it, and yet without exhausting it. Our participation is always partial, and reality is more than just the sum total of its parts."[32] Dialogical thinking embraces the other's uncovering of my own myths because the other helps expose my presuppositions as what they are, and then I can either discard them or incorporate them into my conscious assumptions on which I build. Panikkar urges the use of what he calls diatopical hermeneutics, crossing cultural spaces to seek out what something means for another religious community. Getting glimpses of others' meaning is an urgent task in our own spiritual understanding. For Panikkar, I trust the other not out of an ethical principle of duty, but because I have experienced the "Thou" as the counterpart of the "I." "I discover the Thou as part of a Self that is as much mine as his—or to be more precise, that is as little my property as his."[33]

Dialogical dialogue incorporates the priority of the human other that Emmanuel Levinas prescribes as an ethical-religious principle. All we can access in the other is the face of the other person, which reveals something to us, but which conceals vastly more from us and beyond which we cannot presume access. To attempt to know the other any further would be an act of sheer violence. In the context of an interreligious encounter, this implies not tolerance, but one's accountability for one's religious convictions before the other. It means that I expose my convictions that support me at the deepest level of my being and allow the other to inspect them and to interrogate me because this discourse is itself revelatory.

Pluralism

The word *pluralism* may not be ideal to describe the posture Panikkar prescribes of openness to the mystery and contingency and freedom of reality to manifest itself because its meaning to different thinkers is conditioned on their particular concerns with making sweeping judgments on the truth-value of different religious traditions.[34] Anselm Min identifies several types of pluralism—phenomenalist, universalist, ethical or soteriocentric, confessionalist, and dialectical—and identifies Panikkar's as ontological pluralism. While most other forms, Min says, accept pluralism as a necessary evil that emerges from the inevitable limitation of the human perspective, Panikkar argues for a radical, ontological pluralism of reality itself.[35] For Panikkar, truth is neither one nor many, but pluralistic. Terms like *Trinity* and *Advaita* might for Panikkar better express this nonobjectifiable mystery in orthodox Christian and Hindu language.[36] Panikkar's pluralism is not a theoretical system about the ultimate identity of all religious statements or an attitude that respects the relative value of different religious hypotheses, but an attitude that respects the freedom of sacred reality to transcend our systematizing efforts to contain and define it. It actively resists the tendency to absolutize any claims to validity. While most other pluralisms remain within the dichotomy of absolutism or relativism, assuming the ultimacy and unity of truth beyond diverse perspectives, Panikkar's pluralism deconstructs this will to unity, totality, and universality.[37] Pluralism affirms "there is a fluxos quo which will never permit us to freeze anything real, that reality and the logos itself are open-ended."[38] In Panikkar's use, then, pluralism acknowledges the freedom of sacred reality and becomes an explicit and active rejection of any claims to rationally encompass the sacred.

As Panikkar writes, "pluralism is not a supersystem, a meta-language, . . . an intellectual panacea. Pluralism is an open, human attitude, which therefore entails an intellectual dimension that overcomes any kind of solipsism, as if we—any we—were alone in the universe, the masters of it, the holders of the Absolute."[39] Pluralism becomes then a religious prescription of extreme humility and a reminder to live without total security, to dwell religiously in our vulnerability. He describes this in the paradigm of Christian mysticism as kenosis. "Only when a Man is completely empty of himself, is in a state of kenosis, of renunciation and annihilation, will Christ fulfill his incarnation in him. Only kenosis allows incarnation and incarnation is the only way to redemption."[40] The exercise of self-emptying or deconstruction is a religious mandate, in a sense. It extends in Christian terms of humility, self-sacrifice, or kenosis what Anri Morimoto identifies as a dynamic of self-relativization of believers before the presence of the ultimate that is built into the major religions of the world.[41] A pluralist attitude is predicated on the religious need to correct our inevitably mistaken assumptions and presumptions about the sacred. Panikkar incorporates the religious prescriptions of Christian mysticism in a contemporary posture of Christian pluralism. Engaging in interreligious dialogue is necessary to keep ourselves from falling into complacent reification or idolatry of God. Although Panikkar says that Reality itself is pluralistic, the question remains whether his pluralism is still a perspectivalism that simply articulates humility before a single ineffable Reality. Using the analogy of different religious windows that open to Reality, Paul Williams raises concerns about whether Panikkar speaks from a Christian window alone (which prevents his speech about Ultimate Reality itself) or from a transcendental standpoint (which cannot be justified).[42] Drawing on the dGe lugs tradition of Tibetan Buddhism, Williams criticizes Panikkar's assertion of the transcendence of the Real beyond understanding as a further reification of some transcendent Absolute.

While Panikkar's pluralistic approach insists on humility before the inexhaustibility of divine mystery, it also allows confidence that we can in fact know God, however partially. As Min notes, "Panikkar's ontological pluralism, then, means passing beyond absolutism without falling into relativism with its agnostic tendencies. It does presuppose radical relativity or relationality at the bottom of reality."[43] Panikkar's confidence that we apprehend reality, albeit incompletely and imperfectly, depends on two important components of his theology that remain in tension with his mysticism. The first is the centrality of revelation and incarnation, and the second is a pragmatic realism. The cosmotheandric experience expresses both the interconnectedness of reality and the fact of revelation. This dynamic relationship between cosmos, God, and human reveals itself in every spark of the real and continually manifests itself anew. It is this incarnational, revelational dimension that grounds Panikkar's methodological pluralism that refuses to collapse the very real differences of our religious experiences into a final and higher unity. This coming to presence, or revelation, is most explicitly realized in the Christian incarnation of God in Jesus Christ, but Panikkar locates it also in the Hindu concept of *Isvara*, or personal deity. What is key in what he terms the "unknown Christ of Hinduism" is the revelation of a reality that is inherently mysterious. In some ways, the Hindu concept of Isvara demonstrates a greater fluidity of the divine life than some conventional Christian discourse insofar as popular Hindu theology accommodates quite easily a divine that is always embodying itself, always manifesting itself anew. The many gods of Hindu theism help preserve for Hindus the tension and paradox between divine transcendence of the limits of human discourse and divine immanence whereby the sacred becomes fully incarnate and revealed.

The second component of Panikkar's theology that contributes to the pluralist approach is a kind of pragmatic realism that may be traced to Advaita Vedanta. According to Advaitic epistemology, all knowledge has intrinsic validity, but not ultimate validity. According to Eliot Deutsch, "an idea is held to be true or valid then, the moment it is entertained . . . and it retains its validity until it is contradicted in experience or is shown to be based on defective apprehension."[44] This process of belief is justified because our apprehension is limited to the means by which we acquire knowledge. There is no place outside the knowledge-acquiring process itself where we may look for a way to confirm a judgment. This theory of the self-validity of knowledge enables a pragmatic realism. Because we cannot judge the validity of our judgments by some "objective" or independent criterion, we may provisionally trust our cognitions and our religious systems as long as we do not absolutize them.

Together, the centrality of revelation and incarnation and this pragmatic realist epistemology allow a theological confidence that proceeds in humility. It affirms the inexhaustibility of divine mystery, but then confidently trusts God to faithfully reveal and enact solidarity with us, with *all* of us across our humanly constructed religious and theological borders. It allows God to do the saving beyond whatever we can understand of this ultimate mystery. In conclusion, for Panikkar, we *should* be pluralists to avoid reifying God into an idol of our own theological construction; we *can* be pluralists because God is in charge. Along the lines of Moltmann's theology of hope in God's faithfulness, Panikkar trusts fundamentally in God's infinite activity of incarnation, that God is Immanuel, or "God with us," however much this remains an ultimate mystery to human understanding and an unresolved metaphysics of the sacred. Given his assumptions of a sacred reality that remains mysterious, the question arises: does Panikkar, in the end, actually move substantially beyond John Hick's pluralist hypothesis, which has been criticized as an unjustified claim to transcend all the particular religions, to see more than what the particular religious viewpoints can see? To the extent that he does, it is primarily because his pluralism is not a descriptive account of all the religions coming together beyond our apprehension, and because he consistently upholds a postmodern sense of meaning escaping us even while we continue to seek it and employ it. In this sense, Panikkar's pluralism may echo the movement of continual self-transcendence discussed in chapter 4's analysis of Hindu traditions as much as it resembles too Eckhart's teaching of the spiritual ascent through unknowing discussed in chapter 5.

John Caputo's Postmodern Religion

John Caputo is best known for his deconstructive hermeneutics of religion and theology and his exposition of the work of deconstructionist philosopher Jacques Derrida. Caputo opens his book *On Religion* with a question posed by Augustine in *The Confessions*: "what do I love when I love my God?"[45] By the end of the book, in his proposal of a religion without religion, he demonstrates that not knowing what it is we love when we love God and confessing this lack of knowledge are integral to genuine religion. This final section of this chapter develops two particular components presented in Caputo's short book *On Religion* for how to think meaningfully about religion in today's world. The first is Caputo's answer to the question of what religion is. He argues that religion is the love of God, and he then posits what it means to love, arguing in lovely rhetoric, "religion is for lovers." The second is his proposal for a "religion without religion," in which he develops the religiosity of Derrida. Contrary to the view that religion is under attack in postmodernity, Caputo argues that religious faith is more genuinely possible now because of an antidogmatic rehabilitation.

"Religion is for lovers"

Caputo begins with the simple assertion that religion is the love of God. He argues, "religion is for lovers, for men and women of passion, for real people with a passion for something other than taking profits, people who believe in something, who hope like mad in something, who love something with a love that surpasses understanding."[46] What does it mean to love something? Caputo says that love is "a giving without holding back." "Love is not a bargain, but unconditional giving; it is not an investment, but a commitment come what may."[47] Caputo does not restrict this unconditional commitment of love to one's love of God. Rather, it is the character of love to be excessive and unconditional. Religion is for lovers because "to love deeply and unconditionally is to be born of God."[48] Religion is, for Caputo, not about attending church or believing a certain set of creedal statements. Caputo's definition of religion waylays the trite distinction between the religious and the secular and becomes somewhat postsecular. Religion is about loving deeply, genuinely, and to excess. Therefore, Caputo writes, "the real opposite of a religious person is a selfish and pusillanimous curmudgeon, a loveless lout who knows no higher pleasure than the contemplation of his own visage, a mediocre fellow who does not have the energy to love anything except his mutual funds."[49] So religion is about love, and love has to do with passion and over-the-top excessiveness. One who loves only within measure, or as a fair and even exchange, is not loving another, but is negotiating a deal. For Caputo, religion as irrational love, hope, and optimism is to be contrasted with more moderate, practical, and reasonable self-interest. I return to this opposition with Caputo's distinction between a religious sense of life and a tragic sense of life later. First, I must deal with his linking of the category of the impossible with the love of God.

Caputo notes that the relevant question for religion is not whether one loves God or whether there is a God to love; the relevant question that religion asks is "what do I love when I love my God?" While this question is not supposed to be answered easily, and it is supposed to remain a question that is repeatedly and constantly asked by a religious person, the answer seems to be that what one loves implies a particular way of relating to God, to all that is unknown, to the future, and to the entire category of what is possible and impossible.

Caputo raises Derrida's suggestion that we think of God as the becoming possible of the impossible, and meditates on the gospel assertion that with God all things are possible. What is impossible as far as we humans are concerned becomes possible with God. The faithful are willing to wager passionately on this premise, this promise witnessed in the Christian narrative. In explicating the category of the impossible, Caputo discusses the realm of the future. "The future pries open the present by promising us the possibility of something new, the chance of something different, something that will transform the present into something else."[50] He distinguishes a relative future, which is essentially foreseeable and more of the same, the part that we practically must work to ensure, from the "absolute future." While we can and must plan for the relative foreseeable future, the absolute future requires the more challenging abandonment of control in hope, faith, and love. "With the 'absolute' future we are pushed to the limits of the possible, fully extended, at our wits' end, having run up against something that is beyond us, beyond our powers and potentialities, beyond our powers of disposition, pushed to the point where only the great passions of faith and love and hope will see us through."[51] Caputo explains that the religious sense of life implies a particular openness to the absolute future, by which we must be willing to go with what God provides, ready for anything.

A religious sense of life then is open and willing to go toward this absolute future where there are no guarantees and plenty of risks. (Moltmann might interject here that while we do not have guarantees in our ordinary sense of the word, what we do have are God's promises witnessed to in Christian revelation.) Faith in a promise, however revelatory, is of course precisely not the kind of guarantee we can cite in court like a written warranty. It demands a covenant with the impossible, as Caputo says; it demands a willingness to abide with whatever might come, like the lilies of the field.[52] This willingness to embrace risk, uncertainty, even impossibility, is the religious sense of life. "The Scriptures are filled with narratives in which the power of the present is broken and the full length and breadth of the real open up like a flower, unfolding the power of the possible, the power of the impossible beyond the possible, of the hyper-real beyond the real."[53] Caputo points out that miracle stories of transforming change and the idea of forgiveness itself have to do with lifting the weight of the past and present and granting a new future for people. He calls to mind this prophetic dimension of religion—prophetic, not in the sense of predicting the foreseeable future (like being a weatherman, he says), but rather in the messianic hope and expectation of peace and justice.

James H. Cone in his book, *God of the Oppressed*, argues similarly about the powerful prophetic dimension of the religion of black people suffering in America through the inhumanity of slavery, Jim Crow laws, and segregation. He says that while Karl Marx provided a useful analysis of the economic basis of all ideology, he was wrong about religion. Despite the degree to which religion was an institution like any other and reinscribed and justified the status quo, the religious experience of black people also taught them that they were more than what they were told by everyone around them, that they were loved by God, that they had dignity and spirit, contrary to everything they saw around them.[54] Cone cites the hymns and stories that promise the coming of God to right all wrongs, a future that would put an end to the present of their experience. One can only imagine the sense of impossibility of such a future in which God might right the wrongs of slavery, and the irrationality and risk to life and limb of hoping for such a contradiction to the reality of their experience.

Caputo would agree with Cone that religious faith and hope have not to do with fanciful illusion and wish-fulfillment but with this posture of imagining an alternative future. The religious, those who love, according to Caputo, stand courageously on the threshold between the actual and possible before them and the impossible ahead of them. In his book, *God Has a Dream*, Archbishop Desmond Tutu eloquently describes the bold faith with which black South Africans fought apartheid.

> During the darkest days of apartheid I used to say to P. W. Botha, the president of South Africa, that we had already won, and I invited him and other white South Africans to join the winning side. All the "objective facts" were against us—the pass laws, the imprisonments, the teargassing, the massacres, the murder of political activists—but my confidence was not in the present circumstances but in the laws of God's universe. This is a moral universe, which means that, despite all the evidence that seems to be to the contrary, there is no way that

evil and injustice and oppression and lies can have the last word. God is a God who cares about right and wrong. God cares about justice and injustice. God is in charge. That is what had upheld the morale of our people, to know that in the end good will prevail. It was these higher laws that convinced me that our peaceful struggle would topple the immoral laws of apartheid.[55]

It must have seemed absurd, their faith that the harsh realities of apartheid would be transformed in their lifetime. Archbishop Tutu emphasizes the doctrinal basis for such radical hope in the power of God's transformation of the world. "The principle of transfiguration says nothing, no one and no situation, is 'untransfigurable,' that the whole of creation, nature, waits expectantly for its transfiguration, when it will be released from its bondage and share in the glorious liberty of the children of God."[56] Many non-Christians or nonreligious criticize the seeming ease with which many Christians talk about justification by faith and mock the idea that one can so easily be freed of sinful actions through mere repentance. However, the vision of Christian hope evoked by Archbishop Tutu, Cone, Moltmann, and Caputo is founded on the power and promise of God to redeem and transform the world. For Christians, God has revealed Godself in Jesus as Immanuel, or God with us. God has revealed an uncompromising solidarity with humanity. Justification by faith in God's grace does not naïvely ignore the degree of human sin, but trusts and hopes in God's gracious solidarity as more powerful than any human sin. Christian faith and hope trust that there is nothing in us that is too mean, too low, for God to redeem.

This is a very risky way to live. It is not practical in many respects but the religious sense of life has precisely to do with both letting go of security and becoming vulnerable, on the one hand, and becoming expectant on truth to manifest itself. As Caputo proclaims, "If safe is what you want, forget religion and find yourself a conservative investment counselor. The religious sense of life has to do with exposing oneself to the radical uncertainty and the open-endedness of life."[57] We find in Caputo a postmodern religious apologetics, one that is very different from the religious apologetics of the nineteenth century, for example. Whereas others continue to argue that religion is useful to support morality, that religion is practical because it provides structure and meaning to life, or that belief in the supernatural is a perfectly rational thing to posit, Caputo's apologetic is founded on loving to excess, taking risks by embracing boldly the radical uncertainty of life, and believing that human destiny might be (impossibly) different from everything we know to be present and real. The role of uncertainty gains special focus in his proposal of a "religion without religion."

Religion Without Religion

In *On Religion*, Caputo presents his view of postmodern faith as "religion without religion." What he means by this enigmatic phrase is what he has described as the religious sense of life—the passionate love of God that courageously embraces the becoming possible of the impossible—without the dogmatism that much traditional confessional religion has accrued. Recalling the question he borrows from Augustine—"what do I love when I love my God?"—Caputo stresses the posture of questioning itself as an abiding part of being religious. Religious experience is marked by a radical nonknowing. He says the faithful must concede they do not *know* what they believe by faith. "While faith gives the faithful a way to view things, they are not lifted by the hook of faith above the fray of conflicting points of view. They do not enjoy certain cognitive privileges and epistemic advantages of which others have been deprived, and their beliefs are not entitled to special treatment outside their own communities."[58] Faith is not knowledge and does not yield certainty; faith does not remove doubt. Like Panikkar, Caputo does not see faith as a way to get beyond the inherent conflict between different worldviews. Faith is not faith without doubt, as Tillich argues. With Tillich and Barth, Caputo distinguishes between religion and God. The former is a human practice and "is always deconstructible in the light of the love of God, which is not deconstructible."[59] God and God's revelation always transcend and critically trump religion as human response and representation of that revelation.

Supporting this fundamental sense of nonknowing at the heart of religion, Caputo presents three axioms of a religion without religion: "I do not know who I am or whether I believe in God"; "I do not know whether what I believe in is God or not"; and "What do I love when I love my God?"[60] The first defines human being as a mystery and a questioning spirit. The second confesses the basic phenomenological problem of all religious discourse—we talk about something that we have defined as being radically beyond our knowledge. Caputo therefore reminds us to confess this nonknowing. The lack of certainty does not indicate an imperfect stage of knowledge that we are obliged to master. The lack of certainty is what keeps faith faith. Faith has to do not with the relative future, but with the absolute future, which is the realm of impossibility as far as our understanding goes. The final question is the one that for Caputo best defines a postmodern faith. The posture of questioning *what* it is we love when we love is the religious sense of life. This questioning then is not merely a preliminary stage to religious faith. Religion lies in the questioning, not in arriving at an answer. "So what has dropped from the sky is not The Answer with which I may smite my enemies, but a question with which I am myself put in question! God is a question, not an answer, the most radical thought we can entertain, that exposes the questionability of all the other answers we think we have."[61] Religion is the experience of this questioning and the responsibility to answer over and over again as we question over and over again. Caputo argues that the problem with fundamentalism is that it closes down precisely this question of *what* it is we love. He eloquently proposes that being truly religious requires that we remain desert wanderers, never resting in a final answer about meaning, but always wandering and restless because we do not know.

The discussion of the role of nonknowing in faith reinforces the contrast between a religious sense of life and a tragic sense of life. The tragic sense of life sees reality as it presently is and accepts it as fate, as the way things are. It says "this is it; there is nothing more." Caputo describes it as the sense of an anonymous and loveless force in the world. Such a tragic sense of life captures some of what is commonly attributed by critics to atheism and postmodern relativism—not the sheer denial of a God, but the view that the universe is morally ambiguous or indifferent to human life. This is the claim that most disturbs many of today's conservative evangelical Christians, and some respond by rejecting any and all the peripheral suggestions that religion is largely a human construction. The view that the universe is morally ambiguous is seen as an avenue to utter relativism and meaninglessness, and triggers in some a dogmatic fundamentalism.

Evangelical theologies are by no means uniform in their response to the kind of questioning of traditional ways of thinking about God modeled by Caputo, Moltmann, and Panikkar, as well as by religious pluralists like John Hick and process theologians like John Cobb and Charles Hartshorne. Clark Pinnock's openness theism is a notable example of evangelical theology that sees value in questioning long-held theological assumptions and participates in dialogue with very different and even conflicting theological perspectives, offering options within evangelical theology that are not guided by fundamentalist dogmatism. In these particular ways, the openness theists echo some of Caputo's concern for a readiness to question dogmatism while prioritizing a biblical revelation of God as love. Pinnock describes this open view of God as follows: "God, in grace, grants humans significant freedom to cooperate with or work against God's will for their lives, and he enters into dynamic, give-and-take relationships with us."[62] Openness theists criticize traditional forms of classical theism as articulated by Augustine, Thomas Aquinas, and John Calvin, according to which God has eternally preordained all events. They agree with the classical theist view that all power belongs to God and disagree with process theists' rejection of such an idea of divine power and volition. Openness theism, also called free will theism, challenges the elements of Greek metaphysics that influenced the way early church thinkers conceptualized God. For example, the Aristotelian notion of an unmoved mover adopted by the Roman church supported a classical Christian position of God's impassivity and independence of the world, even though it appears to contradict the biblical experience of God as caring deeply for humanity.[63] The openness theist position has come under heavy fire from traditionalist evangelicals because of its challenge to the Thomistic position of divine impassivity and the Calvinist position of divine sovereignty, but it offers a dynamic engagement with theological tradition that prioritizes scripture as a source and norm for Christian theology. In its normative role as the written witness to God's self-revelation, scripture can be used to criticize the distorting effects of Greek metaphysics on early Christian understandings of God and to retrieve the gospel affirmation of the redemptive and responsive God behind the classical view of a God who is unmoved by human suffering. While questioning the tradition of Christian theology, the openness theists reject any suggestion that the universe is morally indifferent to human well-being, citing scriptural witness to how God interacts with humanity in a dynamic and caring relationship of love.

Openness theists like Clark Pinnock by no means mirror all of Caputo's concerns, but they provide an interesting counterexample to Caputo's postmodern and nondogmatic religious faith, with a very different evangelical perspective that respects God's freedom and unambiguous love for humanity while questioning traditional metaphysical assumptions that may be foreign to the biblical revelation. Caputo's postmodern sensibility does not espouse the ultimate ambiguity of the world. Instead, he says that the religious sense of life is forged over and against this tragic sense of real suffering and death that defines life. The tragic view never goes away; it is never completely refuted and dismissed; it is always right there challenging the religious sense of faith, hope, and love. The tragic does not have the last word, however, but serves as a continuous internal critique in religion. "The tragic keeps the religious honest, keeps it on its toes, and blocks the triumphalism and self-enclosure of [fundamentalism]."[64] Caputo echoes Tillich's view that doubt is a necessary part of faith that prevents faith from falling into idolatry of our own pretend-knowledge. Caputo argues ultimately for the undecidability between the tragic sense and the religious sense of life. In other words, the worry that there is perhaps no greater meaning remains; it keeps alive the questioning that defines religion. It is urgent to Caputo's postmodern faith that "we must all 'fess up' that we do not know who we are or what is going on, not

'Really.'"[65] Faith can be faith only in the face of such persistent doubt and active questioning. It is because of this undecidability between the religious and the tragic that faith is not a simplistic blind belief in a creed or a wishful dream vision that reality is other than how things are experienced. Because faith articulates itself continually in the face of the questioning and doubting and answering that existentially define us, it can be sustainable and dynamic in a world that is more full of questions than easy answers.

Conclusion

This chapter has followed three different proposals of being religious today that move us in different directions beyond a simplistic opposition between faith and doubt, creedal adherence and skepticism. Moltmann relies on the biblical narrative and a rethinking of eschatology to move us to a theology of hope that anticipates the fulfillment of God's promises. He says that God has the last word—that is the promise in Christian revelation. Even God's judgment is not God's last word, however, because God promises beyond that judgment the restoration of all things. Everything else other than that is within time only, not for eternity, and will come to a finite end. Panikkar advocates serious interreligious dialogue as an urgent religious task because of its capacity to move us outside our reified myths. Being religious requires that we enter into authentic dialogue with others beyond our own faith communities because it is the only way we can transcend the partiality and finality of our own understanding. Radical pluralism as an attitude of openness to completely contradictory religious views is essential to experience transcendence and the pluralistic Mystery worshiped as God. Caputo constructs a postmodern apologetic for religion and celebrates the religious dimension of life as one that courageously and boldly inhabits the experience of radical nonknowing and loving without measure. Echoing Moltmann, he suggests that being religious implies a radical optimism by which one trusts that the suffering and evil that are undoubtedly real all around us will not be the last word, and echoing Panikkar's sense of kenotic mysticism, he affirms that faith must proceed by way of radical nonknowing because our very nature is to be restless and excessive in our questioning and loving. All three figures discussed here boldly engage challenges facing religious standpoints that seek to be relevant and sustainable in the contemporary world. They respond not by relaxing traditional religious claims but by truly allowing the religious claims to speak to us and question us in the twenty-first century.

DWELLING IN UNCERTAINTY

The focus throughout this book has been the many dynamic ways in which faith has been described in different traditions. My concern has been to call attention to the resources within our world's abiding religious traditions for a conception of faith that counters a blind acceptance of something that is not understood clearly, that instead acknowledges and embraces doubt in an active process of trust, commitment, transcendence, and self-correction that characterizes a vibrant and honest spiritual questioning.

The components of faith traced here constitute paths that tread deeper into spiritual life than either the fundamentalist religious communities or their staunch atheist critics allow. What characterize both sides are dogmatic restrictions of what is allowed or valid as means of inquiry or criteria for discussion and judgment. Biblical fundamentalists refuse to address any challenges to the literal truth of biblical propositions they selectively propound. Muslim fundamentalists insist that the Qur'an has one single and straightforward meaning—their own—on all matters of religious ethics and human behavior. Hindu nationalists refuse to allow any criticism of oppressive practices from outside the boundaries of native Indian and Vedic tradition. Atheist critics hostile to religion refuse to acknowledge the meaning and value of any faith statements that presume the experience of any unseen reality. Beyond all of these problematic extremes that are unsatisfying for contemporary faith and reason, there lies a promising depth to spiritual questions that must be reclaimed and fortified in order to communicate meaningfully with our religious and humanist neighbors and address more honestly and deeply all of our own lives of spiritual questioning.

This deeper way of a nondogmatic faith that actively engages doubt should not be confused with a contemporary call for so-called moderate religiosity.

To seek to be "moderate" only implies that the clear and forthright direction of true religious faith is dogmatism and extremism. In such an interpretation, to be moderate implies only a watering down of faith or a restriction of faith to the private, seemingly inconsequential sphere of vague feeling rather than the deepest expression of one's humanity, one's engagement with sacred reality, and one's sense of urgent human mission in the world. This book calls not for a moderate, watered-down faith sanitized of passion and urgency, but instead, for a robust, self-examined, and evolving spiritual life. The studies presented in this book illustrate varied articulations of religious faith that actively welcomes self-correction and unknowing in the interest of real transcendence and that is envisioned more as a posture of trust and commitment than as an intellectual assent to creedal formulas.

Many modern thinkers have criticized religion for the damage done in its name. Any brief look at the world's history finds it riddled with religious wars or with one group's persecution or demonization of another on religious and ideological grounds. These historical events and the division and animosity that continue today between many different religious communities undeniably present enormous challenges for the increasingly interconnected contemporary world. The encounter between different religious worldviews and communities of faith is increasingly a fact of daily life. The traditional cultures of the past were shaped by a strict social order that separated different groups of people (some examples include the Hindu Indian caste system, the European feudal system, and racial segregation in the United States and elsewhere). This need to clearly define the boundaries of different groups of people extended quite naturally into religious identity as well for most of human history. However, while we strive to correct many of these strictly delineated norms of traditional societies, we have a great deal of work awaiting us still in the area of religious divisions.

By definition, religion places us in tension between the ordinary finite reality we see and experience clearly and the infinite, ultimate reality that presumably lies outside our concrete experience, between the profane and the sacred. At the interface between finite and infinite, it demands we confront directly the boundaries between what we know and what we do not know, however differently these categories have been defined. The problem with religion is not that it concerns what we cannot see or prove, as many atheist critics would argue. After all, for a religious worldview, this infinite realm is not absolutely invisible or inaccessible. Rather, it is the primary stuff of religious experience. The problem is not that religion engages what lies beyond the world as we see it, but that far too often it is hijacked by dogmatism. As we have seen throughout this book, robust religious faith actualizes the tension of what it means to be human and to confront precisely what is beyond our understanding, to struggle with Paul Knitter to ask "whether there really is a Something More."[1] As we have seen in different traditions, faith embraces quite dynamically the experience of its own uncertainty, its risk of error, and its need to open itself up for criticism and correction. Uncertainty is not the problem with religion. The dogmatic lack of nerve that tries to escape this inevitable uncertainty is the real problem that confronts us today.

As we interact with our neighbors of different religious communities, we clearly need to educate ourselves on each other's views in order to better understand the deeply meaningful beliefs of our neighbors and we need to work on cooperative efforts at increasing peace and mutual well-being among ourselves and our neighbors. We need not agree on doctrine or our collective conceptions of the sacred or the meaning and value of our ritual practices. Our ethical responsibility, which emerges from within our own respective faith traditions as well as from our humanist heritage, is to love and support our neighbors and to guard against any egotistical presumptions that we may already have all the answers. By its nature of engaging with the infinite that lies just beyond the boundaries of ordinary reality at hand, faith must remain open to uncertainty and correction. It must not hide from these challenges by erecting protective walls of dogmatic certitude around itself. These walls can certainly mollify fear, but they will ultimately only trap one inside with no room for growth or transcendence. As Paul Tillich suggests, every faith community must apply to itself the Protestant Principle, the right and responsibility of every individual to radically question and criticize institutionally deemed truths. As Jewish tradition has long held, to be God's covenant partner as Israel requires that one struggle deeply with God, wrestling relentlessly with God and, as God's partner in the world, to struggle mightily to help repair the world and restore it to God. In the nontheistic setting of Hinduism, the ultimate goal for humans is to transcend the limitations of worldly knowledge and thereby achieve freedom from these bonds to the world of suffering and change. Enlightenment requires that one see maya for what it is, a grand illusion with no substantial or independent being. As Buddhists teach, the world is characterized by emptiness, in the sense that nothing has permanent or independent substance, but instead exists only in mutual interrelationship or dependent origination. The key to ending suffering lies in transcending our attachments to things that do not last and to our misconceptions about what we can gain from them.

As we have seen, faith is not uniform, but it is a labor of love that is embodied by trust, humility, belonging, commitment, and responsibility in the world. It involves struggle and risk-taking. The work of spiritual transcendence incorporates active self-correction or self-criticism and even unlearning and skepticism as part of the work of spiritual development that is the life of faith. Far from constructing ever-higher walls of certitude around itself, a truly viable faith for the twenty-first century must balance honest realism about what Caputo calls the tragic sense of life with an idealism that is grounded in hope for what yet may be, and for what is to be brought about in the world. In his book, *God Has a Dream*, Archbishop Desmond Tutu describes the daring hope with which South Africans fought the dismal realities of apartheid.[2] He says no one would have believed it could happen—until it did. In the days of apartheid, the possibility of freedom and reconciliation looked not only improbable, but even impossible. Nevertheless, the activists saw the world as it should be; they saw justice as the truth that was "at hand" even while it was not quite realized. Their faith and hope represents Caputo's sense of the religious dimension of life—that what we see is not the whole story or the last word. There is something better and it is at hand; with God all things are possible. What does it mean to be religious or faithful? For Caputo, it means being optimistic despite the objective facts of suffering or injustice. For Mother Teresa of Calcutta, it meant waiting patiently for the spiritual darkness she experienced to release her. For Archbishop Tutu as for Moltmann, it means having faith in God's faithfulness to every person, seeing justice as something that is already at hand and discerning our role in bringing about the just transfiguration of the world.

Today the polarization between religious fundamentalism and dogmatic atheism is entirely unhelpful and misguided. Instead of dwelling on this polarized climate and retreating into the security of such dogmatic certitudes, we face ever-growing opportunities to dwell in the uncomfortable space of uncertainty and to learn from others what we do not know or see because of our respective complacency.[3] This requires stances of faith that embrace the value of different religious and humanist communities around us and that use their resources to struggle directly with the experience of uncertainty and seek to act faithfully and hopefully in the world today without retreating into the false and lazy security of certitudes. What we find in our religious and humanist traditions is in fact an active rejection of dogmatism in favor of a higher transcendence possible through unlearning or self-correction. It is my very humble yet ambitious hope that the illustrations given in this book begin to connect these vibrant traditions in a contemporary proposal of faith, doubt, and hope that is committed to dynamically inhabiting the all too human place of uncertainty.

NOTES

Introduction: Beyond Fundamentalism
and Atheism

1. Paul Knitter, *Without Buddha I Could Not Be a Christian* (Oxford: One World, 2009), 121.

2. Knitter, *Without Buddha I Could Not Be a Christian*, 121.

3. The New Atheists are a group of contemporary writers who have heavily criticized religion on the threefold basis that it is irrational, unnecessary, and harmful. The label is derived from journalistic treatment of their books. While their arguments are not new, their media impact in generating public controversy is significant.

4. Richard Dawkins, *The God Delusion* (Boston: Houghton Mifflin, 2006).

5. Homepage of Hitchens's website, accessed September 22, 2011, www.dailyhitchens .com.

6. Creationists seeking to influence science education have resorted to raising doubts about the supposedly unquestionable status of the scientific theory of evolution. They argue that evolution is "just" a theory, not fact. They intentionally mislead people about the scientific treatment of fact, theory, and law, all with the intent to convince religious people that they or their beliefs are under attack by nonbelievers using scientific classrooms to indoctrinate children into their own "unfounded opinions." Scientists argue that evolution itself is a fact that has been observed; the theory of evolution by natural selection is a reasoned explanation, not a guess or a hypothesis, of how such change happens; and the theory of evolution is just that, a theory that can be revised with further investigation, and not a dogmatic scientific law, as the creationists attacking it would imply.

7. James P. Carse, *The Religious Case Against Belief* (New York: Penguin, 2008).

8. John Caputo, *On Religion* (London: Routledge, 2001).

9. Brian Kolodiejchuk, ed., *Mother Teresa: Come Be My Light* (New York: Doubleday, 2007).

10. Mother Teresa's letter in Kolodiejchuk, *Mother Teresa*, 210.

11. Mother Teresa's letter in Kolodiejchuk, *Mother Teresa*, 187.

12. Kolodiejchuk, *Mother Teresa*, 195.

13. Letter from Father Neuner reproduced in Kolodiejchuk, *Mother Teresa*, 216.

14. The character of ultimacy in faith is most explicitly developed in Paul Tillich's description of ultimate concern, discussed in detail in chapter 3.

CHAPTER 1. POSTURES OF TRUST

1. Mystical customs are found in all the world's religious traditions. Because of the commonly used techniques of meditation and repetitive prayer, the mystical, or contemplative, paths of different religious traditions often look very similar in their expressions of the search for and experience of unity with the divine. Nevertheless, under closer study, Islamic mysticism expresses a direct Muslim experience of union with God, while Jewish mysticism expresses a direct Jewish experience of union with God, and so on.

2. Bonaventure, *The Journey of the Mind to God*, ed. Stephen F. Brown, trans. Philotheus Boehner (Indianapolis: Hackett, 1993), 5.

3. St. Teresa of Avila, *Interior Castle*, trans. and ed. E. Allison Peers (New York: Image, 1989), 63.

4. St. Teresa of Avila, *Interior Castle*, 65.

5. St. Teresa of Avila, *Interior Castle*, 106.

6. Carol Slade, "Saint Teresa's 'Meditaciones Sobre Los Cantares': The Hermeneutics of Humility and Enjoyment," *Religion and Literature* 18 (1986): 27–44.

7. Slade, "Saint Teresa's 'Meditaciones,'" 31.

8. Julian of Norwich, *Showings*. trans. and ed. Edmund Colledge and James Walsh (New York: Paulist, 1978), 301.

9. Julian of Norwich, *Showings*, 333.

10. See chapter 2 for a full discussion of C. S. Lewis and his theological treatment of good works or moral efforts.

11. For a survey of Islam in historical development as well as its theological, ritual, and mystical traditions, see Frederick Mathewson Denny, *An Introduction to Islam*, 3rd ed. (Upper Saddle River, NJ: Pearson Prentice Hall, 2006).

12. For a helpful discussion of the ways in which oneness and manyness are used in Hinduism and Christianity to articulate divine transcendence and immanence, see Diana Eck, *Encountering God: A Spiritual Journey from Bozeman to Banaras* (Boston: Beacon, 1993).

13. While Islamic theology proclaims God's absolute uniqueness, Sufi mystical poetry proliferates in metaphors that liken the relationship between God and the faithful to that between lovers who thirst for each other, reflecting at least in part the sense in which Sufism represents a higher-order, esoteric spiritual training that must be done with the guidance of spiritual teachers.

14. Musician Joan Osbourne's 1995 song, "One of Us," asks reflectively, "What if God was one of us?" The song lyrics raise the question of how we might relate to

God if, for example, God were "a slob just like one of us," or "a stranger on the bus trying to make his way home." The lyrics also ask what God's face might look like and what it might mean to see God and how this might be related to believing in the Christian creeds. Whereas in the Christian tradition, these can be good theological questions, in the Islamic tradition, God's uniqueness is emphasized.

15. Shi'a Muslims often combine some of these five prayers into three, by performing two consecutively.

16. In many cultures today, men and women are separated during prayer, with the women grouped to the right or to the rear of the men, but this segregation is a matter of interpretation and custom by different communities and is rejected by many in favor of an integrated prayer service.

17. Friedrich Schleiermacher, *On Religion: Speeches to Its Cultured Despisers*, trans. Richard Crouter (Cambridge: Cambridge University Press, 1988), 102.

18. Schleiermacher, *On Religion*, 109.

19. Andrew Dole, "Schleiermacher and Otto on Religion," *Religious Studies* 40 (2004): 398–99. Dole argues in this article against the interpretation of Rudolf Otto as the intellectual descendant of Schleiermacher because of Schleiermacher's resistance to any supernatural origin of religious feeling of absolute dependence and Otto's insistence that the religious feeling humans experience is the result of an encounter with the numinous sacred reality.

20. Friedrich Schleiermacher, *The Christian Faith*, ed. H. R. Mackintosh and J. S. Stewart (Edinburgh: T&T Clark, 1989), 17.

21. Schleiermacher, *The Christian Faith*, 16.

22. Schleiermacher, *The Christian Faith*, 170–71.

23. Schleiermacher, *On Religion*, 221.

24. Schleiermacher, *On Religion*, 222.

25. Georg Behrens contests the uniform translation of Schleiermacher's description of Christian religion as the feeling of absolute dependence, and retrieves the grammatical form translated as an absolute feeling of dependence. According to Behrens, Schleiermacher is arguing for the uniqueness of such a feeling and using the absolute feeling of dependence to found the existence of God. Religious experience, or relation to God, is absolutely and qualitatively different from all other feelings of dependence. Others contest such a translation, however, and point to Schleiermacher's use of both grammatical forms and his reluctance to suggest that religious experience originates in God. See Georg Behrens, "Feeling of Absolute Dependence or Absolute Feeling of Dependence? (What Schleiermacher Really Said and Why It Matters)," *Religious Studies* 34 (1998): 471–81.

26. Puja is a ritual part of the theistic devotional traditions of Hinduism. Whereas mystical texts like the Upanishads see Brahman as a nonpersonal Absolute Reality, the theistic traditions see the many gods and goddesses as emanations of the one Brahman, or representations of what cannot be represented adequately. One way of expressing this dichotomy is through the concepts *Nirguna Brahman* (Brahman without attributes) and *Saguna Brahman* (Brahman with attributes). The many deities

may be seen as part of the Saguna tradition of describing the Absolute in rich and dynamic depictions of personality.

27. Vijay Nath, "From 'Brahmanism' to 'Hinduism': Negotiating the Myth of the Great Tradition," *Social Scientist* 29 (2001): 29. Nath connects the expanding role of the Puranas (Hindu scriptures that narrate a vast Hindu mythology) and watershed economic and political changes to explain the development of medieval Hinduism. For example, because of land grants, the orthodox Brahmins came into much closer contact with tribal peoples and folk religion; as they adopted a more lenient stance toward these religious practices, they began to attach greater efficacy and spiritual merit to those ritual performances that required group participation, like bathing in holy rivers, temple pujas, processions, and listening to the recital of Puranic tales. The result was a narrowing gap between Vedic orthodoxy and diverse folk tales and the emergence of pujas that could and should be practiced with devotion by anyone who desired divine blessings.

28. In the Hindu Trimurti, the three faces of the divine are seen in the deities Brahma (Creator), Vishnu (Preserver), and Shiva (Destroyer). Vishnu, as the preserver of the world, becomes incarnate in the world according to the doctrine of *Dasavatara*, or Ten Avatars. The need for intervention by a personally caring deity is expressed in Vishnu worship in particular, hence the worship of Vishnu or his avatars or his consorts in pujas that accompany major life transitions as well as the everyday pujas that seek to ensure household harmony.

29. Gudrun Bühnemann calls the Satyanarayana puja one of several "trendy pujas" that have only tenuous connections with earlier Hindu rites. See Gudrun Bühnemann, *Puja: A Study in Smarta Ritual*, Publications of the de Nobili Research Library, 15 (Vienna: Institut für Indologie, Universität Wien, 1988).

30. Perhaps this explains the curious and amusing situation where, to the continual consternation of the more devout who plan and perform elaborate pujas at home or at the temple, so many less devout Hindus still manage to arrive late to the temple, just in time to take prasad and derive the benefits of the puja performed by others.

31. The classic articulation of this idea in modern religious thought can be traced to Ludwig Feuerbach's 1841 publication of *The Essence of Christianity*. Feuerbach suggested that our ideas of God emerge from our cultural ideas of what we value most in ourselves and our exaggeration of such desirable qualities as goodness, power, and knowledge to infinite status and divine distance. See Ludwig Feuerbach, *The Essence of Christianity*, trans. George Eliot (New York: Harper, 1957).

CHAPTER 2. WHAT IS OUR SACRED RESPONSIBILITY IN THE WORLD?

1. Lewis was a prominent Christian apologist. Because of his continuing influence in contemporary Christian circles, I have chosen to address elements of his treatment of faith and works and his allegorical fiction of Narnia with the other narrative traditions of sacred responsibility discussed in this chapter. His allegorical

treatment of Christian responsibility provides a helpful but apologetic comparison with the more traditional and narrative treatments of dharma, khalifa, and tikkun olam insofar as each represents an ethical responsibility premised on faith.

2. Bernard Jackson, "From *Dharma* to Law," in *Between Jerusalem and Benares: Comparative Studies in Judaism and Hinduism*, ed. Hananya Goodman (Albany: State University of New York Press, 1994), 184.

3. *Laws of Manu* 2:12.

4. J. A. B. van Buitenen, "Dharma and Moksha," *Philosophy East and West* 7 (1957): 37–38. Van Buitenen notes ambivalence in ancient Brahmanic Hinduism between the goals of dharma and moksha, by which one follows dharma for the good of society but abandons dharma and pursues moksha for the good of the soul. The pursuit of moksha as a turning away from the good life here and now will be considered in chapter 4, which identifies ambiguities of faith and self-correction as part of the work of spiritual transcendence.

5. Arti Dhand, "The Dharma of Ethics, the Ethics of Dharma: Quizzing the Ideals of Hinduism," *Journal of Religious Ethics* 30 (2002): 353.

6. Austin Creel, "The Reexamination of 'Dharma' in Hindu Ethics," *Philosophy East and West* 25 (1975): 165.

7. Ramesh Menon, trans., *The Ramayana* (New York: North Point, 2001).

8. Dhand, "The Dharma of Ethics, the Ethics of Dharma," 354.

9. David Shulman, "Toward a Historical Poetics of the Sanskrit Epics," in *The Wisdom of Poets: Studies in Tamil, Telugu, and Sanskrit* (New Delhi: Oxford University Press, 2001), 21–39.

10. Shubha Pathak, "Why Do Displaced Kings Become Poets in the Sanskrit Epics? Modeling Dharma in the Affirmative 'Ramayana' and the Interrogative 'Mahabharata,'" *International Journal of Hindu Studies* 10 (2006): 141–44.

11. Gurcharan Das, *The Difficulty of Being Good: On the Subtle Art of Dharma* (New Delhi: Allen Lane by Penguin, 2009).

12. This is an area of Hindu ethics and theology that has been heavily criticized. The rules of dharma and karma help justify the status quo by teaching that everyone is currently reaping the fruits of their own actions of previous births. The common question of why bad things happen for no apparent reason is bypassed because the teaching of karma explains that there always is a reason located in the past. In this sense, it is a perfect theodicy, or rational explanation of God's ways or of the existence of evil and suffering. However, the nontheistic operation of Hindu karma explains not why God per se allows evil and suffering but why people suffer, seemingly without reason. Accepting the inequality around us as indeed justified and acting dutifully in our current life is the only legitimate way to improve our standing in future births. The doctrines of karma and dharma justify current inequalities as indeed fair, and therefore can lead to social complacency by promising future reward for one's current patient suffering. Of course, by the teachings of dharma and karma, those who are more fortunate are explicitly obligated to care for others, whatever the rational justification for their suffering.

13. Creel, "The Reexamination of 'Dharma' in Hindu Ethics," 163.

14. Arvind Sharma, "Karma and Dharma: New Links in an Old Chain," *Tikkun* 23 (2008): 14–15.

15. C. S. Lewis, *The Lion, the Witch, and the Wardrobe*, in *The Chronicles of Narnia* (New York: HarperCollins, 1994). See also the movie *The Chronicles of Narnia: The Lion, the Witch, and the Wardrobe*, released 2005.

16. It is a particularly dismal sort of winter that goes on endlessly, without even the treat of Christmas to look forward to. The historic dating of Christmas to coincide with the winter solstice was quite intentional and meaningful, both traditionally and mythically. The winter solstice marks the end of one year and the beginning of a new year, marked by the beginning of the earth's orbit around the sun. As such, it also marks the midpoint in winter. Up to that point, the days have grown shorter and shorter, and after that point, the days will become progressively longer. Therefore, this fictional depiction of a winter without a Christmas represents the continuation of cold and short days with no end in sight, with no trace of renewal or new life. Theologically, it represents a world without the advent of Jesus' birth, without God's promise to repair and transform this dark world.

17. *The Chronicles of Narnia*, movie.

18. This was Barth's playful but telling answer when he was asked during his one and only visit to the United States in 1962 to summarize his systematic theology.

19. Robin W. Lovin, *Christian Ethics: An Essential Guide* (Nashville: Abingdon, 2000), 12.

20. C. S. Lewis. *Mere Christianity* (San Francisco: HarperCollins, 1952), 142.

21. Lewis, *Mere Christianity*, 142–43.

22. Lewis, *Mere Christianity*, 143.

23. Lewis, *Mere Christianity*, 131.

24. Lewis, *Mere Christianity*, 147–48.

25. Abdulaziz Sachedina, "Human Viceregency: A Blessing or a Curse? The Challenge to Be God's Caliph in the Qur'an," in *Humanity Before God: Contemporary Faces of Jewish, Christian, and Islamic Ethics*, ed. William Schweiker, Michael A. Johnson, and Kevin Jung (Minneapolis: Fortress, 2006), 36–38.

26. James Fadiman and Robert Frager, eds., *Essential Sufism* (New York: Harper, 1997), 203.

27. Ijtihad was formally closed in the eleventh century as Sunni legal scholars (*ulama*) worked to systematize the tools of jurisprudence and further limit the authority of individual interpretations that might be subject to whim or self-interest. Many reformers today call for the reopening of ijtihad to allow for more independent and original interpretations that seek to adapt to today's changing circumstances. Ijtihad was never considered closed for Shi'a Muslims, and there traditionally has remained wide-ranging latitude for the independent interpretations of individual legal experts in the Shi'a tradition.

28. Some fundamentalist Muslims today insist that Shari'ah law requires some very particular behaviors that are clearly and explicitly laid out in the Qur'an and Hadith,

even though all behaviors beyond the five ritual obligations require interpretations of the central sources for Islamic religious law. Today, a matter that receives an enormous amount of attention inside and outside the Muslim community is the question of whether women are required, according to God's revelations in the Qur'an, to cover their hair, face, or body. Interpretations vary widely, and this is an incredibly controversial issue, as Muslim legal experts differ on whether the Qur'anic injunction on modesty should be interpreted to mean that a woman should practice restraint, refrain from flaunting her body, cover her bosom, cover her entire body, cover her hair, or cover her face and entire body. Interpretations vary also on whether the injunction on modesty applies equally to men and women. *Hijab* (veiling for modesty) is just one controversial issue that speaks to the extensive role of interpretation in Islamic law.

29. This theological insight of human vulnerability to corruption reflects a concern similar to that articulated in the Christian doctrine of original sin and the Augustinian reflection that the earthly church is a body of sinners, not a communion of saints, in direct criticism of the fourth-century Donatist controversy that tried to equate church membership with holiness. Augustine emphasized that holiness belonged to Christ, not to the church, and to assume some sort of perfect holiness or sinlessness as the basis for continued church membership was to forget the need for Christ in the first place. Whereas a Christian response has been to reinforce human dependence on God's grace and encourage repentance, a Muslim response has been to reinforce the need for continual repentance and vigilant striving to overcome the lower inclinations of the self.

30. Paul L. Heck, "'Jihad' Revisited," *Journal of Religious Ethics* 32 (2004): 95–128.

31. Heck, "'Jihad' Revisited," 99. Heck cites Qur'an 12:53 here.

32. Heck, "'Jihad' Revisited," 108.

33. Eugene B. Borowitz, "Renewing the Covenant: A Theology for the Postmodern Jew," *Jewish Publication Society* (1996): 30.

34. Nicholas Wade, "The Evolution of the God Gene," *New York Times* article online, November 14, 2009. www.nytimes.com/2009/11/15/weekinreview/12wade.html.

35. Gordon Freeman cites Lewis Hyde's discussion of this larger component in covenant as an exchange of gifts. See Gordon M. Freeman, "The Process of Covenant," *Publius* 10 (1980): 71.

36. David Hartman, *A Living Covenant* (New York: Free Press, 1985), 55.

37. Gilbert S. Rosenthal, "*Tikkun ha-Olam*: The Metamorphosis of a Concept," *Journal of Religion* 85 (2005).

38. Because so many of the original 613 mitzvot concerned ritual performance in the life of the temple, which was destroyed in 70 C.E., only about half of them are even applicable today.

39. Martin Buber, "Jewish Religiosity," in *On Judaism*, ed. Nahum N. Glatzer (New York: Schocken, 1967), 86.

40. Martin Buber, "The Silent Question," in *On Judaism*, ed. Nahum N. Glatzer (New York: Schocken, 1967), 209.

41. Buber, "Jewish Religiosity," 85.

42. This arrival of the Messiah is expected by some Jewish communities as an actual person, and by other communities as an impersonal divine act of redemption and restoration.

43. Robert McAfee Brown, introduction to Elie Wiesel's *The Trial of God*, trans. Marion Wiesel (New York: Schocken, 1995), vii.

44. For a discussion of the Book of Job and its legal claims, see Robert Sutherland, *Putting God on Trial: The Biblical Book of Job* (Victoria: Trafford, 2004).

45. *The Book of Job*, trans. Raymond P. Scheindlin (New York: W. W. Norton, 1998), 37:24–25 and 38:1.

CHAPTER 3. CHRISTIAN FAITH
AND THE PROTESTANT PRINCIPLE

1. John Calvin said that the human heart and mind are a veritable factory of idols. Humanity inevitably attempts to refashion God's revelation into something that is humanly imagined.

2. Kierkegaard's view of faith targets many prominent nineteenth-century philosophies. For example, he criticizes G. W. F. Hegel's emphasis on the cosmic dimension of Spirit and focuses instead on the individual alone in her relation to God; he criticizes Hegel's sense that philosophy and religion have the same content, that knowledge is superior to faith as spiritual consciousness. Kierkegaard instead suggests that faith is not a primitive or imperfect knowledge at all, but is an active relation to a truth and a decision on how to relate to that truth. Against Immanuel Kant's rehabilitation of religion and Christianity on the basis of the practical reason of morality, Kierkegaard disputes the pragmatic nature of faith altogether.

3. Søren Kierkegaard, *Fear and Trembling*, trans. Alastair Hannay (London: Penguin, 1985), 51.

4. Kierkegaard, *Fear and Trembling*, 52.

5. Kierkegaard, *Fear and Trembling*, 65.

6. Kevin Hoffman, "Facing Threats to Earthly Felicity: A Reading of Kierkegaaard's 'Fear and Trembling,'" *Journal of Religious Ethics* 34 (2006): 444.

7. Søren Kierkegaard, *Philosophical Fragments*, ed. and trans. Howard V. Hong and Edna H. Hong (Princeton: Princeton University Press, 1985), 62–64.

8. Søren Kierkegaard, *Concluding Unscientific Postscript to "Philosophical Fragments,"* vol. I., ed. and trans. Howard V. Hong and Edna H. Hong (Princeton: Princeton University Press, 1992), 210.

9. See David Wisdo, "Kierkegaard on Belief, Faith, and Explanation," *International Journal for Philosophy of Religion* 21 (1987): 95–114, and Louis P. Pojman, "Kierkegaard on Faith and Freedom," *International Journal for Philosophy of Religion* 27 (1990): 41–61.

10. C. S. Evans, "Is Kierkegaard an Irrationalist? Reason, Paradox, and Faith," *Religious Studies* 25 (1989): 352.

11. Evans, "Is Kierkegaard an Irrationalist?" 354.

12. Steven M. Emmanuel, "Kierkegaard's Pragmatist Faith," *Philosophy and Phenomenological Research* 51 (1991): 279–302.

13. Evans, "Is Kierkegaard an Irrationalist?" 361.

14. 1 Corinthians 13:12.

15. Kierkegaard, *Concluding Unscientific Postscript*, 204.

16. Matthew Gerhard Jacoby, "Kierkegaard on Truth," *Religious Studies* 38 (2002): 29.

17. Kierkegaard, *Concluding Unscientific Postscript*, 204.

18. Kristen K. Deede, "The Infinite Qualitative Distinction: Sin, the Self, and Revelation in the Thought of Søren Kierkegaard," *International Journal for Philosophy of Religion* 53 (2003): 35.

19. Søren Kierkegaard, *The Sickness Unto Death*, ed. and trans. Howard V. Hong and Edna H. Hong (Princeton: Princeton University Press, 1983).

20. Sylvia Walsh, *Living Christianly: Kierkegaard's Dialectic of Christian Existence* (University Park: Pennsylvania State University Press, 2005), 31.

21. Kierkegaard, *The Sickness Unto Death*, 85.

22. Pojman, "Kierkegaard on Faith and Freedom," 44.

23. Emmanuel, "Kierkegaard's Pragmatist Faith," 300–301.

24. Kierkegaard, *Fear and Trembling*, 129.

25. Kierkegaard, *Fear and Trembling*, 129.

26. Most of us responsible adults do not like to remain in anyone's debt, especially in the debt of someone very close to us. We grow resentful of them and despise them for our experience of being beholden to them. It takes great emotional maturity to graciously accept a gift from another with true gratitude, without despising that person for it. The greater the gift, the greater the temptation to despise the giver and the greater the challenge to accept the gift wholeheartedly. For example, the greatest emotional challenges often seem to lie in the survival or rescue after immense tragedy. It is difficult to accept this gift without despising oneself and God or fate or witnesses to the gift.

27. Amy Laura Hall, "Self-Deception, Confusion, and Salvation in 'Fear and Trembling' with 'Works of Love,'" *Journal of Religious Ethics* 28 (2000): 56.

28. Hall, "Self-Deception, Confusion, and Salvation," 58.

29. People often too easily conflate morality and religious faith or obedience. Christianity, like Judaism and Islam, does link the two together through an ethical monotheism, by which the God of these traditions is believed to have particular preferences for human behavior, including morality. God is seen as the definer of the good in these monotheistic traditions. However, Kierkegaard exposes a problem in any simplistic conflation of the two. If we consider morality to be what we in a human community consider good and right (even if this definition is initially given us by God), then many biblical acts of religious obedience must be considered immoral. Abraham's actions of near-sacrifice must be judged immoral by any community. There may not be very many universally agreed-upon norms of moral behavior,

but we generally concur that it is wrong to kill another, and it is most reprehensible and disgusting for a father to kill his own child. The only way it has been judged acceptable is as an act of sacrifice or religious obedience. It may be religious obedience or sacrifice, but it must be judged immoral.

30. Hall, "Self-Deception, Confusion, and Salvation," 58.

31. Karl Barth, *The Humanity of God* (Atlanta: John Knox, 1960), 56.

32. Barth, *The Humanity of God*, 49.

33. Barth, *The Humanity of God*, 47.

34. Barth, *The Humanity of God*, 51.

35. Merold Westphal, *Transcendence and Self-Transcendence: On God and the Soul* (Indianapolis: Indiana University Press, 2004)

36. Ludwig Feuerbach, *The Essence of Christianity*, trans. George Eliot (New York: Harper, 1957).

37. John Glasse, "Barth on Feuerbach," *Harvard Theological Review* 57 (1964): 69–96.

38. *Karl Barth: Theologian of Freedom*, ed. Clifford Green (Minneapolis: Fortress, 1989), 118.

39. *Karl Barth*, 118.

40. Garrett Green, "The Hermeneutics of Difference: Barth and Derrida on Words and the Word," in *Postmodern Philosophy and Christian Thought*, ed. Merold Westphal (Bloomington: Indiana University Press, 1999), 93.

41. Green, "The Hermeneutics of Difference," 95–96. Green is echoing Barth's statement in *Church Dogmatics*, section 17, that no religion is true, but a religion can become true as a matter of grace.

42. Ingolf U. Dalferth, "Karl Barth's Eschatological Realism," in *Karl Barth: Centenary Essays*, ed. S. W. Sykes (Cambridge: Cambridge University Press, 1989), 23.

43. Dalferth, "Karl Barth's Eschatological Realism," 34.

44. Jesse Couenhoven, "Law and Gospel, or the Law of the Gospel? Karl Barth's Political Theology Compared with Luther and Calvin," *Journal of Religious Ethics* 30 (2002): 193–94.

45. Couenhoven, "Law and Gospel," 195.

46. *Karl Barth*, 100.

47. *Karl Barth*, 101.

48. S. W. Sykes, "Authority and Openness in the Church," in *Karl Barth: Centenary Essays*, ed. S. W. Sykes (Cambridge: Cambridge University Press, 1989), 82.

49. *Karl Barth*, 101.

50. Sykes, "Authority and Openness in the Church," 82.

51. *Karl Barth*, 105.

52. *Karl Barth*, 107.

53. *Karl Barth*, 108.

54. This is what we see in the marriage of the Christian conservative circles with the Republican Party. Suddenly, the claim seems to go, there is only one party that believes in God and the Jesus of the Gospels, the right to own guns, family values,

reduced or no taxation at all on investment income, and a strong deterrent military presence around the world, as if these disparate values were somehow part of a divinely ordered system. There are legitimate political values in this list—what is troubling is the automatic assumption that these go together as the only kind of faithful or religious vision of American and Christian citizenship.

55. Paul Tillich, "What Is Wrong with the 'Dialectic' Theology?" *Journal of Religion* 15 (1935): 138.

56. Tillich, "What Is Wrong with the 'Dialectic' Theology?" 142.

57. Robert P. Scharlemann, "The No to Nothing and the Nothing to Know: Barth and Tillich and the Possibility of Theological Science," *Journal of the American Academy of Religion* 55 (1987): 61.

58. Paul Tillich, *Systematic Theology: Three Volumes in One* (Chicago: University of Chicago Press, 1967), vol. 3, 245.

59. Tillich, *Systematic Theology*, vol. 2, 49–51.

60. Tillich, *Systematic Theology*, vol. 3, 224.

61. Tillich, *Systematic Theology*, vol. 3, 224.

62. Tillich, *Systematic Theology*, vol. 3, 207.

63. Paul Tillich, *Dynamics of Faith* (New York: HarperCollins, 2001), 12–34.

64. Tillich, *Dynamics of Faith*, 13.

65. Dirk-Martin Grube, "A Critical Reconstruction of Paul Tillich's Epistemology," *Religious Studies* 33 (1997): 68.

66. John P. Dourley, "Jacob Boehme and Paul Tillich on Trinity and God: Similarities and Differences," *Religious Studies* 31 (1995): 431.

67. Tillich, *Systematic Theology*, vol. 1, 111.

68. Tillich, *Systematic Theology*, vol. 1, 109.

69. Tillich, *Dynamics of Faith*, 15.

70. A former student expressed the danger inherent in our assumptions about revelation as follows: "The most dangerous person is the one who believes God is talking to him, and turns out to be wrong!"

71. Tillich, *Dynamics of Faith*, 18–19.

72. Tillich, *Dynamics of Faith*, 21.

73. 1 Corinthians 13:12.

74. Tillich, *Dynamics of Faith*, 23.

75. John J. Thatanamil, *The Immanent Divine: God, Creation, and the Human Predicament. An East-West Conversation* (Minneapolis: Fortress, 2006), 99.

76. Paul Tillich, *The Essential Tillich*, ed. F. Forrester Church (Chicago: University of Chicago Press, 1987), 4.

77. Tillich, *Systematic Theology*, vol. 1, 205.

78. Tillich defines religion and faith as the state of being ultimately concerned. While people may have any finite thing as their ultimate concern, including wealth, fame, or love, it is only the true infinite, the true sacred, or God that can satisfy this ultimate concern.

79. Tillich, *Dynamics of Faith*, 47–50.

80. Tillich, *Dynamics of Faith*, 48.

81. Tillich, *Dynamics of Faith*, 51.

82. Lewis S. Ford, "The Three Strands of Tillich's Theory of Religious Symbols," *Journal of Religion* 46 (1966): 104–30.

83. Tillich, *The Essential Tillich*, 70.

84. Tillich, *The Essential Tillich*, 71.

85. Tillich, *Systematic Theology*, vol. 3, 245.

86. Tillich, *Systematic Theology*, vol. 3, 207–8.

CHAPTER 4. FAITH AND TRANSCENDENCE IN HINDU TRADITIONS

1. The label "Hinduism" originated as a religious and geographical designation—first by seventh-century Muslim invaders to designate the religion of the people settled around the Indus River Valley and later by the British who used "Hindu" as a catch-all census category to designate virtually all Indians who were not Muslim, Christian, Sikh, or Buddhist. Although scholars of religion often designate specific traditions, beliefs, and orthodoxies like Vaishnavism, Shaivism, and Shaktism for the sake of nuance and accuracy, these three "traditions" and others within the broader family of "Hinduism" or "Hinduisms" have influenced each other so much and are so commonly combined in much (not all) lived religiosity that denoting the particular designations at times may impose a sense of distinct boundaries that is not entirely accurate or helpful. Therefore, there is a case for using the more broad term "Hinduism" despite its problems.

2. For a comprehensive introduction to Hinduism, see Gavin Flood, *An Intro-duction to Hinduism* (Cambridge: Cambridge University Press, 1996), and Klaus Klostermaier, *A Survey of Hinduism* (Albany: State University of New York Press, 1994). For a discussion of the orthodox and heterodox philosophical movements in the Hindu family of thought, see *A Sourcebook in Indian Philosophy*, ed. Sarvepalli Radhakrishnan and Charles A. Moore (Princeton: Princeton University Press, 1957). For a discussion of the ritual practices and vernacular narratives of Hinduism, see *Religions of India in Practice*, ed. Donald S. Lopez Jr. (Princeton: Princeton University Press, 1995), and Alain Danielou, *The Myths and Gods of India* (Rochester: Inner Traditions, 1985).

3. Wendy Doniger O'Flaherty, *Siva: The Erotic Ascetic* (Oxford: Oxford University Press, 1981), 316.

4. Historians and scholars have noted a transformation in orthodox Hinduism that occurred between 800 B.C.E. and 200 B.C.E.. Karl Jaspers called this the Axial Age because simultaneously around the world, religious beliefs and practices were changing radically, shifting from an external sacrificial worship to an internal sacrifice modeled by morality and piety. In India, this shift from Brahmanic Hinduism (in which the primary form of worship was a fire sacrifice presided over by trained priests or Brahmins, with the goal of achieving or maintaining personal, social, or cosmic harmony

and order) to the speculative philosophy of the Upanishads (looking inward to better understand the nature of reality and the self) and the disciplines of karma and bhakti yoga (which focus on selfless action and devotion as the primary avenues to spiritual freedom) coincides with the growing prominence of Buddhism and Jainism. Although Jainism had ancient indigenous origins, probably predating the Vedas, the teachings of both its greatest teacher Mahavira and Siddhartha Gautama, the Buddha, grew particularly prominent after the fifth century B.C.E. and posed a serious challenge to the hierarchical authority of sacrificial Brahmanism. What ultimately developed into orthodox medieval Hinduism represents an evolution influenced in large part by the confrontation of these different strands of Indian religion.

5. In the Hindu view, the Vedas were not revealed by a god; instead, they contain the eternal wisdom accumulated from previous cycles of creation and heard at the beginning of the current cycle. While very different from the Western, monotheistic notion of revelation, what is asserted in the Vedas' status as shruti is that they are not considered by traditionalist Hindus to be of human composition and therefore are given ultimate authority.

6. The heroes of the *Ramayana* and the *Bhagavad Gita*, Rama and Krishna, respectively, are considered avatars of Vishnu, and help shape the immensely popular devotional traditions of Vaishnavism.

7. See Madeleine Biardeau, *Hinduism: The Anthropology of a Civilization* (Delhi: Oxford University Press, 1989).

8. Many modern Hindus commonly emphasize the immense value of inclusivism and tolerance that are supposedly inherent in Hindu tradition. While inclusivist positions purport to see greater value in competing traditions than do the exclusivist positions that insist that one's own tradition is alone true and salvific, Hindu inclusivism, like its counterpart in late twentieth-century Roman Catholicism, can be an imperialistic posture in its own right, as it does claim to contain the greatest possible truth of all the religious traditions or to better understand and express the truth that is only implicitly available in other traditions.

In addition, the claim of tolerance can be traced to a modern Hindu apologetics, by which Hindu thinkers from the late nineteenth century on attempt to defend and support Hindu tradition to a predominantly modern Western audience that values equality, freedom, monotheism, reason, and enlightenment. The result is a skewed modernist emphasis by Western-educated Hindus on precisely those values that Westerners would identify with. The cultural importance of other ideas like caste and the land of India itself as the exclusive place for Enlightenment or liberation, for example, sometimes receive diminished or no attention at all, or they are dismissed simply as part of the older, more primitive society that has supposedly been transcended by today's enlightened Hindu society. In that respect, modern Hindu self-identity may be vulnerable to the same Enlightenment prejudices that plague Western Christian assumptions of having transcended the older, medieval problems of inequality and superstition for a more moral, more rational, and more tolerant religious ethic.

9. Joël A. Dubois, "Each in Its Proper Place: Shankara's Approach to Diversity in Upanisadic Insight Texts," *International Journal of Hindu Studies* 6 (2002): 275.

10. *Mundaka Upanishad* I.i.4–6. All Upanishad citations are from R. E. Hume, *The Thirteen Principal Upanishads*, 2nd ed. (London: Oxford University Press, 1931).

11. *Chandogya Upanishad* II.xxiii.1.

12. Sarvepalli Radhakrishnan and Charles Moore, eds., introduction to *A Sourcebook in Indian Philosophy* (Princeton: Princeton University Press, 1957), xxvii.

13. *Katha Upanishad* IV.2.

14. *Kena Upanishad* II.3–4.

15. *Mundaka Upanishad* III.ii.9.

16. *Maitri Upanishad* VI.7.

17. *Katha Upanishad* VI.9.

18. *Chandogya Upanishad* VI.xiii.1–3.

19. Gerald Larson, review of "The Song Celestial: Two Centuries of the 'Bhagavad Gita' in English," *Philosophy East and West* 31 (1981): 513–41.

20. Barbara Stoler Miller, trans., *The Bhagavad Gita* (New York: Bantam, 1986), 2:47.

21. Miller, *The Bhagavad Gita* 2:51.

22. Christopher G. Framarin, "Good and Bad Desires: Implications of the Dialogue between Krisna and Arjuna," *International Journal of Hindu Studies* 2 (2007): 157.

23. Miller, *The Bhagavad Gita* 9:23.

24. Miller, *The Bhagavad Gita* 9:26.

25. Miller, *The Bhagavad Gita* 9:28–29.

26. Miller, *The Bhagavad Gita* 7:21.

27. Part of this teaching of God's grace that grants unwavering faith to those who trust God influences the turn to theism in classical Hinduism.

28. Shankara is often considered the single most important medieval Hindu theologian. His commentaries on the Upanishads and the *Bhagavad Gita* are most central in articulating what comes to be a classic Hindu Advaita philosophy. Shankara is also credited by many for rehabilitating orthodox Hinduism itself in the face of the immense challenges posed by heterodox Indian movements like Buddhism and Jainism and the consequent stagnation of Brahmanic ritual tradition.

29. See Francis X. Clooney, S.J., *Theology After Vedanta: An Experiment in Comparative Theology* (Albany: State University of New York Press, 1993). Regarding the multiple layers of meaning in the Upanishads, see also Dubois, "Each in Its Proper Place."

30. The *Matsya Purana* is one of the eighteen principal Puranas. It is presented as recited by Vishnu himself, in the form of his first avatar, the fish.

31. Swami Vijñanananda, trans. *Devi Bhagavata Purana*, 3 vols. (Forgotten Books, 2008), vol. 3, book 9.

32. Hugh Nicholson, "Two Apologetic Moments in Sankara's Concept of Brahman," *Journal of Religion* 87 (2007).

33. Thatanamil, *The Immanent Divine*, 31–36.

34. The three broad categories of Hindu theism are Shaivism, Vaishnavism, and Shaktism, in which the Absolute, itself unknowable, is encountered most truly in the figure of Shiva, the various avatars of Vishnu, or in the form of the Great Goddess, respectively. Hindu traditions suggest that the ability to identify the sacred that transcends human understanding requires a relationship to an Ishtadevata, a deity taken to be one's chosen Lord. In embracing different Ishtadevatas, Hindus have articulated in practice what theologians in many traditions have said—that we cannot really ever speak definitively about God because God the Absolute is utterly beyond our ordinary knowledge and must be approached through devotion.

35. Rudolf Otto, *The Idea of the Holy* (London: Oxford University Press, 1958 [1923])

36. O'Flaherty, *Siva*, 6.

37. Wendy Doniger O'Flaherty, "Asceticism and Sexuality in the Mythology of Siva," Part I, *History of Religions* 8 (1969): 300.

38. Don Handelman and David Shulman, *God Inside Out: Siva's Game of Dice* (New York: Oxford University Press, 1997), 57–96.

39. Flood, *An Introduction to Hinduism*, 149–55.

40. Danielou, *The Myths and Gods of India*, 197.

41. Flood, *An Introduction to Hinduism*, 153.

42. O'Flaherty, "Asceticism and Sexuality in the Mythology of Siva," 307 (reference to Mahabharata XIII).

43. Handelman and Shulman, *God Inside Out*, 161.

44. The story is reprinted and discussed in Richard H. Davis, "The Origin of Linga Worship," in *Religions of India in Practice*, ed. Donald Lopez (Princeton: Princeton University Press, 1995), 637–48.

45. Danielou, *The Myths and Gods of India*, 190.

46. Richard Davis, *Ritual in an Oscillating Universe* (Princeton: Princeton University Press, 1991), 19. Davis defends the notion of taking seriously Shaiva Siddhanta as a coherent system of knowledge and practice because the textual sources present a unity of thought and action. I am indebted to Davis's detailed account of the Shaiva Siddhanta system for the following discussion.

47. Davis, *Ritual in an Oscillating Universe*, 27.

48. Davis, *Ritual in an Oscillating Universe*, 25.

49. Davis, *Ritual in an Oscillating Universe*, 29.

50. Davis, *Ritual in an Oscillating Universe*, 83.

Chapter 5. Resisting the Reification of Religion

1. Even though Sam Harris is the most contemporary figure to be discussed in this section, I discuss him first because his view presents such a straightforward introduction to the problem with dogmatism.

2. Sam Harris, *The End of Faith: Religion, Terror, and the Future of Reason* (New York: Norton, 2004).

3. Harris, *The End of Faith*, 43.

4. Sam Harris, National Public Radio's *Talk of the Nation* (originally broadcast October 2, 2006).

5. Friedrich Nietzsche, *Thus Spoke Zarathustra*, trans. R. J. Hollingdale (London: Penguin, 1961).

6. Karl Marx, "Critique of Hegel's Philosophy of Right" (1844), in *Marx on Religion*, ed. John Raines (Philadelphia: Temple University Press, 2002), 171.

7. Marx, "Critique of Hegel's Philosophy of Right," 171.

8. Marx, "Critique of Hegel's Philosophy of Right," 171–72.

9. John A. T. Robinson. *Honest to God* (Louisville: Westminster John Knox, 1963).

10. Robinson, *Honest to God*, 17.

11. Robinson, *Honest to God*, 41.

12. Robinson, *Honest to God*, 71. Verse quoted is 2 Corinthians 5:19.

13. Robinson, *Honest to God*, 74.

14. Robinson, *Honest to God*, 137.

15. Robinson, *Honest to God*, 125.

16. Robinson, *Honest to God*, 125.

17. Robinson, *Honest to God*, 126. Verse quoted is Romans 8:38.

18. *The Cloud of Unknowing and Other Works*, trans. Clifton Wolters (London: Penguin, 1961), 63.

19. *The Cloud of Unknowing*, 64.

20. *The Cloud of Unknowing*, 88.

21. *The Cloud of Unknowing*, 61–62.

22. *The Cloud of Unknowing*, 83.

23. *The Cloud of Unknowing*, 145.

24. *The Cloud of Unknowing*, 67.

25. *The Cloud of Unknowing*, 94.

26. *The Cloud of Unknowing*, 110.

27. *The Cloud of Unknowing*, 111.

28. *The Cloud of Unknowing*, 142.

29. *The Cloud of Unknowing*, 142.

30. *The Cloud of Unknowing*, 61.

31. Bernard McGinn, *The Mystical Thought of Meister Eckhart: The Man from Whom God Hid Nothing* (New York: Crossroad, 2001), 19.

32. Beverly J. Lanzetta, "Three Categories of Nothingness in Eckhart," *Journal of Religion* 72 (1991): 260.

33. Lanzetta, "Three Categories of Nothingness," 252.

34. Charlotte Radler, "Losing the Self: Detachment in Meister Eckhart and Its Significance for Buddhist-Christian Dialogue," *Buddhist-Christian Studies* 26 (2006): 111.

35. *Meister Eckhart: The Essential Sermons, Commentaries, Treatises, and Defense*, trans. Edmund Colledge and Bernard McGinn (New York: Paulist, 1981), 193.

36. *Meister Eckhart*, 180.

37. *Meister Eckhart*, 198.

38. *Meister Eckhart*, 162, 168.

39. Lanzetta, "Three Categories of Nothingness," 256.

40. *Meister Eckhart*, 183.

41. *Meister Eckhart*, 183.

42. Lanzetta, "Three Categories of Nothingness," 252.

43. *Meister Eckhart*, 184.

44. Lanzetta, "Three Categories of Nothingness," 256.

45. *Meister Eckhart*, 188.

46. *Meister Eckhart*, 187.

47. Charlene Burns, "'Soul-less' Christianity and the Buddhist Empirical Self: Buddhist-Christian Convergence," *Buddhist-Christian Studies* 23 (2003): 92.

48. David Kalupahana, *Buddhist Philosophy: A Historical Analysis* (Honolulu: University of Hawaii Press, 1976), 17–19.

49. Kalupahana, *Buddhist Philosophy*, 19.

50. D. T. Suzuki, *Zen Buddhism*, ed. William Barrett (New York: Doubleday, 1956), 137.

51. David Loy, "A Zen Cloud? Comparing Zen 'Koan' Practice with 'The Cloud of Unknowing,'" *Buddhist-Christian Studies* 9 (1989): 45.

52. Loy, "A Zen Cloud?" 51.

53. Loy, "A Zen Cloud?" 50.

54. Kalupahana, *Buddhist Philosophy*, 19.

55. While conventional Christian discourse often privileges immortality and eternal happiness in heaven, some popular thought articulates an ambivalence toward immortality; for example, the fictional subject of vampires. Vampires are depicted as condemned to immortality, unable to grow old or change or die, decade after decade, century after century. They are trapped in this frozen state. Over against such a perpetual doom to more of the same, we mortals, because of the reality of emptiness in Buddhist teaching, are able to grow and change.

56. Burns, "'Soul-less' Christianity and the Buddhist Empirical Self," 96.

57. This focus on interrelationship is not exclusive to Buddhism, of course. Different world traditions teach the multiple ways in which we are constituted and defined by our relationships; the Hindu teaching of dharma discussed earlier, the Jewish sense of covenantal responsibility, and Christian Trinitarianism all emphasize the way in which a person's identity is constituted by one's relations to others.

58. Thich Nhat Hanh, *The Heart of Understanding: Commentaries on the Prajnaparamita Heart Sutra* (Berkeley: Parallax, 1988), 7.

59. Hanh, *The Heart of Understanding*, 3.

60. Hanh, *The Heart of Understanding*, 7.

61. Alice Keefe, "Visions of Interconnectedness in Engaged Buddhism and Feminist Theology," *Buddhist-Christian Studies* 17 (1997): 64.

62. Keefe, "Visions of Interconnectedness," 66.

63. Students first studying Buddhism often focus on the question of what and where Nirvana is and how it is experienced. This is itself to miss the Buddha's lesson about learning to let go of grasping and clinging in order to free oneself from suffering.

64. Paul Williams, *Mahayana Buddhism: The Doctrinal Foundations* (London: Routledge, 1989), 62.

65. Williams, *Mahayana Buddhism*, 167.

CHAPTER 6. FAITH AND HOPE
FOR THE TWENTY-FIRST CENTURY

1. The term *postmodern* is difficult to define, but it identifies a loose set of critical practices that challenge and destabilize several assumptions of what is termed *modernity*, including epistemic certainty, historical progress, the stability of identity, objectivity, universal norms, and a univocal treatment of meaning. Postmodern thinkers do not necessarily reject modern values, but they often see themselves as clarifying the underlying roots of those values. In its critical vein, postmodernity may inject an alternating playfulness and subversion into critical philosophical and theological reflection that mirrors the project of unknowing and transcendence of ordinary understanding discussed in chapters 4 and 5.

2. Jürgen Moltmann, *In the End—The Beginning: The Life of Hope*, trans. Margaret Kohl (Minneapolis: Fortress, 2004), x.

3. Jürgen Moltmann, *The Coming of God: Christian Eschatology*, trans. Margaret Kohl (Minneapolis: Fortress, 2004), xv.

4. Moltmann, *The Coming of God*, 35.

5. See Richard Bauckam, ed., *God Will be All in All: The Eschatology of Jürgen Moltmann* (Edinburgh: T&T Clark, 1999). The contributors to this volume vary on whether there is such a radical change or continuity from Moltmann's early to later views on historical eschatological realization.

6. Wolfhart Pannenberg, "Constructive and Critical Functions of Christian Eschatology," *Harvard Theological Review* 77 (1984): 124.

7. Moltmann, *The Coming of God*, 105.

8. Moltmann, *The Coming of God*, 234.

9. Moltmann, *The Coming of God*, 29.

10. Moltmann, *In the End—The Beginning*, 41.

11. Moltmann, *In the End—The Beginning*, 47.

12. Revelation 21:5.

13. Moltmann, *The Coming of God*, 250–51.

14. Moltmann, *The Coming of God*, 251.

15. Moltmann, *The Coming of God*, 255.

16. Moltmann, *The Coming of God*, 255.

17. Moltmann, *The Coming of God*, 255.

18. Moltmann, *The Coming of God*, 234.

19. Jesus utters these words in Matthew 19:26.

20. Such beliefs in human progress, moral evolution, and universal reason were more characteristic of a nineteenth-century Enlightenment-era optimism. The late twentieth century witnessed a loss of confidence in such "objective" and universal truths, and contemporary people often express a distrust of universal judgments or expectations that we all *must* hold identical values despite our cultural differences. It is in the aftermath of such a postmodern loss of modern confidence that we discern in some contemporary discourse a nostalgic retreat to a seemingly simpler and perhaps clearer time, to the "good old days" of 1950s America, for example. When considered more clearly, however, that decade, for example, was not good for everyone, but instead presumed a security that in many ways was more a cultural construction rooted in a very white, middle-class, suburban-tinged American dream than a reflection of the actual experience of most Americans, including many of those white, middle-class, suburban Americans themselves. Contemporary culture is far more likely to discern the very real differences among us.

21. Joy Ann McDougall, "The Return of Trinitarian Praxis? Moltmann on the Trinity and Christian Life," *Journal of Religion* 83 (2003): 177–203.

22. Moltmann, *The Coming of God*, 234.

23. In the *Bhagavad Gita*, when Krishna urges Arjuna into battle, he does not deny that it will result in death for many. However, cosmic order and justice demand it, and Krishna teaches not only rebirth but a way to free oneself even through concrete worldly action. What Moltmann is suggesting is not the same thing, however. While the *Bhagavad Gita* teaches a means to enlightenment and freedom, it does not share the Christian sense of linear time and Christian hope as forward-thinking. Both suggest a transcendent form of justice, but Christian hope sees it as an advent to be realized historically.

24. Moltmann, *The Coming of God*, 65.

25. Moltmann, *The Coming of God*, 235.

26. Senator John McCain repeatedly made bold promises to follow Osama bin Laden to the gates of hell during his 2008 presidential campaign.

27. Frank Podgorski, "The Cosmotheandric Intuition: The Contemplative Catalyst of Raimon Panikkar," in *The Intercultural Challenge of Raimon Panikkar*, ed. Joseph Prabhu (New York: Orbis, 1996), 107.

28. Raimon Panikkar, "A Self-Critical Dialogue," in *The Intercultural Challenge of Raimon Panikkar*, ed. Joseph Prabhu (New York: Orbis, 1996), 238.

29. Raimundo Panikkar, *The Unknown Christ of Hinduism: Towards an Ecumenical Christophany* (New York: Orbis, 1981), 23.

30. Paul Williams, "Some Dimensions of the Recent Work of Raimundo Panikkar: A Buddhist Perspective," *Religious Studies* 27 (1991): 511–12.

31. Raimon Panikkar, *The Intrareligious Dialogue* (New York: Paulist, 1999), 31.

32. Panikkar, *The Intrareligious Dialogue*, 37.

33. Panikkar, *The Intrareligious Dialogue*, 38.

34. Pluralism means different things to different people. In recent years, it has

been taken to represent the hypothesis offered by John Hick, among others, that the different religious traditions represent different paths or manifestations of one common hidden truth or spiritual goal of moving from self-centeredness to Reality-centeredness. Many theologians have criticized Hick's brand of pluralism for presuming a bird's-eye view of Reality and therefore, claiming special and exclusive access to truth about Reality. Many theologians, including John Cobb and S. Mark Heim, share the concern to value insights offered by different religious traditions, but are troubled by what they interpret as Hick's reduction of real differences among religious teachings to merely superficial differences on a single hidden absolute truth. John Cobb has often spoken of his rejection of a simple pluralism for the sake of a deeper pluralism that balances particularity and difference with the need to affirm the value of different traditions. See S. Mark Heim, *Salvations: Truth and Difference in Religion* (New York: Orbis, 1995), for a critique of the assumption of a single religious end common to different communities. Heim argues that different religious communities do have different ends that are constituted by their respective paths, and that each path requires an exclusive commitment to its truth. See *Deep Religious Pluralism*, ed. David Ray Griffin (Louisville: Westminster John Knox, 2011), for various efforts united in valuing diversity and plurality of human religious life and the particularity of Christian revelation without ending in relativism.

35. Anselm K. Min, "Loving Without Understanding: Raimon Panikkar's Ontological Pluralism," *International Journal for Philosophy of Religion* 68 (2010): 60.

36. Panikkar, *The Unknown Christ of Hinduism*, 24.

37. Min, "Loving Without Understanding," 70.

38. Panikkar, "A Self-Critical Dialogue," 255.

39. Panikkar, "A Self-Critical Dialogue," 257.

40. Panikkar, *The Unknown Christ of Hinduism*, 61.

41. Anri Morimoto, "The (More or Less) Same Light But From Different Lamps: The Post-Pluralist Understanding of Religion from a Japanese Perspective," *International Journal for the Philosophy of Religion* 53 (2003): 176.

42. Williams, "Some Dimensions of the Recent Work of Raimundo Panikkar," 518.

43. Min, "Loving Without Understanding," 66.

44. Eliot Deutsch, *Advaita Vedanta* (Honolulu: University of Hawaii Press, 1969), 86.

45. John Caputo, *On Religion* (London: Routledge, 2001), 2.

46. Caputo, *On Religion*, 2.

47. Caputo, *On Religion*, 4.

48. Caputo, *On Religion*, 6.

49. Caputo, *On Religion*, 3.

50. Caputo, *On Religion*, 7.

51. Caputo, *On Religion*, 8.

52. Caputo, *On Religion*, 8.

53. Caputo, *On Religion*, 15.

54. James H. Cone, *God of the Oppressed* (New York: Orbis, 1975), 113–15.

55. Desmond Tutu, *God Has a Dream: A Vision of Hope for Our Time* (New York: Image, 2004), 2.

56. Tutu, *God Has a Dream*, 3.

57. Caputo, *On Religion*, 14.

58. Caputo, *On Religion*, 111.

59. Caputo, *On Religion*, 113.

60. Caputo, *On Religion*, 132–34.

61. Caputo, *On Religion*, 117.

62. Clark Pinnock, Richard Rice, John Sanders, William Hasker, and David Basinger, *The Openness of God: A Biblical Challenge to the Traditional Understanding of God* (Downers Grove, IL: Intervarsity, 1994) 1.

63. See Clark Pinnock, *Most Moved Mover: A Theology of God's Openness* (Grand Rapids, MI: Baker, 2001). In this text, Pinnock considers the scriptural support for openness theism, discerns the pagan influence on classical Christian theism, and articulates the metaphysics of openness theism in contrast to that of process theism, which he and other openness theists criticize for its collapse of the dynamic relationship between God and the world, which requires real difference between the two.

64. Caputo, *On Religion*, 120–21.

65. Caputo, *On Religion*, 124.

Conclusion: Dwelling in Uncertainty

1. Paul Knitter, *Without Buddha I Could Not Be a Christian* (Oxford: Oneworld, 2009), 121.

2. Desmond Tutu, *God Has a Dream: A Vision of Hope for Our Time* (New York: Image, 2004), 8.

3. A promising development in recent years is the increased cooperation seen among interfaith groups and secular humanist organizations on college campuses.

INDEX

145, 158, 192n63; tradition of, 79,
98–99, 161, 186n1, 187n4, 188n28

caliph, 35, 46–47, 49–50
Calvin, John, 126, 168–69, 182n1
capitalism, criticism of, 82–85
Caputo, John: on love, 163–64; on religion
without certainty, 167–70; on religious
sense of life, 164–66, 168
Carlin, George, 128
Carse, James, 7–8, 10
caste: and dharma, 35, 40, 100, 105, 114;
hierarchy, 29, 99, 127, 172, 187n8
Catholic Church, 43, 63, 94
certainty (certitude): false claims to, 7, 124,
173–74; inward, 100–103; lack of, 123,
167; transcending, 1–8, 96, 146–47,
192n1
Chandogya Upanishad, 101–2
Christ: and atonement, 43–45, 123; Barth
on, 77–80; Christian gospel of, 54,
63, 181n29; as incarnate God, 21, 99,
137–39; Kierkegaard on, 68, 72, 74;
Moltmann on, 150–53, 156; Panikkar
on, 160–61; return of, 149; Robinson on,
129–32; and sacrifice, 42; Tillich on, 94
christology, 136, 138
church: Barth on, 77, 81–86; Catholic, 43,
63, 94; as institution, 123; Moltmann
on, 150; Protestant, 86–87; Robinson
on, 130; teaching, 15, 18, 148–49, 169,
181n29; Tillich on, 94–95
Clooney, Francis, 107, 188n29
Cloud of Unknowing, 131–34, 141
Cobb, John, 168, 194n34
Colbert, Stephen, 128
commandments, 44, 47, 51, 54–56, 58
Cone, James H., 165–66
contemplation, 20, 132–34, 163
cosmotheandric principle, 157–58, 161,
193n27
Couenhoven, Jesse, 81
covenant: Christ and, 77, 80; and faith
commitment, 44, 54, 64, 71; and God's
promise, 151–52; and hope, 164; and
Jewish relationship with God, 35, 51–53,
59–60; and responsibility, 11, 56–58,
150, 173, 191n57
Creel, Austin, 40

Dalferth, Ingolf, 80–81
Dao, 1–2
darsana, 111
Das, Gurcharan, 40
Davis, Richard, 117–18
Dawkins, Richard, 3, 124
death of God, 124, 126
deconstruction, 128, 137–38, 148, 160
dependence, absolute, 11, 16–17, 24–29, 33,
177n19, 177n25
Derrida, Jacques, 148, 162–64
detachment, 49, 105, 132, 135–40, 144–45
devotion: in Christian mystics, 17; in
Christian worship, 87–88, 95; in Hindu
puja, 29–33, 177n26, 178n27; as Hindu
tradition, 98, 100, 105–6, 187n4; in
Muslim worshp, 49–50; as superior to
knowledge, 109, 112, 119, 189n34
Dhand, Arti, 36–37
dharma: as ethical duty, 35–41, 49, 63,
97–100, 179n12; Hindu, 11, 30, 44,
46, 179n1, 191n57; limitations of, 100,
103–5, 113–14, 119, 179n4
dialogical dialogue, 157–59
dice game, 113
discipline: in Buddhist unknowing, 140; in
Hindu dharma, 40–41; in Hindu yoga,
100, 105–7, 110, 187n4; in Islamic
prayer, 22; Teresa of Avila on, 17–19; in
Shaiva Siddhanta, 117
dogmatism: and absolutism, 3, 145, 168,
171–72; doubt and, 12, 32, 126, 174;
protection of, 125–27; resisting, 2, 6,
124, 128, 136, 140; as uncritical thought,
25, 125, 167
Dole, Andrew, 26, 177n19
Dostoyevsky, Fyodor, 123
doubt: as component of faith, 68, 90,
95–98; existential, 90; spiritual function
of, 1–3, 11–12, 94, 115, 124, 136; as
uncertainty, 8, 72, 89, 100, 167; in Zen
Buddhism, 141–42, 145
Dravidian, 98
duty. *See* dharma; responsibility

Eckhart, Meister, 132–33, 135–40, 156, 162
emptiness: in Buddhism, 140, 142–45, 173,
191n55; in Christian mysticism, 134,
137, 139. *See also* nothingness

MADHURI M. YADLAPATI is an instructor
in religious studies at Louisiana State University.

The University of Illinois Press
is a founding member of the
Association of American University Presses.

Composed in 10/13 Sabon LT Std
by Celia Shapland
at the University of Illinois Press
Manufactured by Thomson-Shore, Inc.

University of Illinois Press
1325 South Oak Street
Champaign, IL 61820-6903
www.press.uillinois.edu